playing in such early novels as *The American* and *The Portrait of a Lady*.

James's later works do not, however, share the nineteenth-century novel's fascination with the destructive energy of games; they rely instead on ritual as a metaphor for the resolution of narrative conflict. Morrow argues that both *The Wings of the Dove* and *The Golden Bowl* emphasize the creative and harmonizing power of play—as opposed to the destructive power of competition—thus leading toward the concern with the ontological import of play reflected in twentieth-century fiction. These images of play in James's later fiction help us to understand how his work provides a transition from the nineteenth-century novel to modernist and post-modernist fiction.

Nancy Morrow teaches at the University of California, Davis.

DREADFUL GAMES

Dreadful Games

The Play of Desire in the Nineteenth-Century Novel

Nancy Morrow

THE KENT STATE UNIVERSITY PRESS
Kent, Ohio, and London, England

© 1988 by The Kent State University Press, Kent, Ohio 44242
All rights reserved
Library of Congress Catalog Card Number 87-35902
ISBN 0-87338-358-3
Manufactured in the United States of America

∞

Library of Congress Cataloging-in-Publication Data

Morrow, Nancy.
    Dreadful games : the play of desire in the nineteenth-century novel / Nancy Morrow.
    p.   cm.
    Revision of the author's thesis (Ph.D.)—University of California, Davis.
    Bibliography: p.
    Includes index.
    ISBN 0-87338-358-3 (alk. paper)
    1. Fiction—19th century—History and criticism.   2. Desire in literature.   3. Games in literature.   I. Title.   II. Title: Play of desire in the nineteenth-century novel.
PN3499.M66   1988
809.3'9353—dc19
                                                      87-35902
                                                          CIP

British Library Cataloguing-in-Publication data are available.

Contents

Introduction	1
Chapter 1	
Games and Rituals: Theories of Play and Desire	4
Chapter 2	
Work and Play: The Games of the Novel	22
Chapter 3	
Games of Ambition: Stendhal's *Le Rouge et le noir*	40
Chapter 4	
Games of Revenge: Balzac's *Le Cousine Bette*	65
Chapter 5	
The Play of Fate: Dostoevsky's *Crime and Punishment* and Hardy's *Jude the Obscure*	87
Chapter 6	
Playing by the Rules: Henry James's *The American* and *The Portrait of a Lady*	118
Chapter 7	
Games as Rituals: *The Wings of the Dove* and *The Golden Bowl*	144
Conclusion	
Old and New Novels	168
Notes	177
Select Bibliography	199
Index	202

■ This work began as a dissertation for a degree in Comparative Literature at the University of California, Davis. A number of people have read the manuscript and made important suggestions for revision, including an anonymous reader for the Kent State University Press. I am most appreciative for the assistance and support I received from my dissertation director, Professor Robert Torrance, from Jim Woodress, whose enthusiasm and encouragement never flagged, and from Ruby Cohn, whose practical advice was always invaluable. I would like to thank the Program in Comparative Literature, the Department of English, and the Program in American Studies at U.C. Davis for supporting me with fellowships and teaching and research positions at various stages of my work on this project. A shorter version of Chapter 6, entitled "Playing the Game of Life: The Dilemma of James's Christopher Newman and Isabel Archer," was published in the Spring 1988 issue of *Studies in American Fiction*. Finally, I am especially grateful to my husband, John Anderson, who learned to eat take-out food and listened to the printer run late at night.

Introduction

■ The novel has always been an almost enigmatic literary form, its rules debated and its characteristics enumerated, often without consensus or resolution. Writing in the 1920s, Russian theorist Mikhail Bakhtin defined the novel as a "diversity of languages and a diversity of individual voices, artistically arranged." The "language" of a novel, he claims, "is the system of its 'languages.'"[1] Each novelistic character speaks in a distinctive voice, which addresses itself to the voices of other characters. The fictional narrator speaks as well, often in different voices: sometimes using the language of everyday written or oral discourse, sometimes the language of literary narration, sometimes even the language of "extra-literary" discourse—the languages of philosophy or science or history, for example. Each of these languages uses its own unique and characteristic vocabulary, each of which reflects a different mode of perceiving and speaking about experience. When one "voice" addresses itself to another voice in the text, these vocabularies reverberate across the text. Thus, as Bakhtin says, "the dialogic orientation of a word among other words . . . creates the potential for a distinctive art of prose."[2] Unlike other literary forms, where readers expect to find a distinctive and consistent vocabulary—what is meant, for instance, by "poetic diction"—in the novel, competing vocabularies clamor to be heard.

Fiction differs from other literary genres, from poetry and drama, precisely because it possesses this "dialogic" dimension. And the

Introduction

relationship among the various voices in the novelistic text is often one of strife; voices compete for dominance, one seeking to prevail over another. In the nineteenth-century novel, the voices in the text whose vocabularies derive from the language of games and play often grow louder and more insistent as the novel progresses. Listening to those voices that rely on the language of games, as they address themselves to other voices in the text, often reveals the central conflicts of a novel.

Those who read novels have not always been much concerned with the problem, as Bakhtin describes it, of orienting words among other words. The novel as a form has always seemed to concern itself more with character and event than with the nuances of language. The imagery of nineteenth-century fiction is pervasively, obsessively visual; the Realist text seems to resist linguistic ambiguity and word play. Writing of "The Future of the Novel" in 1899, Henry James was convinced that the novel as a popular literary form would continue to thrive simply because it fulfills "man's general appetite for a *picture*." James worried, though, that a "community devoted to travelling and shooting, to pushing trade and playing football," would not be much interested in experimenting with the "story" a novel provides.[3] Fifty years after James made this prophecy—after film and other visual diversions had begun to offer the public something much different, perhaps much more satisfying in the way of a "picture" than the novel ever could, and after novelists had already begun to experiment with the "story" of the novel, often to their readers' discomfort—literary critic Mark Shorer asserted that criticism of the novel must begin not with the story, or with the "image" of life presented, but "with the word, with figurative structures, with rhetoric as skeleton and style as body of meaning."[4] In his essay "Fiction and the 'Matrix of Analogy,'" Shorer seeks to identify the "dominant metaphorical quality" of classic novelistic texts, looking not only for what he calls "explicit" metaphors, but also for "the buried and dead metaphors, and some related traits of diction generally." Shorer argues that because this kind of metaphorical language "constantly strains toward symbolism," it can provide the structural basis of a novel.

To define "metaphor" in this special way moves the critical discourse about imagery in the novel beyond the specific problems of rhetorical tropes or the subtle distinctions that are often made between "metaphor" and "metonymy."[5] The metaphorical texture of a novel is produced by the play of association among words that belong to either similar or contiguous realms of experience. Even ordinary, "non-poetic" language becomes significant through repetition and opposition.

Introduction

"Word" and "experience" are inextricably bound. The "metaphorical texture" of a work of fiction connects form to story; it makes language the key to the structure of experience as reflected in the text, and experience the key to understanding the special characteristics of novelistic discourse. And in a larger context, fundamental patterns of experience are reflected in metaphorical patterns that recur in a number of different novels.

The "metaphor of the game," as the expression is used in the essays that follow, refers to the metaphorical texture produced by the explicit use of the language associated with games and playing or by implicit references to the structures and attitudes of game playing. The language and structure of games in these nineteenth-century novels is metaphorical in the sense that Todorov defines that process in *The Poetics of Prose:* "the existence of a common predicate permits two subjects to become each other's signifier."[6] To use Todorov's logic, a game is a structure of events governed by rules; social relationships also possess a structure governed by rules; therefore, "game" can signify the social life of human beings. In much the same way, fiction can be described as a "game," in other words, as a pattern of regulated exchange between the reader and the text. As so many novels show, characters often formulate their own "fictions," which play themselves out against the background of the "fiction" conceived and perpetrated by the novelist. The metaphor of the game highlights both the play of fictional characters and the play of the fictional text.

But what makes the metaphor of the game so significant in so many nineteenth-century novels is that the metaphorical equation, "life" to "game"—or even "novel" to "life"—tells either a half-truth or a white lie. Even as both the characters and the narrators assert through word and action that life is a game, to be played and won, the text as a whole repudiates the possibility of such a simple correspondence. The metaphorical texture of these novels illuminates not the similarities between the fictional life of the characters and the logic and structure of game playing, but the essential, irreconcilable differences. The metaphorical texture of a novel becomes, perhaps unwittingly, ironic, demanding that the reader reevaluate and reinterpret the kinds of connections the text suggests. The language of games helps to illuminate this consistent paradox of the nineteenth-century novel. Thus, a theory of play—and of the forces in human experience that motivate human play—can provide a new basis for interpreting some of the classical texts of nineteenth-century Realism.

1

Games and Rituals

Theories of Play and Desire

■ Near the end of Henry James's *The Wings of the Dove,* Merton Densher says to Kate Croy, "We've played our dreadful game, and we've lost." The character refers here not to some conventional game but to a course of action that has become game*like:* Kate and Densher have made moves and countermoves in a scheme to attain both money and each other. As in a game, the characters' actions are strategic, carefully structured, and governed by a specific set of rules. But the expression "playing a game" is an ironic means of describing what happens in the novel. To call what the characters do in this novel a "game" masks the danger and destructiveness of their scheme and seeks to make their actions seem less consequential than they are. Merton Densher is almost unique among fictional characters in recognizing the *unplayful* quality of his actions, since many novelistic characters play similarly "dreadful" games, often blindly and unquestioningly, without such recognition. James's character describes his "game" as "dreadful" precisely because it retains the *form* but not the *essence* of play. The idea of game is used here as a metaphor for actions that possess none of those qualities—like spontaneity, joy, freedom, relaxation, or harmony—that would make them playful.[1]

The notion of "dreadful games" succinctly characterizes the images of play that dominate nineteenth-century European and American novels. The novelists of the Age of Realism turn again and again to the themes of strategy, conflict, and competition, often basing their fictional

Games and Rituals

worlds on the principles of competitive, gamelike transactions. Characters and narrators alike resort to the language of games in their fictional discourse. The desire to "win" becomes for fictional characters an obsession, making them willing to exploit or even to violate the "rules" that govern all kinds of human interaction and that seek to restrain the potentially destructive forces of human desire. By using the language of games to describe what characters do, novelists demonstrate the unplayfulness of competitive games, as well as the dangers of games based on chance, on imitation, or even, to use Roger Caillois's words, on "the pursuit of vertigo."[2] For players driven by the desire to win their "games," cheating becomes an irresistible temptation, and obstacles to victory are eliminated at any cost. Human experience is portrayed as ruthless or futile or both.

The "dreadful games" that play themselves out in many nineteenth-century novels are characterized by meaningless rules, arbitrary choices, merciless fatalism, and destructive competition. Few of these novels ever portray play as an experience that leads to harmony, community, self-awareness, or knowledge—states that even competitive play produces under certain circumstances. A fascination with the divisive and destructive power of games—in other words, a fascination with the way in which playing leads to mutually exclusive distinctions like "winners" and "losers"—often makes for a dismal novelistic world: a landscape of frustrated desire and shattered ambition, a world that ultimately seems to value conformity more than creativity, and aggression more than cooperation. A deceptively simple and straightforward metaphor, "playing the game," as it is used in these novels, provides the novelist with a way of describing the complexity of human psychology and of the dynamics of human relationships.

Understanding the paradox of unplayful games depends on making a careful distinction between activities defined as games and activities characterized by the attitudes of play. Even where the structural pattern "game" is present, the essential qualities of play may be absent. Peter Farb makes this kind of distinction in his study of language "games," *Word Play* (1974). Defining games as "interaction according to well-defined rules, in which something is at stake that both sides are attempting to win," he argues that games are not necessarily "fun."[3] Farb's definition emphasizes both the potential instrumentality of language and the purely formal properties of games. Mathematical "game theory" similarly defines the idea of game by its structure alone. Game theorists devise logical, abstract models of social, political, or economic

5

situations, by exploring the structural relationships between the players, their options, the possible results, and the players' preferences among these results. The "games" devised in this way help describe different kinds of human interaction.[4]

A game, then, has a certain formal *logic:* an order, a sequence of events, a certain way of connecting the elements that constitute it. Just as the "logic" of dreams differs from that of waking reality, games often structure events and relationships differently than everyday experience does. Many games, especially those with more than one player, rely on rules to regulate the structural patterns produced in the process of playing. As events, games are finite and limited structures; they end when players have played for a certain amount of time, scored a certain number of points, or when one player or group of players has achieved some sort of "victory" over the others.

The idea of play, however, describes a much broader range of activities than does the idea of games; play can rarely be defined in terms of its structure, the way most games can. Play has a special logic, a special way of ordering and arranging its elements, but the logic of playing is not always as rigid and prescribed as the logic of many conventional, rule-based games. For example, imitative play, like acting or artistic performance, may structure itself according to a flexible logic, which individual players interpret and "play out" in their own distinctive ways. The idea of play refers not only to human interaction, but to the social relationships of animals, and even to the movement of matter. A recent book on play and games begins by defining play in perhaps the broadest terms possible: "Play is a natural phenomenon that has guided the course of the world from its beginning. It is evident in the shaping of matter into living structures and in the social behavior of human beings."[5] In this sense, play among people parallels the play of energy in the universe, guided by many of the same principles.

Playing is always a dynamic activity. A back-and-forth movement characterizes play, as such figures of speech as "the play of light" or "the play of ideas" suggest. But as these images also suggest, this movement is not finite, in the way that the movement of most games necessarily is. Games are usually finite, goal-oriented events, but play, in this broader sense, continually renews itself infinitely through repetition.[6] To the extent that winning a game ends it, playing without that finite goal at stake keeps the movement of play going. Philosophers as different as Hans-Georg Gadamer and Jacques Derrida have described the open-endedness of play. Derrida describes play as a field of infinite substitutions, always open to new possibilities.[7] Play is not so much about reaching a particular goal—scoring a certain number of points, for instance—as it is about the process by which points are scored. The idea of "winning" is often not even relevant to a discussion of the nature of play. The structure of individual games often remains rigid and closed, but the logic of activities that might best be called "playful" remains flexible and open to a variety of possible resolutions.

Although games are often considered trivial or frivolous, somehow less important than other kinds of activities, "playfulness" cannot be directly opposed to "seriousness." Any human activity—art, religion, language, even work—may embody the attitudes of play. A person may perform "work" as if it were "play." As a result, play describes not only certain kinds of activity, but more significantly, an attitude toward any kind of activity. German philosopher Eugen Fink suggests this possibility, in an essay in which he seeks to develop an "ontology" of play:

> While seeming to be unrelated to our normal life, [play] relates to it in a very meaningful way, namely in its mode of representation. If we define play in the usual manner by contrasting it with work, reality, seriousness and authenticity we falsely juxtapose it with other existential phenomena. . . . Play, so to speak, confronts them all—it absorbs them by representing them. We play at being serious, we play truth, we play reality, we play work and struggle, we play love and death—and we even play play itself.[8]

Fink is not suggesting here that all life is merely play, or even that life is "like" a game—the relationship usually implied by metaphorical language. More precisely, play reflects and represents the whole range of human experiences, which perhaps explains why the problems of play can be studied in so many different intellectual contexts. How thoroughly an attitude of play permeates a game—in other words, how completely an activity embodies and embraces the essential qualities of play, not its special structure or dynamics alone—determines its playfulness.

By creating an atmosphere of enjoyment and relaxation, play seeks to mediate conflicts inherent in human experience, an idea that becomes part of the theory of play at least as early as the eighteenth century. In his *Letters on the Aesthetic Education of Man,* Schiller describes the mediating quality of play. He sees play as an impulse that harmonizes the conflicting forces of the "sensuous impulse" (the physical side of human experience) and the "formal impulse" (the rational side). The "play impulse" achieves this harmony by having both a relaxing effect

Dreadful Games

("in order to keep not only the sense impulse but also the form impulse within their bounds") and a tightening effect ("in order to maintain both of them in their strength").[9] Play dissolves the opposition of mind and matter. For Schiller, play makes the individual most uniquely human: "man is only wholly man when he is playing."[10] Through play, the individual reconciles the experience of the senses with the experience of the mind by balancing the impulses that govern each.

Activities characterized by play—as opposed to those activities merely structured as games—are spontaneous or voluntary, without obligation or compulsion. Players choose to play. For this reason, children instructed to play, or even ordered to play (like Pip and Estella in Dickens's *Great Expectations*), or bullied into playing (like Lewis Carroll's Alice) face an impossible task, based on an insurmountable contradiction. Players are absorbed into the special logic of the games they play only when they respond to their own desires, not when they are coerced or obliged by others to act in a particular way.

Although play must be spontaneous, the force of individual desire may motivate play in a way that an individual does not consciously recognize or control. The connection between desire and play can be seen in the relationship between desire and the special play of language. In his essay "Existence and Hermeneutics" (1969), Paul Ricoeur states that "language is deeply rooted in desire, in the instinctual impulses of life."[11] Language arises from an initial lack or absence, followed by a desire to satisfy that lack. This initial desire for someone or something, this initial absence or lack, links sounds in language to objects in the material world. Moreover, that connection remains, even after the desire has been satisfied. Language ultimately depends not only on the desire that motivates it, but also on the order created by the satisfaction of that desire.[12]

Desire motivates other play activities in much the same way as it motivates language. William James discusses the "instinctive" nature of play in *Principles of Psychology* (1891). In his chapter entitled "Instinct," James identifies two kinds of play: physical games and "ceremonial games," which involve "concerted action as one of an organized crowd." He argues that play responds to some "primitive element in our nature," and he emphasizes the extent to which playing even the most complex of the "ceremonial games" is a motor response, "just as when puppies chase one another and swallows have a parliament."[13] This analogy suggests that play, at its most fundamental level, is a response to an internal or external stimulus.

Playing is often a response to the conflict that arises between desire and satisfaction, between wanting something and being able to have it. Soviet psychologist L. S. Vygotsky has suggested that the activity of play begins when very young children become aware of needs that cannot be immediately satisfied. Play can be defined in this sense as "the imaginary, illusory realization of unrealizable desires."[14] Play provides a kind of "fiction" or "illusion" that compensates for what might be lacking in everyday experience and supplements this lack. Freud also notes that play is compensatory. In his discussion of the "repetition compulsion," in *Beyond the Pleasure Principle* (1920), he explains how children often re-create their unpleasant experiences in play, seeking in this way to "master" them or to "pass them on" to a substitute, like a toy or playmate. Based on his observations, Freud identifies "mastery" and "revenge" as two desires that are often "played out."[15] Henry James dramatizes these responses in his novel *What Maisie Knew* (1897), where, at the end of chapter 5, the child Maisie speaks to her doll Lisette in the same tone of voice and manner that her mother has used with her. Maisie seeks both to "master" her experience with her mother, by re-creating it, and to pass it on by making Lisette suffer as she herself has suffered. Because of its compensatory nature, play helps to resolve emotional conflicts and to comfort those who have experienced pain or loss.

These theories suggest that play is an inevitable response to physical or psychical tension, and furthermore, that play provides an outlet for desires that cannot be satisfied *except* in the special activity of play. As Plato says in the *The Symposium*, an individual does not desire what he already possesses, his "present blessings," but only those things he lacks.[16] Inasmuch as such desire either consciously or unconsciously motivates play, the individual does not play out desires that can be immediately satisfied in other, more direct or immediate ways. Like language itself, all play activities arise from a lack or absence of something—in other words, from a desire for some person or object or state of being. In playing, individuals seek to balance desire and satisfaction; they attempt to reconcile the polarity of wanting and having, through an experience that mediates these extremes. Play thus takes place in a kind of "middle ground."

Although desire motivates play in this way, individuals absorbed into the movement of play—who enter this middle ground—suspend their subjective desires for the duration of play. They surrender their desire to gain and their fear of losing anything that might have intrinsic value for them beyond the moment of play.[17] Play balances desire and satisfaction by absorbing both into its own special logic and movement. James Joyce's Stephen Dedalus offers an explanation of how play suspends desire in this way. In the fifth chapter of *A Portrait of the Artist as a Young Man,* Stephen argues that the possession of an object, toward which desire moves, is arrested in art, by what he calls the "esthetic emotion." By experiencing this esthetic emotion, "the mind is arrested and raised above desire."[18] Play—and the "play" of art—are, according to the theory that Stephen derives from his reading of Aquinas, transcendent experiences, drawing the individual toward otherwise unrealizable possibilities. A game characterized by the attitudes of play, like the kind of art Joyce's character describes here, subordinates the players' individual desires and fears to its own logic, to the demands and rewards of the game itself.

Play is performed only for its own sake, without any other end in mind. The "subject" of play is not the players, but the movement of the game itself; as Gadamer says, "play merely reaches presentation through the players."[19] For Gadamer, this loss of subjectivity provides a basis for the comunicative energy of play, especially of the play of language. Language as dialogue becomes a shared response, an integration of subjective desires, and not an instrument of any one participant's satisfaction. Language communicates, in this special way, only when it does not serve some ulterior purpose. Gadamer's explanation of the "game" of language provides an important contrast to the theories of someone like Peter Farb, whose interest lies in the manipulation and rivalry, not the sense of community, reflected in linguistic interaction. For both writers, language is a "game," but one that plays itself out in different ways and with different results.

Some games might be described as "dreadful," because they fail to balance desire and satisfaction. Paradoxically, though *play* seeks to harmonize conflict, discrete *games* are not always harmonizing activities. Players do not always willingly surrender their subjective interests; desire does not always extinguish itself in the movement of play. Because play arises in desire, an individual may perceive a particular game as simply a means to an end, not as something performed for its own sake. Desires like "mastery" and "revenge" may lead to rather fierce, even vicious games, especially when they occur outside the inherently more protected and neutralized world of the child. Stendhal suggests this possibility in *Racine and Shakespeare* (1823), when he argues that the "element of vengeance" in so much French comedy of his day produces a kind of "affected" laughter, which he finds "devoid of significance."[20] When someone "amuses" himself or herself at the expense of another, or when this "amusement" leads to someone else's misery, the experience fails to achieve the sense of harmony and reconciliation that the play impulse seeks to create.

How individuals identify and articulate their own desires very often determines how they will play them out. As René Girard has illustrated in his study of the novel, *Deceit, Desire and the Novel* [Mensonge romantique et vérité romanesque], desire is often "mediated," originating not from a spontaneous need, but in imitation of the desires of another. The subject of such mediated desire may become the player of a "dreadful game," because he or she can never become the imitated other. As a result, a game arising from mediated desire can never lead to harmony and reconciliation. The rivalry that erupts between the subject of mediated desire and the imitated other often leads instead to irreconcilable conflict, even to violence.[21] The essential attitudes of play are suppressed whenever the player of a game seeks to dominate others and to assert his or her own superiority through play—or, in the example of the gambler who inhabits so many novels, seeks desperately to resolve financial problems at the gaming tables. Rather than resolving inner conflicts, the play of desire may, in some circumstances, generate endless conflicts.

In contrast to such "dreadful games," many play experiences encourage learning, experimentation, and creativity, not only because play is always open to possibility, but also because it minimizes or suspends the consequences that actions might have in everyday experience. Narrative games like utopia, science fiction, or fantasy permit both author and reader to imagine alternative worlds without risk, without altering the structure of everyday experience.[22] Actions performed in the middle ground of play are neither inherently true nor inherently false, and the moral implications of such actions are, in effect, suspended for the duration of play. When an ethical value is attributed to an activity, in Huizinga's words, "it ceases to be play."[23]

At the same time, the freedom implied by the special logic and structure of play may not be justified in those circumstances where actions do have consequences, just as the rules of one game may not apply to another. The board game Monopoly may resemble what some might call the "game" of real estate investment, but actual investors would hardly pursue properties according to the logic by which a player acquires and develops the "fictional" properties. By the same measure, mountain climbers who use their skill and daring to scale high-rise buildings usually find themselves charged with a crime, their actions not recognized by others as "play." To call an activity a "game" often belies the fact that individuals must face consequences for their actions. In contrast to these situations where individuals must accept responsibility for their actions, once the middle ground of play is established, even as players submit to the risk and danger implicit in the process of surrendering their subjective desires, the consequences of their actions are neutralized. Play remains a sheltered realm, its content fictional, premised on an agreement to make believe, for the duration of play, in a collective illusion.[24]

Rules help to maintain the sheltered, neutral quality of play, by controlling and directing the energy of the game. In games with more than one player, rules help to integrate all of the players into the middle ground of play. Even in games of fantasy and imagination, or in role-playing games based on mimicry and imitation, a script or role model functions much as the rules do in competitive games or games of chance.[25] But players may perceive the rules either as "roles," flexible guidelines for action, or as inviolable principles, which prescribe and legislate action.

How players perceive the nature of the rules of a game helps to determine the quality and tone of it. As Piaget has observed, adults are more likely to play rule-based games than very young children, whose play is often more "symbolic." As children adjust to reality, and as they begin to play with one another, they too are more likely to devise rules to regulate the energy of their games.[26] But the symbolic and imaginative power of play may diminish as the rules become more formalized and more complex—in other words, as the game moves further away from its origins in individual symbolic play. Language again provides a useful illustration of how such changes occur. Language as spoken or written discourse relies on certain rules of grammar, style, and syntax. But these rules, which facilitate the play of language, rarely make themselves obtrusive. Speakers of a language rarely think about these rules as they speak; as Wittgenstein notes, "we rarely use language as such a calculus."[27] "Word play" often depends on actually violating rules in various creative ways: A metaphor, pun, or allusion may initially evoke a vivid impression in a listener's or reader's mind, but in time it may lose that power, joining instead the ranks of "dead metaphor," cliché, or truism. For any kind of play to realize its power and its possibility, a balance must be struck between strict adherence to the rules of a game and creative violation of those established rules.

Rules, then, are no more than *conventions,* which players agree to accept when they enter the middle ground of play. Just as players must enter the game without compulsion, rules cannot be imposed upon them. In discourse, speakers and listeners, or writers and readers, agree to accept particular definitions, even, in some cases, a special technical language. Participants in an act of discourse agree to abide by special rules and forms in certain situations. But these conventions are guidelines, not laws, and they need not be rigidly followed or blindly obeyed. In fact, language often seems most playful when it *reverses* a reader's or listener's expectations of what will follow. Along these lines, in *The Critique of Judgement* Kant discusses the way in which a joke produces laughter through the "play of representations." Laughter arises, he says, "from a strained expectation being suddenly reduced to nothing."[28] The joke deceives temporarily, creating tensions, which resolve into relaxation as the deception is unmasked. But both participants in the joke encounter, the joke teller and the listener, must share the deception and its unmasking, or the power of the joke diminishes. The playful text resists the temptation to manipulate the game at the reader's expense.

Just as the playfulness of a specific game depends on more than its structure, the playfulness of language depends on more than prescribed techniques. A spoken or written text that might be called playful, or "ludic," *invites* the listener or reader to participate in its own playing.[29] A speaker can use tone of voice or gesture to invite such play, and a writer may invite the reader's participation in the play of style by exaggeration, emphasis, or incongruity. The self-consciousness of much literature that seems playful, or fun, stems from the writer's attempt to call attention to the flexibility and ambiguity of language as it produces meaning. In order to share in the play of a text, for a text to "gratify" in the way that Kant describes the gratification offered by a joke, a reader must eventually recognize the "deception" that a text has played. Clearly, playful language is neither rigidly bound to rules and conventions, nor excessively literal. Furthermore, the "deception" of a playful text is only temporary; an author seeking to tap the power of play does not seek to confound or to deceive the reader willfully or permanently. As Peter Hutchinson notes in *Games Authors Play* (1983), if the "challenge that a text poses seems too difficult, a reader may

Dreadful Games

refuse to play the author's game"—a risk that any text takes whenever a writer tries to compete, rather than to communicate with his reader.[30]

In other kinds of play activities, the rules may be similarly flexible. In both competitive and noncompetitive games, players must *consent* to follow the rules. When new games are learned—when games are passed from one group to another—players usually accept them as a whole. As a group continues to play that game, however, they may agree to change or to modify certain rules. As Piaget's observations of children at the game of marbles reveals, young children often believe that the rules by which they have learned to play come from some higher authority, from adults or from God. Only as they grow older, do these same children begin to experiment with the rules, acknowledging that rules are no more than conventions, and learning that by establishing appropriate "legal" mechanisms, they can change the rules and create new ways of playing.[31] What Piaget's observation suggests is that rules themselves are not inherently sacrosanct, but that children and even adults often confuse the content of specific rules with the process by which all rules are established. The principles underlying the rule-making process—such as agreement, consensus, consent, and compromise—and not the actual rules themselves, remain constant and inviolable.

Games with rules can nurture the individual values, like fairmindedness, honesty, and respect for authority and tradition, that facilitate social cooperation. Nevertheless, players can become obsessed with rules, which can, in turn, make a game less playful. "Mastering the rules" may become more important than "playing the game," as indeed it was for the younger children that Piaget observed at the game of marbles. Some people may attribute a mystical, inviolable authority to rules whenever others suggest that the rules of a game—or the "rules" of those activities such as commerce or marriage or law, for which "game" often serves as a metaphor—are not sacred, that they do not come from God, that they are mere conventions, and that they can be changed. Furthermore, people who begin to see the rules not as devices or conventions, but as obstacles that prevent them from winning, may cheat in order to secure their own goals, thus tampering with the risk that players accept as a part of playing. At the same time, it is impossible to "playfully" violate rules that others consider sacred. Whatever the case, play begins to lose its ludic power when the rules become the center of interest in game playing.

The middle ground of play remains sheltered and neutral, not only because rules regulate the energy that motivates play activities, but also

Games and Rituals

because all kinds of play and games are characterized by some sort of spatial and temporal boundaries.[32] These boundaries ensure the integrity not only of the middle ground of play, but of the realm of actual experience, which remains separated from the realm of play but always adjacent to it in time and space, always surrounding it. The boundaries of the playing field in football, for example, limit where players may pursue their game, and as a practical matter, protect the spectators who encircle the game from the possible physical dangers of it. Again, such boundaries are not imposed on a game, but rather generated by it. The boundaries of play help to neutralize the consequences of what occurs within the play encounter; as David Chaney explains in *Fictions and Ceremonies* (1979), "play lacks consequences because it encapsulates itself, we can usually choose to end the play and resume conventional responsibilities."[33] By "encapsulating itself," play protects its own middle ground as well as the realm of experience that surrounds it.

Just as the players of a game willingly accept its rules, they negotiate and agree upon the boundaries of play, limiting it to specific places and specific times. In conventional games, sports in particular, the boundaries are rarely ambiguous to either the players or the spectators; they are clearly and precisely defined. Anyone who willingly steps into these boundaries submits himself to the logic of that game. At the same time, the player who steps outside these boundaries leaves behind the neutral realm of play and must acknowledge the consequences of his or her actions.

In some situations, however, and for some players, these "boundaries" are neither clear nor impenetrable; rather, they possess a fluid, even nonexistent quality. Actors, for instance, are not always able to separate their own personalities from the roles they play; the lines between fact and fiction in a novel or film may be disputable. But in most play encounters, the boundaries must be "framed" in some way. Gregory Bateson has described the way in which the message, "this is play," frames such an encounter. This message can be transmitted in a variety of different forms, either explicitly or through gesture, tone, or nuance. Yet as Bateson notes, such messages are often falsified or misinterpreted. A kind of "false play" results, masking unresolved feelings of hostility or enabling one player to manipulate another ruthlessly, all under the guise of play. In effect, one or more players consciously signal to the others, "this is play," when, in fact, the activity is *not* play.[34] For this reason, the idea of "game" sometimes describes a deception, willfully perpetrated, a scheme or a plot, where

15

an individual "pretends" to play in order to secure an advantage over someone else.

Some individuals have difficulty negotiating the passage between play and experience, some unable to move into the realm of play and others reluctant to leave it.[35] It may be difficult to determine when the boundaries of play have been crossed. Instances of play or games like artistic performances, social relationships, or linguistic interaction often have virtually unrecognizable boundaries, compared with the chalked or painted lines in many formal, conventional games. When the boundaries of play are difficult to detect, an activity takes on a different character than when boundaries are more clearly defined and universally accepted. The concerns of daily life and the demands of individual desire may enter the realm of play, as so often happens in professional sports or gambling. The special logic and freedom of play—but especially the rigid logic and structure of formal games—may in turn infiltrate the realm of experience, so that every aspect of human experience becomes a "playing field." The authentic behavior that individuals expect from one another—unless they have agreed to play—becomes virtually indistinguishable from the "fictional" or "make-believe" behavior that characterizes play.

When the boundaries of play are breached, the idea of game comes to stand for any activity based on a set of rules to be mastered and manipulated to achieve an individual goal. Roger Caillois calls this process "the corruption of games."

> The rule of instinct again becoming absolute, the tendency to interfere with the isolated, sheltered and neutralized kind of play spreads to daily life and tends to subordinate it to its own needs, as much as possible. What used to be a pleasure becomes an obsession. What was an escape becomes an obligation and what was a pastime is now a passion, compulsion, and a source of anxiety.[36]

The process that "corrupts" games in this way, that significantly alters them in quality or composition, drains them of the essential qualities of play: lack of compulsion, subordination of individual desires, relaxation of tension, simple enjoyment. Under these circumstances, games become ways to exploit others. Eric Berne has captured much of the sense of Caillois's notion of the corruption of games in *Games People Play* (1964), his study of the motives and dynamics of personal relationships. He defines game as "an on-going series of complementary ulterior transactions" between two people, and argues that such games are

Games and Rituals

essentially disingenuous, that they actually prevent "players" from communicating with one another.[37] What is most characteristic of the "games" Berne describes is the persistent ulteriority of individual action, an ulteriority that characterizes all corrupted games. After games have been corrupted, all that remains is an empty shell, a gamelike structure, which fosters not harmony, but irresolvable conflict, a polarization of desire and satisfaction.

The metaphor of the "dreadful game"—of the games that Caillois calls "corrupted," because they lack the essential qualities of play, and of the "ulterior transactions" that Berne describes—dominates all other images of play in the nineteenth-century novel. The characters who populate these novels are not as a group inherently evil or degenerate (though clearly some do perpetrate evil), nor have they willfully or ignorantly relinquished a more "natural" or "innocent" style of human interaction in favor of those actions and decisions that can be characterized by the expression "dreadful game." The novelists who describe these "dreadful games" do not so much try to define "morality" as they seek to question the logic and the ethics of individual choices. They raise these questions through the language and logic associated with games—that is, by juxtaposing the *structure* of a character's action with the desires and attitudes that motivate it and with the conditions an action promotes in the world of the novel. It is not the content or form of a character's game that makes it "dreadful," but the relationship of those activities characterized as games to the rest of a character's fictional experience. In a novel, when the boundaries between play and experience are breached either because the messages that frame a play encounter are distorted or misinterpreted, or because a character has subordinated the play of desire to his or her own interests—in other words, when play and experience are no longer distinguishable in a character's mind or actions—that novel describes a world of corrupted games.

In these novels of corrupted or dreadful games, even when characters assert that they are "only playing," the consequences of their actions are not minimized any more than had they not characterized their actions as play. To be "only playing a game" in this context is to deceive oneself and others. In a novel like Laclos's *Les Liaisons dangereuses,* a young girl can be seduced and ruined for the sake of amusement; in Balzac's *La Cousine Bette,* a family can be reduced to poverty because the "game" of society calls for exacting revenge; and in Dostoevsky's *Crime and Punishment,* a woman can be brutally murdered to test a

Dreadful Games

theory about the human will. When a character uses the metaphor of the game she or he often seeks to justify action that could not be justified in any other way. Ambitious characters, like Julien Sorel in Stendhal's *Le Rouge et le noir,* devise gamelike strategies to prove their superiority and to defeat all their rivals in order to satisfy their always-escalating desires. And failure, as in Hardy's *Jude the Obscure,* is attributed not to human irresponsibility or weakness but to the inexorable hand of fate. Characters in each of these novels learn the rules that govern "society," and then exploit this knowledge to manipulate others. Victimization is often a corollary to the "win or lose" mentality of corrupted games. Defeat often results from an inadequate understanding of the rules that govern the play of desire, as it does for Henry James's Christopher Newman in *The American.* Characters who embody or attempt to embody the essential attitudes of play in their exchanges with the world around them, like James's Isabel Archer in *The Portrait of a Lady,* find these playful responses to life undermined and suppressed by the manipulatory schemes of others. Each of these novels uses the language of games to describe the fictional experiences generated by the play of desire, as well as to underscore precisely the *unplayfulness* in much of human experience.

In the novels of his "major phase," Henry James finds a way to reformulate the narrative strategy of these nineteenth-century novels and to provide a resolution to the incessant play of dreadful games, as chronicled by these novels. As *The Wings of the Dove* and *The Golden Bowl* demonstrate, games need not end in division and destruction; they need not declare winners at the expense of losers. Gamelike situations are transformed so as to minimize the costs of both victory and defeat. The concept of *ritual,* and especially the distinction that might be made between "ritual" and "game," provides a way to interpret the endings of both these novels and explain how the essential qualities of play might be returned to human activities—how, in other words, games might once again fulfill the possibilities of play.

Like play, ritual has its own logic and structure and remains separate and distinct from the realm of everyday experience.[38] Ritual does differ from play in the sacred character that is often attributed to it but not to other kinds of play. But this sacred character is not essential to all rituals, and the feelings between people that any ritual seeks to foster have the power to transform the destructive forces of the energy released in corrupted games. Participants in both play and ritual share a common "fiction," although in ritual a certain moral value is sometimes associated with that fiction. Nevertheless, in either games or rituals, this fiction serves to integrate individuals into the patterns of events. Just as the rules of a game demand a conformity of action, rituals require that actions be performed in a specific manner. Like corrupted games, rituals can be empty and meaningless, gesture without substance. But rituals can, on the other hand, serve to bring individuals together and to integrate them into some common purpose or goal. Like play, ritual is both an activity, the rite itself, and an attitude toward activity.

In a ritual event, group interests replace individual concerns. In *The Savage Mind* (1962), Lévi-Strauss distinguishes between game and ritual, and as in the distinction that can be made between game and play, he emphasizes attitude and motivation, as opposed to form or rule.[39] Lévi-Strauss describes the way that some cultures will play competitive games, like football, over and over, not until one side emerges clearly as the "winner," but until the opposing sides have each won an equal number of games—until, in effect, the opposition is eliminated. In this way, they play football not as a game but as a *ritual*. Ordinarily, games move from symmetry of relationship, from a situation where all players or teams of players are more or less equal, toward asymmetry, where distinctions, like "winners" and "losers," for example, are established and preserved. Rituals, on the other hand, begin with a situation of asymmetry, where individuals or teams are not equal in their relationships with one another, and move toward a situation of symmetry, where individuals are bound together into a larger community of participants. Simply stated, games have a "disjunctive" effect, while rituals "conjoin" participants.[40]

While game playing often effects categories and divisions, a ritual attitude toward group events seeks to eliminate such distinctions, to make all participants in an activity equal, to depolarize and to balance opposing forces within the group or community, and thus to create harmony and to produce both satisfaction of desire and pleasure in participation. Once the boundaries between play and experience begin to disintegrate, they cannot be simply repaired or reconstituted. But the conflict and polarization that result when these lines are breached can be transformed and the energy of the game redirected by the attitudes that characterize rituals. In this way, games are transformed into rituals.

In *The Golden Bowl*, Henry James portrays in Maggie Verver a character who attempts to "ritualize" the relationships among a group of characters in just this way. The ritualized game that Maggie devises

Dreadful Games

when she begins to suspect the long-standing intimacy between Charlotte and the Prince moves the characters from disequlibrium and a lack of harmony—in which Maggie must somehow "defend" herself from "losing" to Charlotte and the Prince, while at the same time Charlotte must "plot" to ensure the secrecy of her own actions—to a situation where direct confrontation is avoided and the consequences of any defeat are minimized. Maggie achieves her own purpose without securing Charlotte's defeat. Charlotte leaves for America not humbled or castigated but with her pride intact. While Maggie regains the Prince's fidelity and affection, this ritualized game permits both Charlotte and Maggie to participate in the "fiction" of choice and self-righteousness. That it remains, for the characters, "only" a fiction may distress some readers, but that fiction nevertheless offers the characters more possibilities at the ending of the novel than would an ending marked by the defeat or victory of either Maggie or Charlotte. The ritualized game mediates the extremes of victory and defeat by embracing both as the pattern of events plays itself out.

Thus, the ritualized game of this novel, unlike the schemes, intrigues, and plots of other nineteenth-century novels, realigns the characters without destroying, eliminating, or defeating anyone. In *The Golden Bowl,* Maggie resists the temptation to secure a personal victory for herself in the "game" played by Charlotte and the Prince; she does so by refusing to "play a card that she could play," much as characters in James's early novels resist being drawn into the schemes and plots of others. In his last two major novels, Henry James defines a mode of playing not usually found in nineteenth-century novels. It is, in fact, difficult to imagine many of the characters who populate nineteenth-century novels resisting the temptation that Maggie faces when given the knowledge and the opportunity to crush her opponent.

James's later novels mark a departure from the themes and methods of his earlier novels and short stories, but perhaps even more significantly, they mark a departure from the themes and methods characteristic of many classic novels of the nineteenth century. The endings of some of these other novels do, of course, offer glimpses of the harmony and equilibrium that play produces—for instance, the epilogue of *Crime and Punishment,* or the endings of the Dorothea Brooke story in George Eliot's *Middlemarch* and the Levin story in Tolstoy's *Anna Karenina.* These endings do suggest a "transcendental" resolution to conflict, which permits the characters to reach beyond commonplace experience, with its limitations and restrictions. Perhaps even more clearly than the endings of *The Wings of the Dove* and *The Golden*

Bowl, the endings of these other novels suggest a ritual-like solidarity between individuals, and between the individual and the environment, which corrupted games preclude. These endings, are, in fact, opposed to other kinds of endings within the same novels—Svidrigaylov's suicide in *Crime and Punishment,* Anna's death in *Anna Karenina,* and Lydgate's failures in *Middlemarch.* What makes the ritualized games of Henry James's later novels unique is an emphasis on the process through which ritual-like solidarity is achieved. In James's later novels, the initial game, the "dreadful game," is not left behind or mystically transcended, as in these earlier novels by Eliot, Tolstoy, and Dostoevsky. Rather, the ritualized realignment of the characters plays itself out as the novel is resolved. By exploring this process, James suggests new possibilities for relationships, for answering questions of morality, and for the novel form itself.

Whenever the realm of play collides with the realm of everyday experience, as it does in so many nineteenth-century novels, almost irreparable consequences result. For a novelist to use the language of games to describe events does not minimize or trivialize the experience of the characters, just as to speak of language or art or religion as play does not make them less important or serious. That the "game" in these novels so often becomes "dreadful" does not necessarily mean either that human experience is devalued or that play itself is inherently dangerous and destructive. The metaphor of the dreadful game does, however, question the relationship of play to experience and the assumptions behind such mutually exclusive distinctions as winning and losing, success and failure, the moral and the immoral act. The *opposition* inherent in the movement of play becomes *rivalry* in the context of corrupted games; in much the same way, success in corrupted games is defined as victory over another, at the expense of another. Many nineteenth-century novels seem either to deny the possibility of ludic reconciliation, portraying instead the inescapability of conflict, or to resolve such conflict only through some kind of transcendent experience. A possible reason why nineteenth-century fiction seems to preclude the possibilities of play, in other words, why other nineteenth-century novelists do not suggest, as Henry James does in his last two novels, a way of restoring the essential qualities of play to the gamelike structures of experience, may lie in some prevalent nineteenth-century ideas about the nature of play. These general attitudes toward play are, furthermore, reflected in the characteristic play of the text in nineteenth-century realist fiction.

2

Work and Play

The Games of the Novel

■ Novelists often rely on the language of games and play to describe how characters pursue their desires, but rarely is this "plot-game" the only "game" a novel plays. Every novelistic text plays a particular kind of game with its readers: by encouraging them to participate in the play of language and ideas, by making them believe in the imagined world of the text, or even by challenging them to solve a particular problem or puzzle. At the same time, the narrator of a novel sometimes plays a game at the expense of the characters, concealing things from them, revealing things to the reader that characters could never know, sometimes making characters appear ignorant or foolish in the reader's eyes. Although almost every novel plays out these three relationships—character to character, text to reader, narrator to character—some novels emphasize the narrator's game with the characters, while other novels indulge enthusiastically in the play of the text with the reader. The way in which a particular novelistic text balances these three "games" provides clues for interpreting its meaning. The nineteenth-century Realist novel is somewhat unique in its emphasis on the games of the characters—in other words, on the plot-games of the novel—and its apparent lack of interest in, even suppression of games between the reader and the text and between narrator and characters.

The nineteenth-century novel flourishes in an age that values work over play and science over the imagination. For Johann Huizinga, writing in the late 1930s, the nineteenth century seems like a dark and dismal moment in the history of what he calls "Western Civilization *Sub Specie Ludi*":

> [T]he great currents of [nineteenth-century] thought, however looked at, were all inimical to the play-factor in social life. Neither liberalism or socialism offered it any nourishment. . . . Realism, Naturalism, Impressionism, and the rest of that dull catalogue of literary and pictorial coteries were all emptier of the play-spirit than any of the earlier styles had been. Never had an age taken itself with more portentous seriousness. Culture ceased to be "played.". . . Work and production become the ideal, and then the idol, of the age.[1]

Whether or not one agrees with Huizinga's antipathy toward nineteenth-century culture—or even his definitions of "play" and "culture"—two questions emerge from the argument he makes here: did nineteenth-century culture privilege work over play, thus suppressing the "play-spirit"? And is nineteenth-century Realism (especially realist or naturalist fiction) antithetical to the "play-spirit" found in the artistic styles that preceded it? Responses to these questions help to explain the kinds of games that structure the nineteenth-century Realist novel.

Comparing the words of Schiller and Carlyle on the subject of play helps to illustrate the argument that Huizinga makes about the apparent resistance to play in nineteenth-century culture. Near the end of the eighteenth century, Schiller writes that play is the highest expression of an individual's humanity; play, he argues, makes man most completely human. Less than half a century later, Thomas Carlyle, an early admirer of Schiller, would, in effect, turn this thesis upside down. In *Past and Present* (1843), he argues that "the only happiness a brave man ever troubled himself with asking much about was, happiness enough to get his work done. . . . [A] man perfects himself by working."[2] For Carlyle, work, *not* play, which he characterizes as idleness and dilettantism, validates human experience and gives the individual life meaning. He even urges readers to "know what thou canst work at," rather than trying to "know thyself." The concept of the "self" is hopelessly elusive, Carlyle seems to suggest, but work provides the individual with an indisputable identity. The opportunity to validate oneself through work was not restricted to men. As Priscilla Robertson explains in her history of women in the nineteenth century, the "cult of domesticity" that flourished among nineteenth-century women of the middle classes "offered women a duty parallel with the work ethic that the industrial

Dreadful Games

system pressed upon men."[3] Clearly, many people worked simply to survive, to earn the money to feed their families; but arguments like Carlyle's began to confer a value on their efforts that exceeded the monetary compensation they received for working. People began to believe that work is inherently admirable and idleness reprehensible; work is the individual's duty and play what keeps him or her from it.

Although what has come to be called the "work ethic" has its origins in seventeenth-century Puritanism, by the nineteenth century, and even in those cultures relatively untouched by Puritan theology, work attained a greater value than it ever had in the past, a result of both the impact of theology on social life and changes in the economic structure of most Western nations. Differences between conditions in different nations prove less significant than similarities in social life throughout Europe and America. As Max Weber argues in *The Protestant Ethic and the Spirit of Capitalism* (1905), the work ethic is perhaps best understood as a result of the economics of industrial labor and the discipline and conformity it demanded, as well as the rational and ascetic tendencies of Post-Reformation religious beliefs and practices. Even in a country like imperial Russia—where the Industrial Revolution came late, where the Reformation never came, and where Utilitarianism and Positivism remained on the intellectual fringes of philosophical discourse—important and influential books, like Chernyshevsky's *What Is To Be Done* (1863), explored the problems of industrial labor and the lives of the working classes. Progressives like Tolstoy's alter ego Levin in *Anna Karenina* tried, albeit futilely, to make peasant workers more disciplined and more productive. Everywhere the life of work was described and analyzed. As Weber points out, the nineteenth century witnessed a "rationalization" of all aspects of culture.[4] The Reformation stripped earlier forms of Christianity of many of their liturgical aspects; for many believers, religious observance was no longer "played," and a dominant theme in much Protestant theology was that of "play as a sinful waste of time."[5] Work was clearly the more righteous, or "godly," enterprise.

Cut off from play, religion often becomes joyless and dogmatic in its approach to moral questions—an effect that was not limited to the religious observances of Protestants. In the words that Kurt Reinhardt uses to describe the "bourgeois religious experience" of both Catholics and Protestants beginning in the nineteenth century, "the promise of salvation is handled like a business transaction. . . . If they play by the rules, they cannot miss."[6] Thus, for middle-class citizens, both Catholic and Protestant, of many Western nations, belief becomes a contractual arrangement, with rights and duties on all sides. The game metaphor here, as elsewhere, highlights the way an aspect of human experience can be depleted of the essential qualities of play. Play, by definition, mediates the extremes of experience, creates a middle ground where values can be tested. Without this middle ground, values become polarized and ethical choices limited and narrowly legalistic. As theology becomes more rationalized and less playful, religious experience becomes an empty shell of form without essence.

What may make nineteenth-century attitudes even more significant than the value placed on work is the extent to which work and play oppose one another in such philosophies. Many twentieth-century writers have argued that for preindustrial society, the opposition of work and play—especially of work and lesiure—remains an alien concept. Victor Turner shows that in ritual and myth and even in the legal processes of tribal and agrarian culture, "work and play are hardly distinguishable."[7] Where men and women work on the land and derive their concept of time from nature, and where their festivals and rituals and celebrations arise from this work—when they celebrate the spring planting or the autumn harvest, for example—work and play are complementary modes of expression. But in the nineteenth century, more and more people find themselves living not on farms in the countryside but in tenements in rapidly growing towns and cities. For individuals whose lives are no longer ordered by the rhythms of nature—for the bourgeoisie in commerce or in the bureaucracies, or for the growing industrial worker classes—work was no longer celebrated as it had been in the past. Under these new circumstances, workers become "alienated," to use a Marxist term, not only from the products of their labors, but perhaps more significantly, from any kind of play that would celebrate their working experience. In such an environment, work and play both become mediated experiences: in the words of one writer, "one cannot play while he works, but he can play *after* work with the money earned *during* work."[8] Work and play must be pursued at different times, each at the "expense" of the other.

Nineteenth-century attitudes toward work and play influenced the craft of fiction writing. For the Romantic poets, as Lionel Trilling argues, "pleasure was the defining attribute of life itself and nature itself," and pleasure that, according to Wordsworth, constituted "the native and naked dignity of man."[9] Art is valued, according to this principle, precisely for the pleasure it gives and for the feeling and emotion it expresses. Art reconciles opposition, offering the individual a means to resolve the split between self and other. But these attitudes—toward pleasure and toward art—begin to shift by midcentury, just as Realism becomes the dominant mode of literary art. Much as Carlyle urged the ordinary man to validate himself through his work, and steadfastly refused to associate man's dignity with the pleasure principle, Balzac is credited with giving "younger writers the terse advice of a self-made industrialist: 'Work!' "[10] For the novelist so inspired, art becomes a means to an end, not an end in itself. As the nineteenth century progressed, more and more writers earned a comfortable living through writing, in contrast to earlier generations for whom writing either provided little financial reward or served as a pleasurable pastime or passionate avocation. Nineteenth-century fiction developed in the shadow of the work ethic, and writers were not likely to remain untouched by the attitudes like those that Carlyle expressed. Writing became work, not play, validated as such by payment, and writers who wrote in their leisure time, for their own "pleasure," could well be considered dilettantes.

Much in the practice of literary realism seems more "ergic" than "ludic" (to use Victor Turner's distinction[11]), more concerned with the problems of work than with the possibilities of play. And this ergic quality often distinguishes realist fiction from fiction that proves more difficult to classify. Many realist novels convey their earnestness and seriousness in unmistakable ways. This is not to say that other, earlier and later novelists were not "serious" about the novels they produced, but rather that realist fiction is "serious" in different ways and for different reasons. In "The Art of Fiction" (1884), Henry James accuses the English novelist Anthony Trollope of a "want of discretion" in this regard. James argues that fiction should take itself seriously, that the novelist should speak "with the tone of the historian." Trollope, to James's dismay, "admits that the events he narrates have not really happened, and . . . gives his narrative any turn the reader may like best."[12] James suggests that the novelist should resist the temptation to remind the reader that the novel presents a fictional version of reality. In other words, the novelist should resist the temptation to tell readers the truth about his or her fictional enterprise. To follow James's thinking to its logical conclusion, the novelist's success depends on working to deceive the readers—a task accomplished by taking the novelistic project as seriously as possible.

Realist fiction reflects the world from which it arises in a unique and special way, which today's readers may even take for granted, expecting fiction to portray ordinary life and praising plausible and intelligible characters. As Linda Nochlin points out, however, nineteenth-century critics of Realism "frequently berated artists and writers for reducing the great themes of Western art and literature—the transcendental issues of life and death—to the banal level of mere commonplace, everyday reality."[13] Realists explored what most readers considered the traditional themes of "tragedy," but allowed characters perceived as "comic" to play them out, thus attempting to embrace both kinds of dramatic experience in the novel form. The experience of labor and the lives of "ordinary people" became the favorite subjects of nineteenth-century writers and artists. Novelists devoted themselves to presenting precise details about the world often shared by both reader and character. When they wrote about unusual experiences or places, they ensured the accuracy of their efforts with painstaking research and observation. They sought to represent without exaggeration or sentimentality what they considered to be the "facts" of the material world, and to avoid exaggeration and sentimentality, they strove to remain objective about the characters and places and events they described.

The realist novel portrays the fictional world and represents the material world in a way that influences the game that the realist text plays with the reader. Readers are assured of the accuracy of the fictional world before they participate in the experience of the characters. They are persuaded that the events of the novel are not only "possible," but "probable," and the text does not encourage the reader to question the truth of the fictional world. Robert Alter argues that "nineteenth-century novelists are, with rare exceptions (like Gogol, emulating Sterne), disinclined to play with the fictive status of their fictions." Novels like Sterne's *Tristram Shandy* or Diderot's *Jacques le fataliste* portray their fictional worlds as what Alter calls "authorial construct[s] set up against a background of literary tradition and convention."[14] Realists are clearly not less "imaginative" than their predecessors, most having imagined quite believable fictional worlds, but they do avoid reminding the reader that these vast and complex fictional worlds are, after all, products of the imagination. The imagination—so highly valued in itself by the Romantics of an earlier generation—and the play of the imagination that renews itself in endless repetition become for the nineteenth-century Realist almost purely instrumental. Process is subordinated to end result, to product. Realist writers use the fictional imagination as a means to explicate and interpret the "real"

Dreadful Games

world, to present what are, for them, the "facts" about the experiences of their own contemporaries. To do so, they must assert, paradoxically, that their "fictions" are not "fictional" but "factual." Realists are unwilling to risk what Franz Stanzel calls "the playful upsetting of the illusion of the fictional world."[15] The illusion of "fact" must be maintained at all costs.

If nineteenth-century Realists resisted the playful tendencies of the text, they did so not only because so many contemporary voices idealized work, but because the dominant philosophical ideas of the age worshiped "science." Positivism, Utilitarianism, Darwinism, and Marxism all assert to some degree that "truth" arises only from "scientific" experimentation and empirical, verifiable knowledge, especially knowledge acquired by the senses. Knowledge obtained by other methods is suspect, even worthless; the imagination is a source of error. One declaration of this "faith" in the methods of science is found in Ernest Renan's *The Future of Science* (1848–49): "The beautiful is not in analysis; but the real beauty, which is not based on human fictions and fantasies, is hidden in the result of analysis. . . . [T]he true world which science reveals to us is much superior to the fantastic world created by the imagination."[16] Renan argues that "science" can reveal things that the imagination never could, and that science, not the imagination, should be the source of all art, even of poetry. What Renan calls "fiction" fails to reveal, in his mind, any "truth" about the world. Novelists who shared this philosophical viewpoint found themselves compelled to deny the "fictional" or imaginative basis of their novels, simply to ensure the validity of the ideas and experiences they presented. The analogy of art to science was carried to extremes. By the end of the century, Zola had asserted that the novel is a scientific experiment, and that characters could be combined and studied like chemical compounds. Nineteenth-century philosophy placed an unprecedented emphasis on the value of empirical data, and in response to this emphasis, novelists found themselves filling their fictional worlds with all kinds of facts and details taken from the world of everyday experience.

But a novel that somehow denies it is "fictional" must ultimately play a game of deception with its readers. The messages that frame or encapsulate the text and reader in the play of language, idea, and story are, in this situation, inherently confused. The contract between the reader and the text is premised on an almost insurmountable contradiction. The "success" of the novelist's efforts—especially if, as critics often argue, "our highest recommendation for a work of fiction is that it be as unlike fiction as possible"[17]—depends on the ability of the text to conceal something about itself, or more precisely, to conceal its origins in the novelist's imagination. As Marthe Robert says in *Origins of the Novel,* "a novel can only be convincingly truthful when it is utterly deceitful, with all the skill and earnestness required to ensure the success of its deception."[18] The realist novel is, for these reasons, almost inevitably a species of "false play," where the novelist insists to his or her reader, "this is not play."

This problematic position reveals itself in the realist text in different ways. Imagery in realist fiction, as in realist painting, tends to be precise, and more significantly, less symbolic than metonymic, "that linking of elements by sheer contiguity."[19] As a result, the realist text often resists the ambiguity, or "play," of transcendent or multiple meanings.[20] Realist fiction is also highly visual, in a way that contrasts with the play of language in a text by Sterne or Diderot or Gogol, or even with with word play of characters in the earliest novels of manners. In distinguishing between the visual and aural "motives" of fiction, James Guetti argues that "the aural process is so overtly and rootedly the aspect of play. While the visual experience of fiction can be documented and discussed much as fact and ideas can, . . . the aural experience is conspicuously non-progressive and non-productive. So it may seem childish."[21] An "aurally motivated" fiction, which calls attention to its own telling, would no doubt seem distinctly inappropriate to a novelist wanting to produce a more "scientific" fiction. The reliance on visual imagery in the realist novel is analogous to the nineteenth-century scientist's insistence on "empirical evidence." By excluding the aural motive from fiction and limiting linguistic play, the realist seeks to produce fiction with a more serious, less "childish" tone about it— fiction that seems somehow less fictional.

Inasmuch as realist fiction explores the forms and structures of life, character in realist fiction always derives from some force or system that can be defined and analyzed. Characters "perform" their fictional roles against either a precisely detailed material environment, or a fixed, carefully defined system of social behavior, and in some cases, both. Novelists thus make their characters plausible and lifelike, and in doing so, they exclude those implausible or unintelligible aspects of the human personality that earlier fictional styles exploit. Just as the realist must convince readers that the fictional world is factual, she or he must persuade them that the characters are faithful reproductions of "real"

Dreadful Games

people, typical and exemplary, case studies that illustrate some "fact" about contemporary life. And clearly, such writers succeed, since most readers discuss the characters of realist novels as if they had lives and histories of their own outside the fictional world, as if they were "beings" and not as if they were components of a narrative structure.[22]

But "success" in this regard comes, once again, at the expense of the play of the text, in this case at the expense of what Leo Bersani calls "the playful subversion of psychological intelligibility,"[23] which a reader might find, once again, in a novel by Sterne or Diderot or Gogol. For Bersani, characterization in the nineteenth-century novel reveals a fear of what might be called a marginal or fragmented self. If not "fear," the realist novel most certainly reveals a reluctance to subscribe to a perception of human psychology as anything less than stable or consistent or coherent, in other words as something that might be performed and reperformed in a number of different ways, reenacted through the manipulation of language or gesture or role, and most importantly, at the will of the novelist. The realist seems reluctant to present character in terms less scientific than those describing any other phenomenon in the natural world. Characters must be made of something more substantial than words and the author's intentions.

Not only does the textual play of realist fiction differ from that of earlier fiction, but the games that characters play in so many nineteenth-century novels differ as well. Game metaphors in novels bring to mind different kinds of conventional games, based on different skills and prompted by different desires. Huizinga writes that there are two main game motifs in literature: the theme of strife and one that he calls "the game of hidden being."[24] The language of games in nineteenth-century novels more often suggests games of strife and conflict than games of hidden being. In some cases the two motifs overlap, as for instance, when a character plays a game of hidden being as a tactic in a competitive game. But despite its virtual absence from the nineteenth-century novel, the game of hidden being is often played in earlier forms of literature, structuring both narrative and dramatic plots where characters seek to learn something about themselves or another. Shakespeare's *Measure for Measure* and Marivaux's *The Game of Love and Chance* [Le Jeu de l'amour et du hasard] provide examples, from drama, of this game metaphor.[25] These examples help to illustrate how the game of hidden being determines plots, suggesting how novelists would later transform these plots for their own purposes.

The game of hidden being has two related but distinct aspects: first, a character must conceal his or her own identity, then must create for himself or herself a new identity, persuading others to believe it. Thus, mimicry is the instinct that motivates and guides players, but the game of hidden being is also both a game of concealment and a game of deception. Players must re-create the behavior and mannerisms of a role model—either another character, or a type or personality that both the other characters and the audience will recognize. For example, in Shakespeare's play, the Duke conceals his identity by assuming the role of a friar, while in *The Game of Love and Chance,* the characters exchange identities with one another. The game proves pleasurable for both the participants and the observers—that is, for both the characters and the audience—whenever a player captures some nuance of the role model's character, or alternatively, when a participant finds it impossible to duplicate the behavior of the role model, as when Lisette has to play the part of her mistress in Marivaux's play. Since the game of hidden being is a performance game, there are no prescribed rules that must be followed, as there are in competitive games. The imitated roles provide the "rules" of the game. The flexibility inherent in a situation where players must interpret their roles, playing them in their own distinctive ways, makes the game of hidden being potentially "fun."

Along with the possibilities for play, that is, the opportunities for both gaining knowledge and having fun, the game of hidden being is not without risks. For one thing, a character rarely exchanges roles with another or assumes a new identity without having some purpose in mind—some ulterior motive—in doing so. In *Measure for Measure,* the Duke assumes the identity of a friar in order to test the limits of Angelo's moral judgment and also to illustrate to him the harshness and hypocrisy inherent in some of the judgments he has already made. Similarly, in *The Game of Love and Chance,* by exchanging roles with her maid, Silvia can observe Dorante secretly before she consents to marry him. She is unaware that Dorante and his valet have made a corresponding exchange, for much the same reason. In both plays, the game risks becoming too "serious," even dangerous, in direct proportion to how much players are willing to risk in order to obtain the kind of knowledge they seek. The games are inherently dangerous because from the beginning the impulses of play are subordinated to individual goals. The game of hidden being in these plays is, in turn, subordinated to what amounts in both situations to the game of chance, where players wager to gain something even more valuable than what they risk.

Dreadful Games

The game of hidden being is pursued in both plays to elicit knowledge about another, and for this reason, these are not gratuitous games. Silvia risks a great deal in her game; she has much to lose. Instead of revealing her own identity when she learns that Dorante and his valet have exchanged places, she continues playing the part of Lisette. She has already learned how much she loves Dorante; by continuing to play Lisette, she seeks to learn how much he loves that part of herself that playing Lisette does not diminish. The role she plays as Lisette allows her to reveal a "truer," more essential self to Dorante. But in pushing the game that much further, Silvia risks losing Dorante, by allowing him to believe she is only a maid. In Geoffrey Brereton's words, "she stakes relative happiness for the jackpot of total happiness."[26] The Duke's game in *Measure for Measure* becomes somewhat more dangerous as it progresses, not so much for the Duke but for those whom he deceives. Whereas Silvia risks her own happiness in playing the game of concealment, the Duke risks not his own, but other people's happiness in his game of deception. The happiness of Isabella, Mariana, and Claudio, not to mention Angelo, all depend on the success of the Duke's scheme. In fact, the only thing the Duke himself risks in playing his game is being proved wrong about how Angelo and the others will respond in a given situation. The thematic difficulties of this play arise precisely from the degree to which the Duke is willing to risk the happiness and well-being of others in his game with Angelo. Both *Measure for Measure* and *The Game of Love and Chance* involve not only hidden identities but hidden risks as well, which threaten to move each play toward some "dreadful" resolution.

But despite the risks, both games resolve these dangers, each having accomplished pretty much what the initial players had hoped. The possible consequences of having risked one's identity or happiness remain only unrealized possibilities. For Marivaux's Silvia the risk pays off; she ends up with even more happiness than she had bargained for in playing her game. That the potentially destructive energy of these games is never released can be explained in more than one way. First, the conventions of comic drama, even of a "problem" comedy like *Measure for Measure,* preclude the kind of "dreadful" ending that a reader might expect to find in a realist novel, where the traditions of comedy and tragedy are commingled. Furthermore, unlike a realist novel, where facts and details make the fictional world resemble the actual world, these plays perpetuate an air of unreality; the playwrights do not strive to convince the audience that such events or characters exist independently of the shared imaginary world. This air of unreality undermines the anxiety that the character's actions might otherwise engender. Because the world of each of these plays is undoubtedly the dramatist's invention, the characters' actions seem somehow less consequential, less risky. Finally, in playing the game of hidden being, the characters in each play demonstrate a desire to attain an otherwise unattainable knowledge about themselves and others. Consequently, their goal in playing the game of hidden being is consistent with the results that such a game often produces. In contrast to fictional games that seem unlikely to ever satisfy the desires that inspire them, here the game of hidden being resolves the conflict that gives rise to it.

The dramatist's problems with plot making and game playing are not unlike the problems that the novelist faces. In *Don Quixote,* a protoypical realist novel, Cervantes explores some other dimensions of the game of hidden being, as well as many of the risks that arise in the playing of it. Like the characters in *Measure for Measure* and *The Game of Love and Chance,* Don Quixote plays a game of hidden being: he conceals his own identity and creates for himself the identity of a knight-errant. But there are some significant differences in the way that Don Quixote plays this game. He does not play it because he wants to learn about someone or something; his game does not arise from a desire for knowledge or self-awareness. But his game is nonetheless compensatory. He plays because he has read the romances of knight-errantry, and he would prefer that life to the one he leads as a country gentleman. In this sense, he attempts to resolve the conflict between the way he finds the world and the way he would like it to be. Regardless of whether Don Quixote is mad or sane, he seeks to create for himself a world that can exist only in his imagination. And while the Friar/Duke and Sylvia/Lisette are always aware of their other identities—the identities they will reclaim when the game is finished—Don Quixote surrenders his entire being to the game, submerging his own identity in the role he plays. The narrator participates in this aspect of the game by insisting that Don Quixote's former identity is irrelevant. From the time that this country gentleman, who now calls himself Don Quixote, leaves for his first adventures, he is not "playing" Don Quixote as much as he has "become" Don Quixote through an act of sheer will. Cervantes thus illustrates one of the dangers implicit in the game of hidden being: the risk that in playing out an assumed identity players begin to lose their own identities.

Cervantes raises another problem that did not concern either Shakespeare or Marivaux: the rules of the game his character plays. When characters imitate one another or assume some common, recognizable role, their task is much simpler. In creating his new identity, Don Quixote relies on the role models provided by the books he has read. He calls on his memories of these books for the appropriate responses to given situations. But these memories do not provide him with hard and fast rules of conduct; he must recall and interpret the texts he has read in order to forumlate the rules. The novel illustrates again and again how Don Quixote's "rules" can be revised and reinterpreted, as for example, when the innkeeper Don Quixote meets in his first adventures sends him home for clean shirts, calming the knight's fears that such preparations might violate the spirit of the romances. Don Quixote himself is quick to reinterpret a rule when circumstances warrant such expediency.

The problem of the "rules" of Don Quixote's game is the problem posed by all acts of interpretation. When Don Quixote brings Sancho Panza into his game, the rules must be defined more carefully, since Sancho cannot interpret the text to find the rules in the same way that Don Quixote, or even the innkeeper, can. In Part I of the novel, Sancho Panza neither understands nor respects the rules, but he strives to attain a formal understanding of them, so that he can manipulate them to serve his own interests. Sancho consciously seeks material gain in playing Don Quixote's game; he seeks to satisfy his desires for food, money, and luxury. Even that quintessential mediated desire, the island, is, in Sancho's mind, a means to his other ends. He believes that if he can only master the rules Don Quixote teaches him, all his desires will be satisfied. For him, the game is merely a means to an end, and he derives no particular joy from playing it, especially when satisfaction persists in eluding him. In the character of Sancho Panza, especially as he is portrayed in the first part of the novel, Cervantes shows that the player who merely "plays by the rules," without understanding them, risks his own happiness.

Other characters attempt to enter Don Quixote's game, but there is often something contradictory, even "false," about the way they play, since they are often amusing themselves at Don Quixote's expense. Others often subordinate Don Quixote's game to their own desires for amusement, self-satisfaction, or personal gain. Many of the conflicts in the novel arise from the collision of Don Quixote's "game world" with the "real fictional world," in which the events of his game take place. The metaphor of the game helps Cervantes to emphasize the conflict of values, sparked whenever past and present clash. Whenever Don Quixote tries to apply the rules of his game to a world that does not acknowledge those rules, as he does again and again, the results are potentially disastrous.

The dangers inherent in the game of hidden being reveal themselves not only in Don Quixote's game, but also in the way Cervantes narrates the story. The text itself plays a game of hidden being with the reader, attempting to conceal its identity as fiction. The narrator "pretends" to acknowledge and to conform to the rules and conventions of other narrative genres, when in fact, Cervantes has created a novel that catalogues the weaknesses and deficiencies of all those earlier genres.[27] The narrator pretends many other things as well: he pretends not to know about Don Quixote's past, he pretends to lose part of his story, to follow and to comment on inconsistent (and, as the reader cannot help but suspect, imaginary) versions of the story. All of his pretending proves to be a double-edged sword: paradoxically, it calls attention to the telling of the story, to the author's and the reader's awareness that this is fiction, even as the narrator seems to be trying to give the story an illusion of "authority," by denying his own responsibility for its creation. Thus by hyperbole, by arguing that his novel is factual, the narrator makes the novel seem even more fictional. The intensity with which he maintains this illusion of fact and authority is precisely what eventually convinces the reader that it is an illusion. In this way, Cervantes playfully anticipates the problem of the realist who must somehow deny that his novel is fictional, in order to make the image of life it portrays more valid.

The second part of *Don Quixote* illustrates as well how diffuse the boundaries between fiction and "real life" might become. From the beginning of the novel, Don Quixote, the fictional character, seeks literary fame; he wants to find his place among the heroes of chivalric romances that he so admires. The character is granted such fame in the second part, a fame that he has achieved in the "real historical world"— the world outside the game of the text—by the time Cervantes writes part II ten years later. Don Quixote's desire for literary fame is satisfied in the author's own world, a fact that the text seeks to affirm in the episode where Don Quixote meets the Duke and the Duchess. These characters, the narrator asserts, have read of Don Quixote and use their knowledge of his character and exploits to amuse themselves. The boundaries that separate the imaginary world of the literary text from events that happen in the real world begin to crumble, and once again,

Cervantes suggests a problem that the nineteenth-century Realist faces. The more believable (and famous) that novelistic characters become, the more they take on lives of their own. The question of a character's "existence," even of his or her "credibility," becomes more and more confused. The novels of Balzac—who is said on his deathbed to have summoned his own fictional creation, Dr. Bianchon—show how the Realist "tends to make the frontiers of fiction vaguer still."[28] As Marthe Robert points out, Balzac populates *La Comédie humaine* with recurring characters who contribute nothing significant to plot or theme—who seem to exist simply to create the illusion of real life. But because of their privileged status, these characters make the characters who *are* essential to the events and themes of the novel seem like mere inventions, like figments of the novelist's imagination. The novelist whose characters assume lives of their own unwittingly risks alerting the reader to the status of his or her novel as a product of fiction.

In *Don Quixote,* the game of hidden being eventually becomes less important than the games of strife that are played as conflicting interpretations of the world compete for dominance. Competition eventually becomes more important than pretense. The novels of Jane Austen suggest the way in which Huizinga's other game "motif," that of strife or competition, eventually supplants the game of hidden being in the nineteenth-century novel. As the opening pages of *Pride and Prejudice* (1813) reveal, Jane Austen's world is highly competitive in many ways, as characters compete for the prizes they want and play to win. Austen still uses the motif of the game of hidden being to highlight the way characters often conceal their true identities from one another; the structural and verbal irony of her novels often arises from the unmasking of characters' "fictions" about themselves. But as *Mansfield Park* (1814) shows, the risks of the game of hidden being may outweigh the gains. The novel vindicates those characters who eschew playfulness, while assigning appropriate punishments to those who engage most enthusiastically in the "play" that leads to all the major conflicts in the novel.

The central events of the novel concern the presentation of amateur theatricals by a group of virtually unsupervised young people. The novel makes it clear that this activity is unquestionably improper given the circumstances of the participants and the nature of the play chosen for presentation.[29] First of all, Sir Thomas Bertram, the master of the house, has been called away on business, so as a practical matter, his permission cannot be granted. But more importantly, the instigators of the project have selected a play whose characters enter into romances that prove to be disconcertingly similar to the romantic liaisons of Austen's own characters. Maria Bertram, whose engagement is kept secret pending Sir Thomas's return, finds herself playing opposite someone far more exciting and attractive than the man she intends to marry. Edmund Bertram finds himself rehearsing love scenes with a woman for whom he has a growing infatuation. The play thus becomes a way of acting out the love scenes about which the characters might fantasize but could never attempt outside the context of these rehearsals. As a consequence, the play becomes a vehicle through which the characters can pursue their most selfish and self-destructive—and "improper"—desires, as well as a vehicle to further the naturally competitive instincts of the Bertram sisters and Mary Crawford. In this novel, perhaps more clearly than in any of her other novels, Austen is less a novelist influenced by Romantic ideology than she is a Proto-Realist. The process of playing, which, as the Romantics believed, should help to resolve the conflict arising from wanting and not having, here not only fails to resolve conflict but also makes those conflicts virtually irresolvable. Playing is not only risky, but dangerous.

Critics have called *Mansfield Park* Jane Austen's least playful, least ironic novel.[30] Its somber and serious tone contrasts sharply with that of Austen's other novels. Fanny Price is a boring little heroine in comparison to witty, headstrong characters like Elizabeth Bennett and Emma Woodhouse. Fanny, who is ultimately rewarded for her good judgment in refusing to participate in the theatricals, is considerably less charming and sophisticated than any of the novel's other characters, for whom she hardly exists. The novel appears to take a rather prudish view of such frivolous activities as play making and amateur theatricals. But the novel in fact suggests not so much the impropriety of acting per se, as the dangers of playing the game of hidden being in the social world. The role playing in the novel casts an aura of fantasy and romance on the characters' experiences, creating the illusion that their actions have no real consequences, that they are merely playing a pleasantly diverting game to be abandoned at any time. As Martin Price says of the schemes in which Jane Austen's characters involve themselves, "games have every charm until they are used to displace broader awareness and deeper feeling."[31] The games in *Mansfield Park* make the characters less insightful and less self-knowledgeable than they were before they began to play.

In *Mansfield Park,* play acting encourages the characters to idealize

Dreadful Games

one another, all their human faults masked under the romanticized roles they play. Edmund Bertram, for instance, fails to recognize the superficiality of Mary Crawford's moral judgment, while his sister Maria fails to detect Henry Crawford's irresponsibility and lack of commitment. The characters who are unable to shake the illusions fostered in this way pay a heavy price for having played the game. Unlike Austen's other novels, *Mansfield Park* finds no way of resolving conflict, no way of reconciling characters to some common perception, some useful fiction of life. Despite the ostensibly "happy ending," the happiness of some is purchased with the misfortune of others. The ending of the novel includes the disturbing image of a disgraced Maria Bertram, exiled from Mansfield Park along with her foolish Aunt Norris, for sins she cannot completely comprehend. This resolution conforms to the logic of competitive games, where some players emerge triumphant and others retreat, defeated. As they do in other nineteenth-century novels, the games played at Mansfield Park have unmistakably "dreadful" results.

In other nineteenth-century novels, the game of hidden being similarly becomes subordinated to some more clearly competitive goal. In playing games, characters seek to achieve some tangible, valuable goal. Characters recognize that those skills essential to the game of hidden being—for example, an ability to imitate behavior, to manipulate language and gesture, to convey a convincing illusion of some useful "fiction"—might be used to satisfy ambitions that could not be realized otherwise. Some characters educate themselves to the forms of social behavior, learning the "rules" of different "games," much as Sancho Panza does, without any real sense of what the rules mean or of what values they promote. Characters who insist on the truth of an imagined, often intensely desired, but nonetheless illusionary vision of the world often find themselves playing out their desires in a game that leads toward some "dreadful" conclusion. Like Don Quixote, characters often come to believe those illusions they have fostered and find themselves "competing" against those who do not share these visions.

The imagery of conflict and strife is pervasive in nineteenth-century Realist fiction; images of competitive games dominate even those novels that seem more textually "playful"—such as Lewis Carroll's *Alice in Wonderland,* Mark Twain's *Adventures of Huckleberry Finn,* or Gogol's *Dead Souls*—novels that somehow manage to escape the formal paradoxes of classical Realism. F. D. Reeve has noted that in Gogol, the game between the reader and the text often becomes a way for the

Work and Play

author to show his superiority to the reader: "Gogol set up his literary traps with precision. . . . [T]o deceive a reader confirmed his own power."[32] Like other nineteenth-century novels even these more playful novels share the same vision of life that folklorist Thomas Burns finds reflected in a popular nineteenth-century board game, The Checkered Game of Life. This game portrays life as "a very individualistic, competitive, anti-social adventure. . . . Encounters with others are to be avoided unless they are self-controlled and then only when one desires to injure another. While one is encouraged to create such encounters and so to hamper other players when they are more successful than oneself, one is almost never forced to behave aggressively toward others."[33] The creativity essential to the game of hidden being is of little advantage in such a game. A polite, fair-minded parlor game thus conceals a subtext of self-interest, in which success can be achieved most effectively by hindering the progress of another. So too, the "manners" of society, the code of gentlemanly behavior, or the etiquette of business life frequently conceal the amoral ruthlessness of individual goals and efforts.

In the context of social life, as reflected in the Realist novel, strategy replaces performance, and even the performance of self becomes a kind of tactic in some larger scheme. In such a world, even an individual's pursuit of leisure becomes, as Veblen shows in *Theory of the Leisure Class* (1899), a form of competition.[34] Characters' voices, ideologies, and moral values all compete for dominance in a world where winning the game is often preferred to speaking the truth; success is measured mathematically, a ratio of victories to defeats. Characters in nineteenth-century novels devise games or, where expedient, participate in those devised by others as a means of ensuring their own successes. They are often more than willing to injure another to achieve a victory. And the novelist underlines these "facts" of life by the words he chooses. The language of games in the nineteenth-century novel suggests a world where strife is inevitable, and hypocrisy easily justified.

3

Games of Ambition

Stendhal's *Le Rouge et le noir*

■ The person driven by ambition—the *ambitieux,* to use Stendhal's own word—craves distinction. Convinced of his superiority, he pursues any course of action, acts out any plausible strategy, to ensure that others recognize and appreciate his talents and merits. Pursuing one's ambitions often becomes a means of self-validation: success confirms what the *ambitieux* already believes about his abilities. The *ambitieux* often combines vanity with the most unmitigated self-interest. Since "the world has limited prizes to offer,"[1] an ambitious person finds himself locked into endless rivalries, competing with anyone who seeks the same forms of recognition. He often wants what others already have; his desires frequently are, in René Girard's term, "mediated." Hoping to acquire distinction, he may pursue social status, political power, wealth, or romantic conquest—whichever "prizes" his world offers, whatever possessions those around him value. Limited only by the imagination and daring of the *ambitieux,* and by his ability to transform and manipulate his own image, ambition often remains both insatiable and all-consuming, ultimately embracing and reflecting all other desires.

Ambition plays itself out in different ways and with different results. Individuals formulate unique strategies in the effort to realize their ambitions. Hard work, skill, and fortuitous timing are often enough to ensure that individuals will rise in life, particularly where they can apply themselves to some business or trade, where they find appropri-

Games of Ambition

ate outlets for their energies. Examples from nineteenth-century novels illustrate this type of ambition: Balzac's Père Goriot makes a fortune selling vermicelli; William Dean Howells's Silas Lapham develops and markets a new type of paint; and Henry James's Christopher Newman puts his energies into a number of ventures, making a great deal of money. But significantly, each consolidates his gains before the novel begins. Most nineteenth-century novels do not prescribe for success so much as they describe the patterns of failure. Goriot's obsessive love and ambition for his daughters ruin him; Silas Lapham's carelessness brings his unfinished house to the ground; Christopher Newman fails to win the woman he loves. In each novel, the course of ambition runs past success toward failure, suggesting not only the risks but also the limits of action motivated by ambition.

As much as these three novels differ in tone—Silas Lapham's business defeat is, after all, portrayed by the optimistic Howells as a moral victory—the intensity of the character's ambition makes each one vulnerable to failure. These novels also suggest that hard work and good timing are not always enough to ensure lasting and continuing success. Perhaps most clearly in *The American,* the character's failure demonstrates that all things are *not* necessarily possible. Christopher Newman's experience before the novel begins has taught him that hard work and good fortune make for success; but the events of the novel show that others often realize their ambitions not through such concerted efforts, but by means of deceit, duplicity, intrigues, and plots. There are some things that a man of integrity, such as James has portrayed in Christopher Newman, cannot bring himself to do, even in order to realize clearly defined ambitions. The confirmed *ambitieux,* in contrast, is willing to take any steps, ruthless or deceitful, to secure the prize. Simply stated, ambition wears two faces: in some circumstances, it can inspire individuals to tap their own most valuable resources, to achieve greatness through their own efforts; in other circumstances, however, ambition sanctions duplicity of all kinds and fosters the kind of self-interest that devalues and distorts human relationships. The *ambitieux* who believes that the goal justifies any means required to reach it often resorts to such duplicity. In the novel, the language of games often highlights the duality of ambition, suggesting the deceit and self-deception, even the potential violence, of action motivated by personal ambition. And the way in which these metaphorical games subvert the spirit of play shows how easily games of ambition become dreadful.

That the end justifies the means is an enduring theme of novels that

Dreadful Games

chronicle the exploits of an *ambitieux,* and it is often an acceptance of this principle that leads both character and narrator to use the language of games. In *The Aspern Papers* (1888), Henry James explores the effect of what might be called "blind ambition" and in doing so helps to explain how the play of the character and the play of the narrator sometimes intersect in novels of ambition. By absorbing the game of narrator and character into the game between reader and text, this short novel balances the games of the novel more skillfully and imaginatively than many longer novels do. *The Aspern Papers* provides an archetypal model for all novels of ambition.

The narrator-protagonist seeks to succeed where others have failed in obtaining the private papers of a long-dead poet. To do so, he must persuade an old woman, who had once loved this poet, Jeffrey Aspern, to surrender her treasured mementos. The narrator enshrines his ambition in lofty language: he and his "fellow-worshipper" of Aspern have "appointed themselves" the "ministers" at the "temple" of the dead poet's reputation.[2] Even in his own mind, the narrator seeks to vindicate his cause; this crusade for "truth" and "knowledge," especially the truth about the poet's romantic affairs, justifies all his efforts to obtain the papers. And yet, his own language frames his actions as a game. While admitting to the "personal, delicate, intimate" nature of the documents, he tells his confidante that "hypocrisy, duplicity are my only chance"; to take a direct approach, he argues, "should certainly spoil the game." He makes his intentions clear: "I'm sorry for it, but there is no baseness I wouldn't commit for Jeffrey Aspern's sake" (475). In this way, he justifies in advance any action that he may take, but he does so in a paradoxical fashion: games, of course, have no ethical value, but he insists that what he calls his "game" does. Although he argues that his cause is noble, almost sacred, he characterizes his project as a "game" of strategy, cunning, and skill.

To accomplish his goal, the narrator conceals his true identity and his goals from the old woman—in other words, he plays the game of hidden being in service of his ambitions—and secures lodgings in her palatial house. She accepts his intrusion because of the extraordinary sum he agrees to pay her, ostensibly for the pleasures of her garden. He is willing to invest this large sum of money in his project, assuring himself, "I would make it up by getting hold of my 'spoils' for nothing" (486). He sees in old Miss Bordereau an opponent, a rival for the precious papers, an obstacle to realizing his ambitions, whom he will outmaneuver with skill and cunning and deception. By trying to convince both the reader and himself that she too is a strategist, he seeks to guard against any suggestion that he victimizes her. Even though he deliberately deceives her, he seeks to create, for himself and for the reader, the illusion of fair play.

As weeks and months pass without much "success," he attributes to her actions all the gamelike ulteriority of his own. As he sees it, she seeks to extort as much of his money as she can without offering anything in return. He takes pleasure meanwhile, in his own patient tactics, such as sending flowers to the old woman and her niece, seeking to ingratiate himself with both of them, waiting for an opportunity to pursue his ambitions more directly. He finds satisfaction in these actions at first, explaining to the reader that "the sense of playing with my own opportunity was much greater after all than any of being played with" (496). But his desire for the papers grows more intense as success continues to elude him. His moves in the game become bolder, and in the process, he underestimates what his ambitions might ultimately cost.

His "monomania" blinds him to every possible consequence of his actions. The telling of the story is itself transformed, as the narrator focuses more and more intensely on his own desire. Old Miss Bordereau dies, and the papers pass to her niece, who offers them to the narrator in return for marriage. He is stunned. Where he had sought to cultivate an ally, he finds yet another opponent, another obstacle to surmount. Horrified at the unexpected turn of events, he withdraws and considers his actions: "I had said . . . that I would make love to her; but it had been a joke without consequences and I had never said it to my victim" (560). He has done nothing wrong, he insists, in manipulating his "victim," the desperate and dependent Miss Tina; he has merely followed a carefully plotted strategy and adhered to his own rules. Like many an *ambitieux*, he follows a rigidly legalistic view of right and wrong, based on the premise that his actions do not actually transgress any moral code.

Rather than account for the pain he has caused Miss Tina, not to mention her aunt, the narrator remains consistently self-centered: "I grew to wish I had never heard of Aspern's relics. . . . We had more than enough material without them, and my predicament was the just punishment of that most fatal of human follies, our not having known when to stop" (562). But his apparent moment of insight is short-lived. By morning he has had a change of heart and longs once again to obtain the papers: "The condition that Miss Tina had attached to that act no longer appeared an obstacle worth thinking of" (562). It is too late, however, to reconsider his options. Miss Tina, having nothing more to gain from the papers, has honored her aunt's request to burn them. James's choice of a first-person narrator makes the implicit indictment of the character's thought and actions more acute: in this character, hypocrisy and self-deception merge. The narrator's last words to the reader are, quite characteristically, of his own defeat: "I can scarcely bear my loss—I mean of the precious papers" (564). Any remorse he feels is that of someone who wishes he had played a better game, been even more ruthless and committed in achieving his goal.

In the way that *The Aspern Papers* shows the escalation of desire and the blindness of the *ambitieux* to the destructiveness of his own actions, James's *nouvelle* provides, retrospectively, a concise outline of the unique patterns that other novels about ambition trace. The protagonist of *The Aspern Papers* is no doubt modeled on earlier versions of the *ambitieux*. Stendhal's Julien Sorel—the quintessential man of ambition—proves himself similarly blind to the consequences of many of his actions, and like the narrator of *The Aspern Papers,* he insists that his ambitions are holy. Julien goes even further, dressing himself and his ambitions in the garments of a would-be priest. Early in *Le Rouge et le noir,* during his tenure with M. de Rênal, Julien tells his friend Fouqué that he cannot accept a partnership in the older man's lumber business, because he must remain true to "his sacred mission [*sa vocation pour le saint ministère des autels*],"[3] which at that precise moment involves the seduction of Mme de Rênal. Although Julien's professed vocation is the priesthood, he is, in fact, seeking something that proves no less an egotistical obsession than the desire, in James's *nouvelle,* for Jeffrey Aspern's papers; for Julien, the priesthood is merely a means to some more "heroic" end. In rejecting Fouqué's offer, what Julien fears is that "eight years spent in securing my daily bread will rob me of the sublime energy that goes into the doing of extraordinary deeds" (I:VII). Julien seeks "distinction"; he seeks not to make money but to make a name for himself. And his attempts prove more ironic than tragic, because he finds so few appropriate outlets for his "sublime energy," and even fewer opportunities to perform "extraordinary deeds."

Julien always measures his own success against the distinction earned by his earliest inspiration, Napoleon. That by 1830 Napoleon's ambitions had long since played themselves out does not diminish Julien's enthusiasm for his accomplishments. As historian Christopher

Games of Ambition

Herold explains in *The Age of Napoleon,* the Napoleonic legend lived on, somehow separate from the story of the real Bonaparte: "The gift he had made to mankind, the gift of his example, could no more be suppressed than could Prometheus' gift of fire: no goal was impossible of attainment."[4] The *ambitieux* can write and rewrite his script at will. Exiled to Saint Helena, Napoleon attempted, in Herold's words, "to create an imaginary Napoleon whose sole aim it had been to lead humanity into the light of reason."[5] And as Stendhal's novel shows, the legacy he left the Julien Sorels of the nineteenth century was something more than a model of heroic action directed toward impossible goals. Napoleon also proved himself a master opportunist, a consummate strategist, in effect, a *game player* of legendary proportions. It is, consequently, not the least bit inconsistent with his imitation of Napoleon that Julien views his opportunities for advancement as more or less arbitrary—as moves in the game of life.

Even as a child, Julien's notions of his own glory are acted out with a flair for the expedient. He imagines himself one of the dragoons who tie their horses to his father's grilled windows, and he thrives on stories of Napoleon's victories. But when a magnificent new church begins to rise at Verrières, he devotes himself to memorizing the Latin Bible and to building an arsenal of "pious sentiments" (I:V). Julien's ambition—his desire for distinction—always remains an end in itself. The "red" of the Army and the "black" of the Church are mere tactics. Red and black are, for Julien, two equally acceptable ways of realizing his ambitions, and he always considers them in the same context: "When Bonaparte made himself known, France was threatened by invasion: the military profession was both necessary and fashionable. Today, one finds priests who draw salaries of a hundred thousand francs, three times that of Napoleon's famous division commanders." Thus, Julien concludes, "The thing is to be a priest."[6]

Julien reiterates this proposition many times in the novel. Contemplating his initial successes at the seminary, he makes the same kind of connection: "Under Napoleon, I would have been a sergeant; among these future priests I will be a grand vicar" (I:XXVI). But when he is exempted from a conscription call during his stay at the seminary, he laments that twenty years earlier he might have begun a life of "heroic action" (I:XXIX). When a king comes to Verrières, Julien appears to present a ludicrous figure, with the uniform of an honor guard visible beneath his cassock (I:XVIII), but later on, the Marquis de la Mole easily transforms the aspiring seminarian into M. le chevalier Julien

45

Dreadful Games

Sorel de La Vernaye, lieutenant of hussars (II:XXXIV). Julien's "choices" are dictated solely by the opportunities that arise, often through no skill or effort on his part. He has not formulated a coherent master strategy; his actions are almost purely responsive. Not unlike Napoleon in the early stages of his career, Julien takes advantage of his opportunities and revises his tactics as circumstances demand.[7]

Although the rituals of the army differ from those of the Church, and each demands a different style of action, both the "red" and the "black" of the novel follow the same logic. Both the army and the Church are "artificial groups": highly disciplined, highly structured bodies, each governed by precise rules, which are strictly enforced.[8] Only those who adhere to the rules may advance within these structures; even those with special talents must integrate themselves into the group. Leaders must earn the respect and admiration of those who follow them. In *Le Rouge et le noir*, for example, the young Bishop of Agde wins Julien's admiration with "charming good manners" and "skillful tact [*avec l'adresse*]" (I:XVIII). Julien's admiration of Napoleon is momentarily eclipsed by this new example of what he himself might become. In this sense, the army and the Church are both "game worlds": closed, regulated, with a special structure and logic of their own, distinguishing them from everyday experience. Julien must intuit the structural similarities between the two groups, because he always sees them as interchangeable fields for the play of ambition.

Julien does not, as some readers interpret Stendhal's enigmatic title, embrace the priesthood as the only option "open to a youth in his circumstances."[9] His options are simply not that limited, except in his own imagination, as the narrator's ironic treatment of the character helps to confirm. The novel shows that at each stage of his career he is provided with an alternative to pursuing his ambitions in either the army or the Church. Julien confronts and rejects several opportunities, each of which would provide him with a modest, though unmistakable measure of distinction. Fouqué offers him business success; Mme de Rênal's maid Elisa offers him financial security through marriage; Abbé Pirard offers him a post as vicar and half his income; a Russian prince even offers Julien his cousin's hand in marriage. But these particular options are never seriously considered, not because Julien scorns financial success or because he has any moral reservations about doing any of these things, but rather because they are inconsistent with Julien's image of himself. These opportunities are without much risk—reason enough for him to reject them as too easily won—and they are clearly independent of the gamelike logic of the "red" and the "black." Such opportunities are, in effect, independent of those game worlds dominated by ambition. Julien's perception of himself and the world he inhabits is a product of his own imagination; it is a "fiction" against which he judges everything around him. His ambition is "napoleonic": it is virtually insatiable; it will eventually bring him to his own version of Waterloo, at the Church at Verrières, and afterward, he will, like Napoleon, strive to create his own legend of himself.

The novel exploits the character's peculiarly "fictional" view of the world. René Girard compares Stendhal to Balzac, noting that where Balzac often treats very seriously the oppositions he sees around him, Stendhal, like Flaubert, "always point[s] out their futility."[10] This futility, expressed in the unresolved play of possible meanings in the text, presents itself not only in the title of the novel, but also in the author's conception of his character. Although Stendhal draws from the contemporary world—and like most later Realists, from true stories and actual people—in defining his character's situation, his attitude toward Julien resembles that of most eighteenth-century novelists, for whom the character is not a human personality but a product of fictional discourse, assembled and reassembled in the play of language. In this sense, Stendhal's attitude toward character is much different than those of novelists like Balzac, Dostoevsky, Hardy, even Henry James, and more like those of novelists who elude the label "Realist." Stendhal refuses to take his characters too seriously. As Leo Bersani says, "if Stendhal likes to think of the novel as a mirror held up to reality, he can also qualify or even dismiss realism when he speaks of his heroes and heroines."[11] Even if Julien's character is generally "believable" or "lifelike," Stendhal never presents him as a stable or coherent personality. Unlike most Realists, the author seeks again and again to remind the reader of Julien's status as a product of fictional language.

The narrator of the novel maintains an ironic distance from the character—though certainly a more playfully affectionate distance than Flaubert's from Emma Bovary, for instance, or even Hardy's from Jude—which serves both to call attention to the telling of the story by someone other than Julien and to illustrate the superficiality of Julien's own analysis of people and events. As the narrator claims, Julien possesses "one of those astonishing memories so often joined to stupidity" (I:V). And yet, Julien's utter lack of insight into the feelings of others, along with his lack of self-knowledge, is sometimes part of his "charm." This charm, though, is that of a fictional character and not of a human being, since the reader often perceives and enjoys Julien's blindness in a way that no other character can. What the narrator calls "stupidity" often leads to mistakes in Julien's performance of self, and Stendhal invites the reader to laugh at the character's errors in style or judgment. By encouraging the reader to make Julien an object of humor, Stendhal neutralizes some of Julien's potential danger; he downplays the threat of the "monster" always lurking beneath the surface of his character. It is not until the climax of the novel that the reader more clearly recognizes, by sharing in the Marquis de La Mole's perception, the "appalling" quality at the root of Julien's character (II:XXXIV). Once he ceases to be an object of humor in the game between the reader and the text and becomes part of the pattern of games that characters play with one another in the text, Julien becomes someone who is not simply foolish, but positively dangerous.

The play of Julien's various selves is ultimately all that is revealed of him in the novel. His hypocrisy does not seem to conceal anything more "authentic" than egotism. Like the narrator of *The Aspern Papers,* Julien plays the game of hidden being to further his ambitions, but in Julien's case, somewhat like that of Cervantes's Don Quixote, any "original" self becomes submerged, indistinguishable from the various assumed roles. Julien's character demonstrates the open-endedness of play itself. As a result, Stendhal's technique invites a special kind of textual play, not typical of most nineteenth-century Realist novels: the text invites the reader "to react and collaborate in the process of creation."[12] The novel does not merely narrate the historical "progress" of Julien's career—a career that is more circular, more the result of coincidence, than a linear progression from one place in the world to another. Rather, the events of the novel merely postpone the inevitable "novelistic" conclusion to this career—a conclusion that comes somewhat earlier in what Julien calls his "novel" than in Stendhal's own novel.[13] What effects this deferral are the "plots" of the novel, both Julien's and Stendhal's, or to use D. A. Miller's words, "little else than the incessant play of conspiratorial forces."[14]

Stendhal sets this play of conspiratorial forces into motion even before introducing his character. The novel explores what might be considered three distinct fields of play: the bourgeoisie of Verrières, the seminary at Besançon, and the Hôtel de La Mole in Paris. Significantly, as Julien moves further away from the world of his childhood, his encounters with others become increasingly more hypocritical, his actions more clearly ambitious, and his performance of self less spontaneous. Julien's movement from one field of play to another results most directly from a number of "plots" quite apart from his own. Significantly, such coincidences can be distinguished from the sense of "fate" that compels a character like Dostoevsky's Raskolnikov to murder the old pawnbroker in *Crime and Punishment*. Julien is an opportunist, not a gambler; he benefits from the strategic moves of others who are as ambitious as he is. He does not knowingly risk anything that he actually possesses, and he considers each decision, each action, as a tactical move. His first opportunity comes as a result of M. de Rênal's vanity—his desire to see his children out walking with a tutor—and his rivalry with M. Valenod—who has new horses but no tutor for his children. This rivalry ensures Julien's continuing "success," despite all he does that would seem to preclude it, since M. de Rênal lives in fear that Valenod will lure Julien away, a humiliation too great to bear. M. de Rênal thus rewards Julien in order to protect his own vanity and to minimize any risks to his own competitive position.

Julien's own ambitions are fervent, but without a clearly defined objective at first. He knows only that he must leave his family: physically unsuited to the world of his birth, the narrator explains, "in the Sunday games in the public square, he was always beaten" (I:IV). Much more suited to working with children than at his father's sawmill, Julien is intrigued by M. de Rênal's offer. Hypocrisy seems to serve Julien less at this point than does fidelity to his fiction of himself. He initially refuses to accept the offer, unless M. de Rênal guarantees his status in the household: Julien will not eat with the servants, a notion he takes from Rousseau's *Confessions*. When Julien's shrewd peasant father manages to secure this concession, Julien finds himself "surprised that he hadn't been beaten" (I:IV). But as so often happens in the novel, Julien has misinterpreted the nature of his success. The victory belongs not to Julien but to his father, who skillfully manipulates M. de Rênal's vanity.

Julien's belief that he is a man destined to perform extraordinary deeds leads him to seduce Mme de Rênal. Seduction proves, quite simply, the only opportunity Julien finds in M. de Rênal's house that is worthy of his efforts. But it is also quite consistent with Julien's "napoleonic" ambition. If a "quixotic" character logically seeks his Dulcinea, a "napoleonic" character logically seeks his Josephine, as Julien himself is reminded.[15] At the same time, though, the seduction of his employer's wife also offers the advantages of great risk as well as the bitter satisfaction of revenge—that characteristic response of the indi-

Dreadful Games

vidual whose ambitions are otherwise frustrated. In this way, even though Mme de Rênal sees in him only a pretty, girlish young man, the narrator suggests those "appalling" aspects of Julien's character that will emerge more vividly later in the novel: an eagerness to attempt even the most ridiculous or dangerous actions, along with a deeply rooted desire to obtain revenge from those who have, in his mind, obstructed his progress in life.

But Julien's actions at this point seem more harmless than they do later on, because he remains so painfully inept, a fact that the narrator attributes not only to his provincial inexperience, but also to his lack of an appropriate fictional model. Neither he nor Mme de Rênal have, the narrator says, read enough novels: "Novels would have outlined for them the roles to be played, would have shown them the model to imitate. And sooner or later—and without any pleasure, and perhaps even reluctantly—vanity would have forced Julien to follow this model."[16] As is frequently true for the *ambitieux,* games of ambition provide Julien with little pleasure or amusement; they are more like work than play. The playing of one's part takes considerable effort, even for someone as talented as Julien at slavish imitation.

Julien emphasizes the idea of "duty [*devoir*]" as an integral part of the role he has chosen to play with Mme de Rênal: "the role of a man accustomed to triumphing with women [*à subjuger des femmes*]" (I:XV). Even when Julien does win himself a place in Mme de Rênal's bed, his keenest feeling is the letdown that often follows great efforts: "that state of surprise and uneasy discontent that befalls the spirit when it has satisfied something it has long desired." Julien's uneasiness follows no doubt from the self-consciousness that leads him to ask himself, "Did I forget anything that I owe myself? Did I play my role well?" Despite the letdown of victory, Julien's love for Mme de Rênal and what seems like a genuine affection for her provide an antidote to what the narrator calls the "black ambition" that haunts him as he learns more about the political world of Verrières.

For her part, Mme de Rênal is not ambitious, but she learns to be ambitious *for* Julien and to take risks of her own in response to her desire for him. With what the narrator calls "a skill [*une adresse*] truly admirable in a woman so natural," Mme de Rênal arranges for Julien to be in the honor guard for the visiting king, so that she can see him in a blue uniform (I:XVIII). But unlike Julien, Mme de Rênal cannot sustain the belief that her ambitions are part of some game without consequences. Like Mme Arnoux in Flaubert's *L'Education sentimentale,* when her son falls ill, Mme de Rênal suddenly recognizes "the enormity of the fault into which she had allowed herself to be led," and she finds in Julien's reasoning to the contrary, "the language of Hell" (I:XIX).

Through Mme de Rênal's fears, Stendhal offers the first clear indication that the play of Julien's ambitions will have some decidedly "dreadful" outcome. Julien's response to his mistress's crisis resembles the self-interest of the narrator of *The Aspern Papers* when Miss Tina proposes marriage. Julien thinks most clearly at this point of how the events affect him: "She believes that in loving me she is killing her son, but the unhappy woman loves me more than her son. . . . [H]ow could I have inspired such love, me, so poor, so badly taught, so ignorant, sometimes so crude in my manners."[17] Amidst the desperation of Mme de Rênal's feelings of love and guilt, Julien prides himself on a personal victory. In much the same way, he later discovers victory in the shame of Mathilde's pregnancy.

Despite her reluctance to continue her intrigue with Julien, Mme de Rênal proves herself quite capable of participating, with skill, in the "plot" that makes it possible for Julien to move on from Verrières, thus postponing the consequences of their affair. When M. de Rênal receives an "anonymous" letter about his wife from his rival Valenod, Mme de Rênal encourages Julien's natural hypocrisy, suggesting that he court M. Valenod's favor and ingratiate himself with everyone else in town. Mme de Rênal understands, as Julien does not, that they have bruised the vanity of both her husband and M. Valenod. Where Julien would no doubt have made some dramatic and ridiculous response to the anonymous letter, Mme de Rênal has the presence of mind, and tactical intuition, to protect them both from a confrontation. Although Mme de Rênal's words show that she takes this risk out of guilt and fear—as she tells Julien, "it is a minor thing in my eyes if I pay with my life for the hours spent in your arms" (I:XX), and later, "if this turns out badly . . . I lose everything" (I:XXI)—for Julien, the scheme is just another game to be played: it is "with the pleasure of a child" that he cuts and pastes words to create Mme de Rênal's own "anonymous" letter. For her, this scheme is an act of survival, not of pleasure or even of competition. Hers is not a game that demands winners and losers, but one that seeks to avert the consequences of a more decisive defeat on either side.

Julien's "success" in the Rênal household results from his sense of "duty" to his own self-image. But when he enters the world of the "black," at the seminary at Besançon, he astutely realizes that hypocrisy will serve him best, and that his fiction of himself will be of little use to him, and indeed, must often be completely suppressed. His carefully feigned act of contrition, when he arrives downstairs late his first day, earns him the respect of the more skillful seminarians: they recognize him as a man who already possesses the "rudiments of the profession."[18] But this early success, along with his feeling that he is inherently superior to his fellow seminarians, gives way to a series of "false steps." The narrator explains why such mistakes prove inevitable for Julien in this particular "game world": "The important actions of his life had been managed wisely, but he was not careful with details, and the most skillful seminarians pay attention only to details."[19] In order to succeed in the seminary, he needs to master the rules and rituals that govern this world.

Whereas Julien can maintain some of the grander fictions about himself, he finds it more difficult to maintain the little fictions of everyday life, what the narrator calls the "hypocrisy of gesture." The piety of Abbé Chelan, the priest at Verrières, has raised Abbé Pirard's hopes for Julien. But when Julien tries to obtain the appearance of "blind and fervent faith," he thinks not of any living models but of faces like those in ecclesiastical paintings (I:XXVI). Julien's inability to see beneath the surface of human emotions—his willingness, in this case, to convey only the vaguest illusion, the "fiction" of piety—often serves him poorly in the seminary.

But if his special brand of hypocrisy often fails him, his astonishing memory, which enables him to memorize long passages from any book, especially the Latin Bible, leads to his first promotion: Abbé Pirard makes him tutor in the Old and New Testaments (I:XXIX). Abbé Pirard clearly has many reservations about Julien—the promotion is postponed when spies discover Amanda Binet's address written on a playing card among Julien's personal effects—but he believes that Julien has a superior mind, and he sees in Julien "a spark that should not be neglected"—a "spark" that is clearly that of Julien's boundless ambition. The Abbé attempts to "test" Julien's merit, linking merit with performance: "Does a man have merit in your eyes? Put obstacles in front of everything he desires, everything he undertakes. If his merit is real, he will be able to overturn or get around the obstacles."[20] Although Julien and Abbé Pirard undoubtedly define "merit" in very different ways, the Abbé's principle, at least in practice, is not unlike Julien's own idea of how a man succeeds in life: by confronting all obstacles, even if they are "self-imposed challenges."[21] Consequently,

Julien performs well on the Abbé's "test," maintaining what seems like a clear sense of purpose in the face of misfortunes.

Although Abbé Pirard's encouragement makes Julien's life at the seminary easier, it also exposes him to a number of different schemes and schemers, just as had his affair with Mme de Rênal. During examinations, a clever questioner traps Julien into discussing profane authors. The Grand Vicar, the Abbé Frilair, uses this mistake "to humiliate" Abbé Pirard, "his old enemy": he ranks Pirard's favorite student number 198 in the exams, even though Julien had been a sure bet among the other seminarians to place first. Abbé Pirard is distressed, then "overjoyed" to discover that Julien does not plan "a project of vengeance." Yet Julien is no stoic; he has accepted his ranking primarily because he recognizes "the skillful strategem of which he had been a victim" (I:XXIX); he recognizes Abbé Frilair as a superior player. Nevertheless, Abbé Pirard rewards Julien for what he perceives as his tough-mindedness: when the Marquis de La Mole offers Abbé Pirard a chance to leave the world of the seminary behind, the priest secures a place for Julien at the same time.

The novel is structured according to a curious kind of parallelism. The circumstances under which Julien leaves the seminary are much like those under which he leaves Verrières. And just as Julien fails to understand the seriousness of Mme de Rênal's position, Julien takes lightly the events surrounding Abbé Pirard's departure from the seminary: "He saw in the whole affair a well-played game [*un bien joué*] which put him in good spirits and gave him the highest opinion of the Abbé's talents."[22] The confidence and good spirits inspired by his own participation in this "game" inspire Julien to return to the scene of his earlier "success," spending the night with Mme de Rênal on his way to Paris.

From Abbé Pirard's advice to him, Julien might reasonably expect his position as secretary to the Marquis de La Mole to provide him with great opportunities to pursue his ambitions. The Abbé assures him that "there is no fortune, for a man of our cloth, except that of the great lords. With that indefinable—at least for me—quality in your character, if you do not make your fortune you will be persecuted; there is no middle course for you."[23] But Julien's position in the household of the Marquis de La Mole proves no less artificial or equivocal than his position in the household of M. de Rênal. His association with Abbé Pirard confers considerable status on him in the eyes of the Marquis, but it means little to anyone else. Julien remains an outsider, neither an equal nor a servant. When he listens to the conversation of Mathilde de La Mole and her friends, he thinks of it as "a foreign language, which he could understand, but which he could not speak" (II:IV). At the same time, however, he becomes one of the "most distinguished pupils" at the theological school he attends at Abbé Pirard's suggestion, and after some initial errors, the Marquis signs most of the letters that Julien composes for him. But Julien cannot consider these accomplishments "success"; as the narrator explains, these tasks are each pursued "with all the energy of stifled ambition," and Julien soon loses "the fresh coloring he had brought from the provinces" (II:IV). His physical pallor reflects the fading of his ambitions. Whereas he had played out his ambitions—a playing that had energized and invigorated him—the tasks he undertakes now can only be called work, which drains and fatigues him.

Julien's experience in the Hôtel de La Mole shows him that he needs something more than hypocrisy and a good memory to succeed. Clearly, he lacks certain social skills, as suggested by his inability to participate in any of the conversations. He is simply not refined enough to succeed in this game world. If vanity is the motivating principle of the world of Verrières, and vengeance that of the seminary, then the Hôtel de La Mole is ruled by the desire for amusement. But as Julien's experience shows, the inhabitants of this world think of "amusement" in only its most self-interested sense—as "amusing" *oneself,* often at the expense of another, and often in a hollow, mirthless fashion. The Marquis comes to value Julien not because of his skill at letter writing, but because their relationship is conducive to his own amusement. Julien first rearranges the Marquis's financial affairs to make conducting business more amusing for him, because, as the narrator explains, "Rich men with high spirits [*le coeur haut*] look to business for amusement, not results" (II:VI). The Marquis gives Julien a blue suit, which like the black suit M. de Rênal purchases for him, represents not Julien's own ambitions, but his employer's desire, in this case, for entertainment.

Thus the Marquis delineates two separate roles for Julien in his household: the public one of work and the private, confidential one of play. And Julien performs admirably in each role. Suffering from an attack of gout, the Marquis asks Julien to entertain him. He invites Julien to describe the details of his life "with no other purpose than to tell the story clearly and in an amusing fashion." The Marquis explains

Games of Ambition

to him that "one must amuse oneself . . . it is the only real thing in life" (II:VII). But when the Marquis makes this assertion, he speaks of his own amusement, not Julien's. When Julien wears the blue suit, the Marquis treats him as an equal; but this choice remains the Marquis's to make. Julien remains the object of play, the source of amusement.

Perhaps because Julien is of the lower middle classes and not of the aristocracy, he almost always concerns himself not with "amusement" but with "results." For this reason he believes at first that the Marquis is making fun of him. But he gradually comes to value this "man in the blue suit," whom the Marquis has created. The foundation of the Marquis's relationship with Julien nonetheless remains that of "amusement," not "results," even after the Marquis rewards him with a decoration for his diplomatic efforts on the Marquis's behalf. The Marquis tells Julien in the clearest terms that their relationship will *not* help Julien to advance, assuring him that "I do not at all want for you to rise from your present situation." Instead, he tells Julien he will provide for him in other ways: "When my lawsuits bore you, or when you no longer suit me, I will request a good living for you, like that of our friend Abbé Pirard, and *nothing else.*"[24] Julien does not seem much deterred by these words, however. The decoration itself bolsters his pride and confidence. In his attempt to continue amusing the Marquis, Julien inadvertently injures M. Gros, a poor but kind man of Verrières. Julien dismisses his initial concern for the man, noting that he might have to commit other "injustices" in becoming "successful." Despite what the Marquis says, Julien makes a connection in his own mind between amusing the Marquis and pursuing his own ambitions. He seems not to realize that the Marquis has prescribed a limit to his ambitions—a limit that Julien will transgress, somewhat unwittingly even, in his affair with Mathilde. Julien ultimately refuses to play the part the Marquis has assigned to him.

What Julien is unable to do in his relationship with the Marquis— turn "amusement" to profit—he achieves almost by chance in his relationship with the Marquis's daughter. Julien's affair with Mathilde differs significantly from his earlier seduction of Mme de Rênal. Here, of course, Mathilde, not Julien, initiates the affair, and rather than being instantly attracted to Mathilde, as he is to Mme de Rênal, Julien finds her unattractive, and even actively dislikes her at first. Futhermore, Julien genuinely respects and admires the Marquis de La Mole—in business matters he had become the Marquis's "second self" (II:XIII)—whereas he had often felt contempt for M. de Rênal, con-

55

Dreadful Games

sciously seeking to injure him through his wife. The seduction of Mathilde is something Julien's imagination has never contemplated. When she begins to pay him an unusual amount of attention, his thoughts link the idea of "amusement" to the vanity that his dreams of "success" foster. He thinks that "it would be pleasant if she loved me," and remembering that Mathilde is to marry the Marquis de Croisenois, he takes pride in concluding that she must prefer him to "that exceedingly agreeable young man" (II:X). On other days, though, Julien distrusts his own perception of Mathilde's actions and thinks that "this girl is making fun of me. . . . She is in agreement with her brother to trick me." Julien's affair with Mme de Rênal is modeled, somewhat vaguely, on the romance of novels, but his affair with Mathilde arises out of pride and an increasingly unsatisfied lust for power. He plays a game not of imitation or mimicry but of strategy. With Mme de Rênal, Julien considers his "duty" to seduce her, but with Mathilde, his thoughts turn to tricks and schemes that might secure his power over her.

Julien's pride and his ever-present fear of being ridiculed by those associated with Mathilde prevent him from responding to her initial advances. He grows increasingly suspicious of her actions: "nothing was too low or too wicked [*trop profond ou trop scélérat*] for the character with which he credited her" (II:XIII). Even when she insults her friends, Julien believes that she has conspired with her brother and the Marquis de Croisenois to make a fool of him. He arranges to leave Paris, hoping to spoil any such conspiracy. He tells himself, "When all is said and done, they won't have trapped me. . . . Whether Mlle de La Mole's sarcasms toward these gentlemen are real or designed solely to make me over-confident, I have amused myself with them."[25] His "amusement" nevertheless seems completely joyless. When Mathilde grows bold enough to write him a letter describing her feelings, Julien feels a twinge of guilt mixed with pity for the Marquis de La Mole. But comparing his own options to the Marquis's actions in business, he instantly chides himself as "stupid" for having such scruples.

Mathilde's letter transforms both Julien's ambition and his character. He suddenly becomes almost demonic; the narrator describes him as "laughing like Mephistopheles" (II:XIII). His ambition is "redoubled" and all scruples abandoned. Julien still fears that Mathilde's actions are "all nothing but a game [*un jeu*]," a game to which he fears becoming vulnerable by postponing his intended departure (II:XIV). He begins to monitor all of his actions more carefully than he has before, not simply as a *vaniteux,* an individual motivated by obsessive vanity, but as someone who seeks through his actions to manipulate the emotions of others. He attributes his success with Mathilde to the "cold looks" he has given her, and in the narrator's words, such logic leaves him "more cold and calculating than he had ever been in his life" (II:XIV). Julien refuses to let even vanity lead him into error. He is uncharacteristically shrewd—making a copy of Mathilde's letter and sending it to Fouqué for safekeeping—in contrast to the Julien who had followed Mme de Rênal's scheme with "the pleasure of a child." Julien exploits the opportunity he sees in Mathilde's infatuation with him and contemplates where such power over her might take him. There is nothing childlike or innocent or provincial in what he is becoming.

Once again, Julien's "career" parallels that of Napoleon. In 1810, Napoleon divorced Josephine in order to marry the Hapsburg princess Marie Louise—a marriage based not on passion but on political power and the desire for an heir to the empire he had created. In *Le Rouge et le noir,* Mme de Rênal functions as Julien's Josephine, his first and most enduring love. But at this particular point in his career, the young man who had wept the tears of "true passion" at Josephine's Malmaison (II:I) now enters into an alliance, like Napoleon's with Marie Louise, through which he seeks personal power and social privilege and finds, in Mathilde's pregnancy, a potential heir to his own fortunes. Thus, Julien's relationship with Mathilde signals not only a widening field for the play of ambition, but also the beginning of a course of action based not on passion but on the desire for power. Julien begins "playing a game," rather than "playing a role," as he had done in the beginning of the novel—and in the process, his actions become riskier and more dangerous for himself and others.

Not Julien, but Mathilde de La Mole, determines the logic that governs this game. She proves herself bold, and not unlike Julien, she maintains a distinctly anachronistic vision of the world. She has formulated a nostalgic fiction that insulates her from what she perceives as the weaknesses of her own world. She believes that she is dying of boredom, and that "her condition in life has given her all the advantages—rank, wealth, youth—everything, alas, except happiness" (II:VIII). Like Julien, Mathilde longs for a world that has long since passed away, an age of heroic action: Julien keeps a portrait of Napoleon hidden in his mattress; in much the same way, Mathilde wears mourning for Boniface de La Mole, an ancestor beheaded in the sixteenth century. Both Julien and Mathilde worship the past, though

Dreadful Games

clearly, at different altars. Mathilde points to the difference between their "fictions": in the sixteenth century, "a man fought to obtain the one thing he desired—in order to make his party victorious—and not to obtain some dull decoration, as in the time of your Emperor. You must agree that there was less self-interest and pettiness then."[26] Mathilde argues that, in the context of *her* fiction, heroic action is an end in itself, not an effort calculated to ensure advancement.

Mathilde imagines an age in which a man risks his life to save a friend, as Boniface de La Mole once did, and a woman has the courage to ask for her decapitated lover's head, like Marguerite de Navarre. She finds no such heroism in her own world, lamenting that even duels have become "mere ceremonies" (II:XIV), as the absurdity of Julien's own duel has already demonstrated for the reader (II:VI). Mathilde takes pleasure in "playing with fate [*jouer son sort*]" (II:XI), and like her father, she gives "amusement" central value in her life, often equating it with "heroism." She sees her relationship with Julien as more "heroic" than the legal arrangement her family has made with the Marquis de Croisenois: with Julien "everything was left to chance [*tout sera fils du hasard*]" (II:XII). When she tells her father that she carries Julien's child, she argues that "this young Sorel is the only person who amuses me" (II:XXXII)—a statement that seems odd given how much they have tormented one another. But Mathilde believes that anything done purely for its own sake—like marrying Julien—is amusing. Mathilde believes, moreover, that "good birth destroys the strength of character without which a man can never have himself condemned to death" (II:VIII)—the death sentence, in her mind, having become the only source of distinction left in the world. In choosing Julien, Mathilde has chosen the one man of her acquaintance who does manage to get himself condemned to death. The final stage of Julien's career enables Mathilde to play the role of Marguerite de Navarre.

From the moment he begins his affair with Mathilde, Julien begins to form his own "plots." In the atmosphere of intrigue that dominates the first several chapters in book II of *Le Rouge et le noir*—the game world of the Marquis de La Mole—Julien's role is that of an observer, or when called upon, an instrument of plot. But as his obsession with Mathilde grows more intense, he becomes more calculating, devising an intrigue of his own, and more ruthless than he has been earlier in the novel, where his fiction of himself more directly motivates him. The reader is consequently forced to see Julien in a different, more menacing light: As a character, Julien has more charm when his schemes fail than he does when he begins to master the art of manipulation. Even the authorial voice which controls, even neutralizes, the character's actions, begins to recede in the second half of the book.[27] Julien's success with Mathilde robs him of the "warmth" and "passion" that characterizes his earlier ambitions. The game he plays to achieve this success seems devoid of any playfulness, any spontaneity, any creativity or imagination. When he finds himself locked into a power struggle with Mathilde, his actions become "monstrous"—cold and calculating, degraded and degrading.

Up to this point in the novel, Julien has intuitively practiced hypocrisy, but the Russian Prince Korasoff shows him how to exploit this hypocrisy more advantageously. "Remember the great principle of your century," he tells Julien, "always be contrary to what people expect" (II:XXVI). Korasoff urges Julien to appear pleasant to the woman he seeks to conquer, but openly to court another woman, without the slightest appearance of passion. Korasoff even provides Julien with six volumes of love letters designed to accomplish the latter task. Julien remains mechanically faithful to the plan of conduct dictated by Prince Korasoff (II:XXV), never questioning either the methods or the principles on which they are founded.

As Julien patiently copies the tedious and incomprehensible letters, sending them to Mme Fervaques, the narrator compares him to "all those mediocre creatures who accidentally find themselves involved in the maneuvers of some great general" (II:XXVIII). Stendhal is still making fun of his character here, but his tone is more bitter, more clearly ominous. Mindlessly, Julien follows the rules of the game outlined by Korasoff, but he succeeds in spite of his stupidity. As Mathilde watches Julien's performance, she finds herself "captivated" by the "perfect insincerity" that allows him to contradict his own opinions on every subject (II:XXVIII). As it becomes increasingly clear that Mathilde imagines herself in love with him, Julien never allows himself to express any feelings of love for her. In contrast to the moments of joy he had felt with Mme de Rênal, Julien only "abandons himself" to such feelings "in those moments where Mathilde was unable to read the expression of them in his eyes" (II:XXXII). While Mathilde allows herself to be swept up in her love for him, Julien guards against revealing any passion for her.

In following Korasoff's instructions, Julien strives to maintain a position of power over Mathilde, a power that he attributes to his coldness and cruelty. But when Mathilde announces her pregnancy,

Dreadful Games

Julien suddenly finds himself without "the courage to address her using those cruel words, which in his mind were so indispensable to their love" (II:XXXII). Mathilde suddenly reveals herself to him not as a rival, a competitor in Korasoff's game, but as an ally in the conflict that is certain to arise when the Marquis de La Mole learns the news. The balance of power shifts. Mathilde is willing to sacrifice everything for the man she considers her "husband"; even Julien agrees that their destinies lie together. Julien has always valued Mathilde because she is wanted by someone else, the Marquis de Croisenois, and the sacrifice that she is now willing to make flatters his vanity even more and increases her value in his eyes. Just as he had with Mme de Rênal, Julien follows Mathilde's lead, allowing her to formulate their strategy.

While the Marquis de La Mole considers his own options, Julien contemplates three possible solutions to the conflict, none of which includes a marriage to Mathilde. The Marquis might kill him, covering such action with a suicide note provided by Julien himself; Mathilde's brother might shoot him in a duel; or the Marquis might send him away and conceal Mathilde's condition (II:XXXIII). Julien speaks here as an individual who has learned the logic and principles of strategic game playing. He evaluates the Marquis's possible "moves," trying to reason how his opponent might maximize his own interests. When he identifies these three alternatives, Julien is not overestimating the magnitude of the Marquis's rage or his desire for the kind of solution reflected in these three alternatives. The Marquis's imagination has, after all, "left him prey to an insane passion for seeing his daughter possessed of some fine title" (II:XXXIV)—a dream that Julien has shattered. But Julien has misjudged the stubbornness of Mathilde's love for him—she simply refuses to compromise in any of her demands—as well as the ameliorating effect of the Marquis's love for his daughter—he is unwilling to lose her even if he must accept Julien in the bargain. When the Marquis does finally make his decision, Julien once again reveals his vanity and his egotism. As always, the real battle has taken place in Julien's absence, but he claims the victory as his own: "Finally, he thought, my novel is finished, and to myself alone goes the credit. I have made myself loved by that monster of pride, he thought, looking at Mathilde; her father cannot live without her nor she without me."[28] Julien believes that he has finally distinguished himself; Mathilde's passion for him has won him a new name and new position in the world. The fiction that has sustained his ambitions throughout the novel has, he believes, reached a conclusion.

Stendhal, however, has not finished *his* novel, and he seems intent on calling his character to account for all that he has done in the name of ambition. If his "novel is finished," Julien's ambitions are far from dead. Success simply inspires greater ambition. He is "drunk with ambition," and thinks "of nothing but glory and his son" (II:XXXV). And his redoubled ambition makes him stupider than he has yet been. He even suggests that the Marquis write to Mme de Rênal, who, he believes, will provide a personal reference for him. But on receiving the letter of denunciation from Mme de Rênal, the Marquis swiftly and, it would appear, irrevocably rescinds the distinction he has conferred on Julien. Even the resolute Mathilde believes that "all is lost." Julien's actions from this point forward are perplexing: the man who has most recently acted in the narrowest of self-interest suddenly seems to act almost without volition, and clearly against common sense, in attempting to assassinate Mme de Rênal.

But the logic of a fictional character—and Julien is "fictional" in two senses, as the hero of his own "novel" as well as that of Stendhal's novel—does not always correspond to the logic of human possibilities. In both "novels" of *Le Rouge et le noir,* the character's action does make sense in the context of the various roles he has played. Despite his apparent success at Korasoff's game—his success in winning Mathilde's love—Julien is never a particularly skillful strategist.[29] The cold, calculating Julien, who manipulates Mathilde and Mme Fervaques simultaneously, is an aberration. A shrewd competitor follows a carefully formulated strategy, which is revised as needed—a strategy that has no intrinsic value. But Julien remains faithful not to a strategy but to a fiction of himself, which cannot be revised because it does have intrinsic value for him. As his career begins, Julien approaches every task as if it were part of some larger project. He perceives the seduction of Mme de Rênal as part of his duty to himself: it is an opportunity for heroic action, it is filled with risk, and he must therefore attempt it. Even in the seminary, Julien strives to maintain the illusion of his superiority. What sustains Julien's career, even in the wake of failure, is his fidelity to his image of himself. His actions are always intended to make others believe what he believes about himself.

But when the Marquis de La Mole gives him a new name—something he does not for Julien but for Mathilde, to save her from the name Sorel—Julien is no longer playing out his own fiction. He is magically reborn, in his own eyes, and in the eyes of the world. He has accomplished what he set out to do: to make a name for himself. But having done so, having finished his own novel, Julien becomes part of a new fiction, where success is measured in other than "napoleonic" terms. Julien is destined, in the last chapters of the novel, after his own "novel" is finished, to play out the role that Mathilde has imagined for him. That is the price he pays for pursuing his own ambitions. Julien's own fiction, his "novel," may be complete, but Mathilde's fiction remains unresolved. The hero of Mathilde's "novel" is her idea of Boniface de La Mole—not a self-serving *ambitieux,* like Napoleon, but a man who acts out of passion, a man with the strength of character to get himself condemned to death.

If Julien seems more "authentic," more passionate, than he has previously been when he returns to Verrières to shoot Mme de Rênal, this perception can be explained in several ways.[30] First, Julien returns in this episode to the world in which his "game" has been most creative. His desires in the early chapters are not particularly "spontaneous" but rather "mediated" by his fiction of Napoleon. Yet he interprets this fiction with creativity, acting according to his own idea of the "duties" this role demands, and not according to a rigid set of rules like those of Korasoff's game. Furthermore, the fiction he plays out at the end, Mathilde's fiction, is only subtly different from his own "napoleonic" idea of heroism. Both fictions privilege individual action and glorify the passionate response to event and circumstances. But in Mathilde's fiction, the hero acts out of passion without considering what he might gain in the process. Significantly, vengeance serves a more important function in Mathilde's fiction of heroism than it does in Julien's. Just as Julien, seeking to emulate Napoleon, believes it is his "duty" to seduce Mme de Rênal, the "reborn" Julien, Mathilde's man of passionate, heroic action, believes he must assassinate Mme de Rênal to avenge himself. Since in both instances, Julien is playing a role, he is no more intrinsically "authentic" at the end than he is in the beginning of the novel.

Julien sees his final act as a way of "settling his score with humanity [*avoir soldé mon compte envers l'humanité*]" (II:XXXVI). By using this expression, Julien reveals his view of the world as an ongoing struggle against an endless series of opponents, the futility of which he fails to see, but Stendhal does not: the circularity of Julien's career denies the possibility of an individual's "progress." After his final act, Julien begins to see death not as "horrible" but as the inevitable conclusion to his career. At the thought of death, "each of his ambitions was being successively ripped from his heart," and he concludes that

Games of Ambition

"all of his life had been just one long preparation for misfortune, and he had not overlooked the one which passes as the greatest of all."[31] Julien's fate implies that all ambition ends in death, the "greatest misfortune of all." But his choices at the end of the novel allow him to play out this inevitable conclusion on his own terms.

The irony of the conclusion lies in the response of other characters to the final events of Julien's life. His goal has been to make himself a "napoleonic" hero, just as Don Quixote tries to re-create himself as a knight-errant. In the end, though, Julien's "attempted self-creation becomes an act of self-destruction."[32] Only through a criminal act that demands he be executed does he accomplish his goal. By virtue of his final actions, everyone comes to recognize Julien's superiority, his "heroism." Mathilde argues, rather tautologically, that Julien has committed not a crime but a "noble act of vengeance, which shows me the nobility of the heart that beats in your breast" (II:XXXVIII). He has unintentionally made himself more heroic in her eyes than even Boniface de La Mole. And as Julien's confessor tells him, "Everything has contributed to making you the hero of all the young girls in Besançon" (II:XLV). Julien has even been reconciled to Mme de Rênal, who forgives him everything; he even makes her promise to care for "Mathilde's son." He makes all the final arrangements, including the selection of his burial site. He rejects all possible avenues of appeal, not because he wants to be punished for his crime, but because he is ready to die; as he tells Fouqué, "No one will ever see me grow pale." Julien seeks more than material wealth and worldly success, and that distinguishes him from Balzac's more materialistically ambitious characters like Eugène de Rastignac and Lucien de Rubempré, who would never have chosen the fate Julien chooses.[33] But stoicism and fatalism in death are consistent with the ambition and hypocrisy of Julien's life, because "in both cases he proves capable of creating a public self by sheer force of will."[34]

For any *ambitieux* this "public self" is ultimately everything; all that matters in the end is the impression one leaves on the world, the name one makes for oneself. The *ambitieux* places supreme value on self-image and finds a rationale for any action that furthers self-interest. Julien's "noble act of vengeance" becomes a way of perpetuating his image of himself. Julien shocks us most, as Robert M. Adams says, "by dealing good and evil blindly."[35] Even as a condemned man, in complete isolation from the world, Julien contemplates the game of hidden being. Laughing, once again, like Mephistopheles—perhaps the great-

Dreadful Games

est *ambitieux* of all, willing in Goethe's version of *Faust* to challenge both man and God to his game of power—Julien admits that even alone, "I am a hypocrite, as if there were someone to hear me" (II:XLVI). He thinks that if he met God he would admit his guilt, but at the same time ask "great God, good God, kind God, give me back the woman I love!" Julien demonstrates in these final moments the insatiability of ambition: the *ambitieux* can never be satisfied; he can never attain enough wealth, enough love, enough power. He desires everything, attempts anything worthy of his talents, and competes against anyone who stands in his way. The desire for a life of heroic significance makes the play of ambition an endlessly futile cycle of successes and failures.

4

Games of Revenge

Balzac's *Le Cousine Bette*

■ Literary critics sometimes use the idea of game as a metaphor to describe some special quality or idea that a text expresses. In a 1935 essay on Stendhal and Balzac, Georg Lukacs uses a game metaphor to contrast the two novelists' perception of human nature. Both writers, in Lukacs's words, compare social life to "a game of cards," in which "one must not question the justice or the moral value of the rules." Furthermore, both Stendhal and Balzac involve their principal characters in "games of ambition and corruption."[1] But, as he goes on to explain, while the experience of Balzac's characters demonstrates how such participation in the games of social life perverts and corrupts human beings morally and spiritually, Stendhal's heroes manage to escape the most profound degree of corruption. When all has been said and done, Stendhal's *ambitieux* manages to retain an integrity of self, a purity of conviction, that Balzac's characters—even those motivated by ambition, like Rastignac or Lucien de Rubempré—can never quite grasp.

The distinction that Lukacs suggests here reveals itself not only in the way each author portrays human nature, but also in the way each dramatizes social conflict. In *Le Rouge et le noir*, for example, Julien's ambition, along with the steps he takes to realize it, remains the central focus of the text, even though other "plots" and "intrigues"—the petty jealousies of the provincial bourgeoisie, the bitter conflicts of the seminarians, the manipulations of the Marquis de La Mole's business af-

Dreadful Games

fairs—play themselves out on the fringes of Julien's "career." Through the character of Julien, Stendhal identifies ambition as a powerful, motivating force in human experience, but in these various "subplots," he implies that individual action is frequently motivated not by the desire to succeed, as in Julien's case, but by the more insidious and destructive desire to see others fail. The themes of ambition and revenge often overlap, since frustrated ambition can lead to acts of revenge, but in *Le Rouge et le noir,* Stendhal emphasizes games of ambition. Stendhal's *ambitieux* desires to become someone more noble or famous than himself, and even in moments of failure, he remains faithful to this image of what he might become. His own imagination sustains him.

Balzac's characters, however, seek a different kind of power. They desire less to be something than to possess something, and significantly, they are willing to destroy the very thing they desire, rather than allow a rival to possess it. Balzac's characters concern themselves less with self-image than with the rights of ownership. Stendhal and Balzac produce such different kinds of texts, because where Stendhal sees the desire for revenge as peripheral or secondary to the real issues of his novels, Balzac places the play of revenge at the center of his novelistic world. The language of games highlights the energy of revenge as it spreads out across the world defined by the text. Despite the titles Balzac gives his novels, no one character ever emerges as more important in the play of revenge than the others; no "hero" or "heroine" emerges. The "plot" of a novel by Balzac is ultimately the sum of its many "subplots," which trace the complicated patterns of jealousy, envy, and spite in human relationships.[2]

The desire for revenge may smolder for long periods of time, as it does in Balzac's *La Cousine Bette.* Characters watch those around them prosper, for no apparent reason, until, finally, some specific transgression—in Balzac's novel, Hortense's "theft" of the man Bette cherishes as if he were her child—compels such a character to take retributory action. Even though characters motivated by these feelings argue that retribution is justified under the circumstances, they most often act surreptitiously to exact vengeance, concealing true feelings or disguising the true nature of their acts beneath a veneer of hypocrisy, always ingratiating themselves with those they secretly hate. Unlike the *ambitieux,* who often acts impulsively or boldly, who demonstrates pride in himself and in his desire for success, the character inspired by the desire for revenge is more likely to act prudently or cautiously, more carefully calculating every move and countermove. Characters may *pursue* their ambitions, but they must *plot* their revenge, and the novelists' textual strategies often highlight this difference.

Because revenge proves so much more destructive and dehumanizing a force than ambition, it is tempting to interpret Balzac's conception of human experience "as a struggle among wild animals, between beasts of prey and their victims."[3] But Balzac himself distinguishes, in the "Avant-Propos" to *La Comédie humaine,* between the social life of human beings and that of animals. Like animals, humans pursue and attack one another, "but their varying degrees of intelligence render the combat more complicated" than that of the animal species they resemble. Animal life is more simple, Balzac argues, because animals have fewer needs than men and women; only humans shape their material world, reflecting in it their habits and thoughts.[4] Only men and women are obsessed and dominated by the patterns of the material life they create for themselves. Balzac is clearly not willing to see in human experience the conflict of *"les bêtes humaines."* Thus, to read Balzac as essentially a precursor of Zola[5] distorts his ideas about human relationships, as expressed in the intrigues and plots that structure his novels. The games that play themselves out in a Balzac novel, however twisted and malicious they seem, are *human* games, the expression not of animal instincts, but of human intellect in the service of human passions. Only human beings could find satisfaction—by expressing the grim pleasure that Balzac's characters derive from their schemes—in the subtle and intricate manipulations aimed at securing revenge.

The plot of *La Cousine Bette,* composed of a number of interrelated and overlapping games of revenge, more closely resembles Laclos's *Les Liaisons dangereuses* (a novel that precedes it by more than half a century) than it does any novel by Zola. Like Laclos, Balzac senses the potential threat of frustrated desire and thwarted ambition. Both novels chart the progress of schemes designed to secure power over others, to negate the power that others possess, or to ruin their happiness. For the manipulative figures of both fictional worlds, "success" is defined only in terms of the defeat of their rivals or opponents. Furthermore, in both novels, the power that men possess in social life is played off against the more limited power of deception and subterfuge that women exercise against them. It is more than coincidence that in both fictional worlds, women emerge as the master manipulators, generating the destructive energy of the games characters play. Female characters, in both novels, manipulate others to achieve their own ends.

Dreadful Games

André Malraux has called Laclos's novel "a game of cards with only two colors: vanity and sexual desire."[6] All events arise from Mme de Merteuil's desire to punish the Comte de Gercourt, who has abandoned her for another woman. To destroy the man she believes has betrayed her, Merteuil enlists the aid of the Vicomte de Valmont, whom she secretly hates, much as she does Gercourt, for breaking off an earlier affair. In seeking revenge, Merteuil looks to others to do what she cannot do herself; acts of revenge are often mediated through a third party. Instead of taking direct action against Gercourt—over whom she no longer holds any significant power—she persuades Valmont to seduce the young girl Gercourt has chosen for a bride, thus hoping to wound Gercourt's pride as he has wounded hers. Merteuil promises Valmont that her project is "deserving of a hero," and that he "will serve both love and vengeance" (Letter 2).[7] Perhaps most importantly, she promises time and again that her project will be "amusing" for both of them. In this way, play and destruction are inextricably linked.

Valmont agrees to her plan for more than one reason. First, he is an indefatigable egotist: the seduction of Cécile de Volanges is an exercise in power motivated by sexual desire. It proves an easier task for him than his frustrating attempts to seduce the prudish Mme de Tourvel, whose passions are less malleable than those of Cécile. But Valmont is neither a mere libertine nor a pawn in Merteuil's scheme. He seeks to injure Mme de Volanges, who he believes has injured him in his pursuit of Tourvel. Like many who seek revenge, he pursues his vengeance in a roundabout way, not by injuring Mme de Volanges directly but rather by using her daughter as an instrument of his vengeance. However persuasive Valmont's rationale for vengeance seems, Mme de Volanges has, in fact, done no more than caution Tourvel, telling her that "of all the women he has pursued, successfully or not, there is no one who has not had a reason to regret it" (Letter 9). Valmont nevertheless claims grounds for revenge when his desire for Tourvel is thwarted by the truth Mme de Volanges speaks, and he joins forces with Merteuil. Vanity and sexual desire complement one another, finding expression in a project of revenge.

As their scheme plays itself out, however, the conspirators almost forget about avenging the alleged treachery of Gercourt and Mme de Volanges. The conflict narrows, and the real question of power comes to rest between the conspirators themselves. Merteuil and Valmont become both villains and victims in the events they have orchestrated. Merteuil asks Valmont, as their game nears an end, "which of us will be

Games of Revenge

charged with deceiving the other?" (Letter 131). She reminds him of the story of two gamblers, who, recognizing each other as sharks, agree to abandon their game. "We must," she urges him, "remember their prudent example." Using the language of games here, Merteuil demonstrates that she knows that neither of them will emerge as a winner in this game, but neither can stop what has begun. Valmont exacts revenge by seducing both Cécile and Mme de Tourvel. Merteuil manages to "punish" not only Cécile—in whom she sees nothing but "stupidity," nothing that would make her valuable in future intrigues—but even more decisively, her ally Valmont, by provoking a fatal duel between Valmont and the young Chevalier de Danceny, whom she herself has seduced. But, as one critic has said about *La Cousine Bette*, "feminine power" in Laclos's novel is more of a nightmare than a reality;[8] Merteuil only exercises power up to that moment where her victory seems certain, up to that moment where her satisfaction seems nearly complete. Laclos brings the pattern of revenge full circle when Danceny exposes Merteuil's intrigues: stripped of her possessions, she also suffers the disfigurement of smallpox.

The ending of Laclos's novel is bitterly pessimistic. The events of the novel show that a game of revenge produces no winners; nothing occurs without far-reaching consequences, and no one is safe from harm. All the players stand defeated in the end. In playing the Merteuil-Valmont game, no one wins: everyone loses what they have cherished most—virtue, beauty, fortune, reputation, love, life itself. As Mme de Volanges says at the end of the novel, "I see that in all this the wicked are punished; but I can find no consolation for their unfortunate victims" (Letter 173). Everyone pays for what the forces of vanity and sexual desire have set in motion. Despite Mme de Volanges's sympathy for the "victims," the text itself questions whether either Cécile or Danceny, who participate so willingly in their own victimization, possesses the guiltlessness that "victim" connotes. Laclos has not pitted good against evil in this novel, but rather, stripped both notions of any clear meaning.

In the world Laclos describes, outward behavior is carefully legislated. Rules govern projects like those of Mme de Merteuil and Valmont, just as there are rules for the epistolary discourse that structures the novel. Merteuil and Valmont "educate" Danceny and Cécile in the rules of both games. But the "rules" of the "game" of sexual intrigue are neither moral principles nor social values; they have no intrinsic meaning or value. The rules perpetuate hypocrisy, in that they govern relationships that society officially condemns but secretly rewards and

Dreadful Games

encourages.[9] With all the concern for preserving appearances, there is little concern for preserving the integrity of individual feelings or for punishing violations that are not easily observed. To call this life of intrigue and deception a "game," as Merteuil does, not only protects the manipulators from ever revealing their deepest feelings about others, even to themselves, but also releases them from their ethical responsibilities to one another.

Because Merteuil and Valmont *exploit* the rules of their society, without *violating* them, no one in the novel argues that they are immoral, only that they are "dangerous." Everyone is fair game for the forces of Merteuil and Valmont. For example, when Cécile de Volanges leaves the protective walls of the convent and becomes a part of this society, she becomes subject to the rules that Valmont and Merteuil manipulate so skillfully, and neither innocence nor virtue protects her from those who value neither. In this world, only the *appearance* of virtue is valued, and Merteuil easily abandons Cécile to her fate when her protégée fails to master it—in other words, when Merteuil realizes that "while trying to form the little girl for a life of intrigue, we have only made her a woman of easy virtue" (Letter 106). In the end, Laclos demonstrates that, in playing themselves out, projects of revenge often degenerate into acts of generalized violence, where participation, even as a "victim," is incriminating. Merteuil puts it best when she says, "once incited to the game [*une fois piquée au jeu*], one never knows where one will stop" (Letter 20).

As he shows in *La Cousine Bette*, Balzac shares with Laclos the conviction that the energy unleashed by games of revenge threatens to become uncontrollable, irrational, and destructive. Desire and vanity breed more desire and vanity, since the will to power is insatiable. In the process, the master manipulators risk losing control of their own project, as Mme de Merteuil does to Danceny at the end of *Les Liaisons dangereuses*. The problems of controlling the game are more apparent in Laclos's text, where the characters play out their own fears and desires in their own words, without a narrator to mediate or explain. Readers must fill in any blanks in the text themselves; the text remains open to the play of possible meanings. Laclos's characters create for themselves the narrative context that Balzac insists on providing for his. Valmont and Merteuil must not only deceive others; they must deceive each other and even themselves in order to execute their plan. The epistolary form allows all the characters, the manipulator and the manipulated alike, to author and to critique their own destinies—to create, in effect, their own "plots"—by reflecting in each letter their ideas and images of themselves and others.[10] It is left to the reader of *Les Liaisons dangereuses* to organize the details, to distinguish the true from the false, and to find words for the unspoken.

Balzac permits his characters fewer opportunities for creating and defining themselves in this way; he reserves the privilege of authorship for himself as narrator. And at the same time, he offers his reader fewer opportunities to interpret what he means. In this sense, Balzac's text is more closed to the play of possible meanings than not only *Les Liaisons dangereuses* but *Le Rouge et le noir* as well. Balzac is less comfortable than either Laclos or Stendhal with all kinds of ambiguities. It can even be argued that Balzac has produced a text that "deemphasizes its need for interpretation by systematically interpreting itself."[11] But while Balzac's method appears less effective at exposing the lies buried in a character's heart, it enables him to analyze more systematically the forms of social intercourse that these lies perpetuate. Balzac's explanation of why the patterns of revenge proliferate in the society he portrays is not always entirely satisfying. But he does offer compelling evidence of how patterns of revenge evolve.

Desire in Balzac is never vague or generalized or imagined; it is always expressed as the desire for a particular object. Perhaps as a result, Balzac's characters do not seem fully capable of the compensatory, "useful" fictions that sustain and console the Stendhalian *ambitieux* even in moments of failure or frustrated desire. The Balzacian text grants its characters no access to an inner life, where these fictions might be formed. Desire becomes an issue for Balzac's characters only when it plays itself out in the material world.[12] If Laclos suggests that social alliances—the *liaisons* of the title—are "dangerous" because one risks losing oneself in them, Balzac proves that such affairs are dangerous because they are ultimately very costly, as the worn and faded furnishings of Adeline Hulot's drawing room demonstrate. One risks losing one's possessions, which are often, in Balzac's world, signs of the characters' inner selves.

Characters are defined in two ways in *La Cousine Bette:* by their membership in a social or historical group and, more significantly, by the passion that most often moves them to act. Balzac does not make enigmas of his characters; he imparts his knowledge about them. None of the characters escapes the narrator's "generalizing mania."[13] Thus, Bette is referred to as *"la sauvage Lorraine,"* whose appearance alone explains the treatment she receives from others. "Jealousy," Balzac

Dreadful Games

asserts, "forms the base of her eccentric character" (9:59).[14] Like all of the characters in the novel, she is carefully identified and labeled, given all the desires and abilities of a particular class, a specific group. In contrast, Mme de Merteuil's wounded pride and jealousy reveal themselves more slowly, in what she says and in what she does not say. Characters must be seen as representatives of a class and not as individuals—as members of a team rather than players in their own right. In Balzac's novel, once the character has been analyzed and categorized, the narrator no longer has any reason to play the game of concealment with the reader.

But in the context of the "plots" that structure the novel, games of concealment do take place; every character must conceal something from someone at one time or another, and no one does this more carefully or consistently than Bette. Because it is to her advantage, she conceals her deepest feelings from those around her—her hatred, her rage at the injustice of her position, her jealousy of her cousins' position, and her envy of their possessions. Significantly, what the reader knows about Bette, about her capabilities and passions, from the beginning of the novel—what Balzac explains about her—no one else ever knows. The reader thus shares in the author's superior knowledge. On her deathbed, Bette has the "supreme satisfaction" of seeing those whom she has tried to destroy, "mourning her as the angel of the family" (131:466). And Bette is not the only one who must conceal the truth. Hortense conceals from Bette, with Adeline's assistance, her plan to marry Steinbock, until it is virtually a fait accompli. The first episode of the novel establishes the importance of concealment and sets the tone of secrecy that pervades so many of the encounters that follow: Adeline ushers Crevel into a *salon de jeu* off the main drawing-room, taking elaborate precautions to ensure their privacy. The emphasis on privacy here helps to frame Crevel's actions as a game. And by joining him in this "game room," Adeline implicates herself in his scheme.

The first thirty-six chapters, approximately one-third of the novel, forms what Balzac calls the introduction; as he feels compelled to explain to the reader, "this narrative is to the drama which completes it, what the premise is to a proposition, or what exposition is to classical tragedy" (36:175). This "introduction" also establishes the rules that govern the characters' games. Hortense Hulot's wedding marks the end of the introduction, and by the time this event occurs all the various projects and schemes, which will play themselves out in the rest of the novel, have already been laid in place.[15] Balzac uses the introductory section of the novel to identify what motivates each character; he provides the *logical,* if not the *psychological,* grounds for their actions. Balzac is concerned less with why Hulot and Crevel are driven to compete with one another for young mistresses, than with how this fact will inspire Crevel to seek revenge and provide Bette with the means to injure Adeline and Hortense. Similarly, it is less important why Bette wants to control Steinbock's life, keeping him to herself like a cherished pet—or why Hortense, who has everything Bette lacks, feels compelled to take him from her—than how Bette actually goes about avenging this act of treachery. Balzac is fascinated by the power his characters exercise over one another, but he gives less consideration to why they must exercise it, as if the answers to these questions were obvious or irrelevant.[16] As a result, it is often difficult to evaluate the characters' actions, to separate the villains from the victims. The characters' motives are rarely as clear as the author seems to think they are. Just as in the world Laclos describes, virtually everyone is implicated in some way in the pattern of betrayal and revenge.

Bette states the principle on which all human action in the novel seems to be based: "In Paris, most kindness is a shrewd investment, and most ingratitude is an act of revenge" (27:135). People seek either to benefit from others or to injure them, and these two purposes often overlap. Crevel decides that he will avenge Hulot's theft of his mistress Josépha. Since Hortense's marriage has robbed him of power over Adeline, he must find another way to accomplish his goal. Bette is similarly committed to a project of revenge, vowing to punish not only Hortense but Adeline as well, for her part in Hortense's treachery. These two schemes intersect—and the two major plotlines made to connect—in the person of the selfishly calculating Valérie Marneffe, who becomes the object of Hulot's desire. Bette hopes to ruin Hulot, with Valérie's help, and Crevel, in turn, seeks to steal Valérie from him. Bette and Crevel plan revenge through Valérie, who, in turn, uses them both to her own benefit. Once these projects are set into motion, the other characters must act to protect their own interests and to minimize the risks they face. The novel portrays a world where the potential losses always far exceed the possible gains.

The actions of both Hulot and Crevel are framed, in implicit ways, as a game. In the characters of Crevel and Hulot, Balzac illustrates the effects of ambition grown old, ambition that can no longer be expressed in any meaningful way. This fact is, once again, a way of understanding how Balzac's novelistic interests diverge from those of Stendhal. By the

Dreadful Games

time the novel begins, Hulot's lasciviousness has already brought his family to the brink of financial ruin. The narrator explains what Hulot has once been: a soldier of the Empire, a protégé of Napoleon, a man who had won as his wife a woman of rare beauty and grace. His past glory is reflected through Adeline's eyes; to his wife, he was "from the beginning a kind of God, who could never fail" (7:54). But with the fall of the Empire, and with no wars to fight, the Baron had begun a conquest of women, which Adeline recognizes but chooses to ignore: "Madame Hulot traced her Hector's first infidelities to the final moments of the Empire" (7:55). In this way, Balzac suggests that the energy that had been directed toward serving the Empire, toward building a reputation, is now directed toward acquiring ever younger women at ever higher prices. As his affair with Valérie leads Hulot closer to the brink of destruction, he abandons all scruples. As the narrator rather ironically describes the progress of Hulot's recklessness, "people do not use as much energy, intelligence, or daring in the effort to make an honest living as the Baron was using to plunge head first into a wasps' nest" (34:167–168).[17] Hulot is one of the few characters in the novel who is not motivated primarily by a desire for vengeance. But because he has pursued his own destruction with such heroic fervor, he can never be viewed as victim of the plots directed against him. Even if Hulot is not guilty of seeking revenge, he is guilty of inspiring it in others.

Just as Hulot pursues women for lack of anything else to accomplish, Crevel finds in sexual conquest an outlet for the kind of energy and ambition that has already made him a wealthy man. But Crevel's ambition is more Balzacian than Stendhalian in nature—prudent and acquisitive, without the "napoleonic" flair of Hulot's ambition. A truer *ambitieux* than Crevel, Hulot commits himself wholeheartedly to the mistress game, risking financial ruin, boldly pursuing his desires at all costs. His sexual desire will take him to any lengths, as the Algerian swindle finally reveals. Crevel, on the other hand, always keeps the cost of his desires in mind and proceeds more cautiously. Josépha describes Crevel as a man "who always says 'yes,' but then does whatever is in his head. . . . He is vain and passionate, but his money is cold" (98:366). When Hulot steals his "property," the mistress he has bought and cultivated, Crevel takes immediate, well-considered steps to get even with him: he prevents Hortense Hulot's marriage to M. Lebas and threatens Adeline with her daughter's ruin if she refuses to become his mistress. His chagrin at losing Josépha seems to arise as much from the knowledge that, at fifty-two years old, "love costs thirty thousand francs a year" (4:43), as from the loss of "love" itself. He calculates what he is willing to pay for both his pleasure and his revenge.

The price Crevel puts on revenge in the beginning of the novel is three hundred thousand francs, the amount he offers Adeline for Hortense's dowry. But when she rejects his proposition, he finds that he must raise the stakes. Valérie proves herself equal to his shrewdness, and she manages to extract much more from him than he would have paid to Hulot's wife. Mistresses, in Balzac's world, are always more expensive than wives. For Crevel, there is as much pleasure to be found in pursuing revenge as in obtaining it. He knows what he wants and he takes direct steps to achieve it. Crevel's motive principle is summed up best by what he calls his "idée fixe": "I don't wish him any harm, but I want my revenge, and I will take it" (30:146). Both Hulot and Crevel are monomanical, but in different ways. Hulot acts blindly and often stupidly, never recognizing that he is ensuring his own destruction through his actions, whereas Crevel "plays" at monomania. It is a role he has chosen for himself, and he performs it skillfully.

For this reason, Crevel rather than Hulot, always recognizes the gamelike quality of their obsessions and uses the language of games to describe his goals. Crevel, who finally convinces Hulot that he has lost Valérie, is distressed that this defeat seems to touch Hulot so deeply. "We have each won a hand now," he says, "let's play the deciding round [*nous sommes manche à manche, jouons la belle*]" (51:226). When Crevel uses these sorts of game metaphors he appears almost childlike. With what seems like naïveté, Crevel tells Hulot that they can play out their desires without causing any real harm to one another. In this regard, Crevel is either totally lacking in self-knowledge or trying desperately to convince himself of his own innocence. In everything he does, Crevel is a master at rationalizing his actions: in the narrator's words, "the immorality of his situation was justified by reasons of great morality" (29:145). For Crevel, the play of desire is beyond the scope of ordinary moral judgment.

Unlike most of the characters in Balzac's world, Adeline Hulot finds sustenance in compensatory fictions, not so much because she has more imagination than the others, but because, as the narrator asserts again and again, she is more virtuous. He labels her "virtuous," just as he labels Bette "jealous" or Hulot "lascivious"; she belongs in a particular class. She has chosen to play the role of Josephine to Hulot's Napoleon, and where other characters express sexual desire, Adeline expresses maternal instinct, for her husband as well as her children. She preserves an almost irrational belief in her husband's sterling qualities. Her faith in him is, presumably, as strong as her faith in God, and when on her deathbed she finally offers a word of reproach—when the "savagery of Vice had finally conquered the patience of the angel" (128:469)—it is like witnessing someone experience a loss of faith. This faith in God and family, this ability to nurture a fictional view of life, leaves Adeline outside that group of conspirators whose shrewdly calculated projects generate the events of the novel.

Adeline seems immune to the temptations of the games that others play, perhaps for the same reason that she seems almost beyond desire, with the exception of that passion that expresses itself as maternal concern. In Adeline Hulot, Balzac has created a character who bears a strong resemblance to Stendhal's Mme de Rênal. Like Mme de Rênal, she is ambitious not for herself but for others; her desire to see Hortense married is both as compelling and selfless as Mme de Rênal's desire to see Julien Sorel in the uniform of an honor guard. In Balzac's novel, what makes Adeline so unique, so "virtuous," in the narrator's terms, is not only that sexual passion never moves her, as it does Mme de Rênal, but more importantly, that she is not even tempted by the desire for revenge. Born of the people, "she has in her veins what remains of the blood of the earliest martyrs." She never demonstrates the "need" that other women have "to torment their husbands, to score points against them as if in a game of billiards" (7:55).[18] She never seeks revenge for Hulot's infidelities, never seeks to settle the score between them. She never plays the game that, as Balzac assumes, other wives play with their unfaithful husbands.

But even though Adeline is never moved by passion or revenge, she stands willing to sacrifice her virtue when two hundred thousand francs are needed to protect those she loves from the disgrace of the Algerian swindle. The instinct to protect, the same maternal instinct that moves her to assist in Hortense's betrayal of Bette, drives her to offer herself to Crevel, for a smaller sum than the one he had originally offered her. But Crevel does not accept her offer. Adeline does not lose her virtue; she retains her purity, because, as the narrator claims, "the majesty of virtue, its celestial light, had swept the fleeting impurity from her" (89:334). She submits herself to God's will: "If He wills the death of two beings worthy of going to Him, let them die. . . . If He wills the humiliation of our family, let us kneel before the avenging sword" (333). Her moment of temptation has passed, and she has already begun to atone for her weakness.

Balzac has given this episode, no doubt unintentionally, a degree of moral ambiguity. Regardless of what he *tries* to show here, what he tries to prove about the triumph of virtue over vice, he makes more of a statement about the arbitrary, gamelike nature of human experience. Adeline's "moral victory" over Crevel is highly questionable. Rather, what seems clear from this episode is that Crevel is simply no longer a threat to Adeline's virtue, because he has nothing more to gain from her. When he offers her, at the beginning of the novel, the three hundred thousand francs for Hortense's dowry, he sees her as the instrument of his revenge. But when Hortense marries Steinbock, Crevel has nothing more to negotiate with her. And by the time Adeline reaches this moment of weakness, when she is ready to do anything to avert disaster, Crevel has already exacted vengeance, by means of Valérie. Adeline declares that she is ready to become like Valérie, but Crevel has no need for an imitation when he possesses the original. He explains the rules of his game with Hulot to her: "My dear child, I have had my vengeance; your husband knows it. I showed him categorically that he was duped like a fool [*il était dindonné*]" (88:330). Crevel continues to play with Adeline's feelings, to tease her by suggesting, only half-seriously, that he knows someone else who might want her as a mistress at the price she proposes.

Crevel is certainly cruel here; he is, in effect, exacting his revenge for Adeline's rejection of his earlier advances, but as he sees it, he does so in a harmless, amusing way: he "wanted only to penetrate the secrets of Adeline's heart, in order to laugh about them with Valérie" (89:332). As so often in Balzac's world, amusement comes at the expense of another's pain and humiliation. In the end, having had his fun, and willing to pay both for her distress and for her astounding demonstration of religious fervor, Crevel gives Adeline the money unconditionally. It is not a moment of revelation for him, and the moment of revelation that she experiences comes somewhat too late to be exemplary. The gamelike quality implied in all Crevel's actions works against what Balzac tries explicitly to say in this episode. Because the encounter itself is framed, in Crevel's mind, as a game, Crevel emerges less evil, and Adeline less virtuous, than Balzac seems to have intended. Like all of those "unfortunate victims" in Laclos's world, Adeline implicates herself in the game between Crevel and Hulot, while Crevel merely reasserts the rationale he has used all along—it is all "fair play."

Valérie, like Crevel, finds pleasure in revenge, and she possesses skills for playing out projects of revenge that he does not. Crevel is master tactician, astute at making advantageous moves, but Valérie is a

Dreadful Games

skillful performer, who manipulates feelings and emotions to achieve her ends. When Crevel rushes to tell her about his confrontation with Adeline, she satisfies her wounded pride—she exacts her revenge—by putting on her own performance of piety and self-righteous dignity. So convincing is this display, that she brings Crevel to tears, fearing that he has lost her to her own virtue. At this point, Valérie rips away the veil of hypocrisy, and exposes Crevel for fool. "Here you see the method," she tells him, "that pious women use to swindle you out of two hundred thousand francs" (90:340). In tormenting Crevel, Valérie illustrates her own motivating principle: men can be manipulated into believing almost anything. Valérie's own skill, of course, lies not in giving the appearance of virtue, but in creating the illusion of love, and in this sense, she plays the game of hidden being in the service of her own ambitions.

She is an opportunist, an *ambitieuse*, who relies on the special talents of a beautiful woman to advance her cause. Like all Balzac's characters, she belongs to a particular class, in her case that of "women who decide to make use of their beauty and market it" (37:175). Like Crevel, she is skilled at rationalizing her own actions. She justifies her actions by arguing that she has no choice: except for her beauty, life has dealt her a bad hand. In using her beauty, she merely exploits what she has been given. The power she wields over men also gives her a special power over those women whose status she envies. In seducing Steinbock, she takes pleasure in the pain she causes her rival Hortense. She skillfully manipulates her own appearance to produce different results, to cultivate certain responses, and to nurture certain desires, which she can in turn manipulate further. She recognizes that she must above all else entertain and amuse. The ability to please others grants her a power in society that she would not otherwise have: "the world is always very indulgent toward the mistress of a salon where one amuses oneself" (38:180). But Valérie never succumbs to the illusions she creates, but rather, maintains an ironic distance from them, constantly reminding herself of the lies she promulgates. This cynicism—her refusal to see any good in the world—is as much a distortion of people and events as Adeline's refusal to acknowledge evil. But, perhaps because Valérie's assessment of human nature is closer to Balzac's own than Adeline's is, Valérie manages to be more successful than Adeline in the world that Balzac portrays; she assures herself a significant degree of material success by encouraging the illusions of others.

Valérie's relationship with Bette offers another kind of self-gratification as well. Not only does she create and perform an image of herself for others, she also creates a new identity for Bette, educating her in the nuances of self-image. The acts of revenge that Valérie plots encourage her own illusions of the power she has over others. And at the same time, Valérie provides Bette with a vicarious kind of power: power over men and the ability to compete with other women. She is the instrument of Bette's project to wreak vengeance on Adeline and Hortense. Then too, as time goes on, the power that Bette draws from Valérie gradually becomes more than just vicarious. Valérie's influence transforms Bette physically, making out of her "a black diamond, the rarest of all, cut by a skillful hand, mounted in the most suitable setting" (40:186). Having thus uncovered Bette's hidden strengths, helped her to discover for herself the power of appearances, Valérie helps her to plot a marriage to Hulot's loved and respected brother, the Maréchal, which would, in the narrator's words, "render Bette's vengeance complete" (186). In the process, Valérie finds an outlet for her powers of creativity: she *creates* Bette, transforms her, just as Mme de Merteuil had hoped to *create* Cécile de Volanges. Both Balzac and Laclos suggest in this way that frustrated creativity in a woman becomes diabolical. And, once again, the spirit of play inherent in the creative process is subverted. But Valérie also gains in Bette someone with whom to share the grim pleasures of her various schemes, someone to appreciate the nuances of her various conquests.

The character who plays the deepest game of concealment and the costliest game of revenge is, of course, Bette. As much as Balzac emphasizes the schemes and desires of all the other characters, Bette remains the silent and almost invisible force at the center of this novelistic world, dark and unfathomable, the purest expression of the forces of passion and revenge that move everyone else in the novel. Her presence is what binds all the various schemes together and gives them direction. In practical terms, Bette is a "poor relation," someone who must rely on the kindness of her family, and as Bette herself acknowledges, all kindness is an investment, designed to reap future dividends. Hulot's kindness to her, after he meets Valérie, is just such an investment. She perceives a kind of self-serving ulteriority in the acts and words of everyone she encounters. She is treated without ceremony in her own famly and serves as the object of polite amusement to others. Perhaps more significantly, though, Bette is fundamentally and inescapably an outsider, a primitive force, attempting to comprehend the civilized world.

Dreadful Games

Orchestrating most of the novel's events, then, is the character whose game is the most instinctual and the least amusing. Bette might be contrasted most directly to Crevel—for all that they are allies—since Crevel remains so lighthearted and confidently open about his game playing. As Balzac explains early in the novel, primitive man is "capable of only one idea at a time," in contrast to civilized man, who has "a thousand interests and many emotions." Bette's primitive single-mindedness, which might have led her to kill her cousin in a fit of jealousy, is held in check "only by her knowledge of law and of the world" (9:64).[19] At the same time, it is this "knowledge of the world"—combined with what Balzac calls the "profound insight" possessed by "people consecrated to a life of true celibacy" (9:62)—that permits Bette to manipulate the schemes of others in order to satisfy her own desire for vengeance.

Bette is doubly bound to her position as outsider: as a woman, she cannot act directly to satisfy her desires, and as a woman who does not possess beauty, she is denied even those more indirect, more manipulative methods that women like Valérie and even Hortense have at their disposal. Her initial response to this situation is one of resignation and withdrawal from the social world. As the novel begins, Bette has made a peace of sorts with her position in life, a position that has always been inferior to that of Adeline. Bette brings a lifetime of jealousy to her unspoken conflict with Adeline. The narrator indulges again and again in making the contrast that has shaped Bette's life: Adeline is fair, graceful, and kind; Bette is dark, peculiar, and vaguely malicious.

Over time, Bette has learned to suppress the most obvious expressions of jealousy and anger, with what Balzac suggests is only a thin veneer of civilized behavior. Recognizing the futility of competing with Adeline, Bette has created for herself a position of some importance in the Hulot family. Calling herself "the family confessional" (9:63), Bette has learned how to ingratiate herself with everyone, by "discerning and promoting their desires" (9:63). Thus, even before she joins forces with Valérie, Bette has learned how to share the thoughts and desires of others, and how to benefit from these confidences. Even so, Bette shares in Valérie's triumphs and successes with genuine affection, because Valérie has shown her what she believes is unqualified kindness. In contrast, the affection she shows the Hulot family is never quite genuine; it disguises a deeply held but carefully concealed contempt. Bette continues to harbor a generalized sense of resentment toward those she ostensibly seeks to oblige: "Envy remained hidden at the bottom of her heart, like the germs of a plague that can burst out and ravage a city, if the fatal bale of wool in which it rests is opened up" (9:61).[20] Balzac suggests here that Bette's latent hatred, which erupts into a project of revenge when Hortense marries Wenceslas, will infect all those touched by the evil it generates.

Although Bette finds ways to conceal her feelings of envy and jealousy, she finds it more difficult to resist the temptations of vanity: "However secretive an old maid is, there is one emotion that will make her break her silence, and that is vanity!" (10:66). The romantically imaginative Hortense—who has reached the age, her mother fears, where her passions may lead her into disgrace, if she does not find a husband—has tried to tease from her cousin the admission of a secret lover. In a moment of the kind of playfulness that Bette can never quite comprehend, she gives Hortense the means to injure her. Worn down by Hortense's rather relentless "battle of wits [*guerre de plaisanteries*]," Bette finally reveals what she has hidden for years, the existence of the artist she has fed and nurtured in her own dismal lodgings. But Bette must pay dearly for the moment of vanity that prompts this revelation. The pleasure she feels in detailing the facts of Steinbock's life, or in showing Hortense the letter seal he has made, proves to be short-lived. Bette has, in effect, provided Hortense with an object of desire, a means of realizing her romantic fantasies: "For ten months she had created a real being from the stories of her cousin's imaginary lover . . . this phantom had become Count Wenceslas Steinbock; the dream had a birth certificate, and the haze had taken the form of a young man of thirty years old" (11:73).[21] Ironically, had Bette resisted the temptation to silence Hortense's playful teasing, resisted the temptation to gratify her own vanity, she would most likely have kept her secret safe. In this sense, Bette implicates herself in the act of treachery that Hortense commits; in effect, she brings betrayal upon herself by playing Hortense's teasing game, nourishing the younger woman's fantasies.

So complex is the pattern of betrayal and revenge this novel presents that the point of origin for all these schemes is difficult to detect. Hulot is responsible, in part, for the human tragedy that ensues, because his lust and the reckless and unscrupulous means he takes to satisfy it make his family vulnerable to the machinations of others. Crevel is guilty on two counts. His competition with Hulot over Valérie brings the family closer to ruin. Furthermore, the proposition he makes to Adeline, and the fear it instills in her, makes Steinbock a more attractive prospect for marriage than he otherwise would have been; Crevel thus

Dreadful Games

implicates himself in the treachery and revenge that follow his overtures to Adeline. For her part, Adeline encourages Hortense in her pursuit of Bette's "lover," with an enthusiasm founded on desperation. And however noble Adeline's reasons for participating in this scheme, however strong her maternal instinct, her desire to protect the very idea of "family," she is only slightly less guilty of treachery than Hortense herself. Then too, Valérie's envy of women like Adeline and Hortense and her willingness to "market" her beauty, selling herself to the highest bidder, certainly lead to much of the misfortune and unhappiness that the novel chronicles. Virtually all the characters appear to bear some responsibility for the events that occur.

Even though Bette remains an outsider to these schemes and projects, she is the force that encourages all of them. Bette is both present in the world described in the text and absent from it. She initiates events and then removes herself from them. The games she plays are both vicarious and destructive, the expression of negative desires. She is the one who helps put all the events into motion. She plants in Hortense the seeds of desire for Wenceslas; she aids and abets Hulot's headlong pursuit of Valérie, knowing what it will cost the family; and she gives Crevel the idea of seeking revenge against Hulot through Valérie. And she becomes Valérie's alter ego, relishing every success as if it were her own.

And at first there are many such successes to relish. Valérie manages to destroy Steinbock's marriage by pretending that he is the father of her unborn child. She then plays out a scheme with Marneffe and the police, which even the police recognize as a trick, forcing Hulot to give Marneffe a promotion. Then, by dismissing Hulot, she secures from Crevel a promise of marriage, a marriage that threatens to rob the younger generations of Hulots and Crevels of their future inheritance. Each of the four men Valérie manipulates—Crevel, Hulot, Steinbock, and the mysterious Brazilian, Henri Montès—believes that he is Valérie's true love, and each believes he is the father of Valérie's unborn child. Valérie seeks to have her husband's pension when he dies, to obtain Crevel's fortune through marriage, and to retain Steinbock's passionate love, all at the same time. She even hopes that Crevel will die soon, permitting her to marry the wealthy *and* passionate Montès. Her desire for power, money, and passion appears almost unlimited.

For her part, Bette sees in the despair of Adeline and Hortense the fruition of all her plans. Just when Hulot's debts to the moneylender Vauvinet come to light, Bette manages to install herself in the Maréchal's household, and the marriage between them seems certain. This moment, just before the Algerian swindle is revealed, is Bette's greatest moment of triumph: "Adeline and Hortense would finish their days in distress, combatting misery, while Cousin Bette, received at the Tuileries, occupied a place of honor in society [*trônerait dans le monde*]" (85:316). Bette imagines her revenge complete, by "saving" the family she has secretly and relentlessly tried to destroy.

But Bette has savored her victory too soon, and it is at this point in the novel that the pattern of revenge moves beyond the control of those who initiate it, just as it does in *Les Liaisons dangereuses*. No longer do Bette and Valérie manipulate events so successfully. Like Merteuil and Valmont, they begin to lose control of events, and it is only a matter of time until they suffer from the schemes they themselves have begun. The disgrace of the Algerian swindle kills the Maréchal before he and Bette can be married. This death is, for Bette, "like the bolt of lightning that consumes the crops already gathered into the barn"—in other words, like the hand of fate. Bette has succeeded too well in her project of revenge. Much as she did when she enabled Hortense's treachery, Bette brings this disaster on herself: "The Maréchal was dead from the blows struck against the family by Mme Marneffe and herself" (96:360). With the Maréchal's death, Bette's vengeance remains incomplete. To make matters worse, the family's financial situation begins to improve: Victorin receives enough money to pay off his mortgage, along with a position in government that offers an attractive salary. Her own ambitions crushed, Bette looks to Valérie's marriage to Crevel as the only means left to injure the Hulot family.

But although Valérie is successful in this project, like Bette, she proves to be too successful. In achieving her end, she incurs the wrath of both Victorin Hulot and the Brazilian Montès. Balzac seems to have included Montès in the novel not only as a convenient agent of vengeance—his role in the novel is not unlike that of the smallpox that strikes Mme de Merteuil down in *Les Liaisons dangereuses*—but also because he displays the most extreme expression of revenge in the novel. The mysterious venereal disease with which he infects Valérie and Crevel—and Balzac describes all the symptoms in precise detail—becomes almost a symbol of the dehumanizing evil of revenge, with which these two, with Bette's help, have infected their society. Somewhat like Bette, Montès is a primitive, from a half-civilized world. But he proves both more dangerous to betray and more effective at exacting his revenge than any other character in the novel. When he an-

Dreadful Games

nounces—at a party given by Jenny Carabine, one of Hulot's former mistresses—his intention to kill Valérie if her betrayal of him can be proven, his companions respond, "Kill her? We do not do that sort of thing here." Montès's reply is unequivocal: "I am not from your country. I live where I control everything, where I simply laugh at your laws" (115:428).[22] Through him Balzac demonstrates, in effect, the outermost limits of the play of revenge, the most unadulterated expression of this desire. He shows how far someone with power, but without rules, without the sense of "fair play" that a Crevel always demonstrates, will go to accomplish his revenge.

But while Montès's role in the novel seems clear, Victorin Hulot is a much more puzzling character. Clearly intended, by everything the narrator says about him, to serve as a figure of virtue and righteousness, his major narrative function in the novel is that of an agent of vengeance.[23] Victorin is contrasted to both Hulot and Crevel: he is steadfast and hardworking, a man whose misfortunes strengthen him, unlike his irresponsible father and insincere father-in-law: "his mind infatuated with politics, always showing respect for his own hopes and covering them up with solemnity, very envious of established reputations, choosing ponderous statements instead of the incisive words that are the diamonds of French conversation, but with a sense of his own bearing and taking arrogance for dignity" (12:78).[24] While Victorin may appear pompous and self-righteous to the reader—he clearly lacks the charm that both Hulot and Crevel possess—Balzac unmistakably applauds him for supporting the family and for trying to fill the vacuum left when his father abdicates his position of authority. After the death of the Maréchal, the Prince de Wissembourg appoints Victorin to watch over Adeline and Hortense, calling him "a wise man, the worthy son of your noble mother, true nephew of my friend the Maréchal" (100:372), effectively denying the influence of his father. Victorin insists that it is honor, not money, that makes him try to prevent Crevel's marriage to Valérie. He flourishes under the load he bears and exemplifies those qualities that Balzac seems most to admire.

Victorin nevertheless becomes a significant character in the novel only when he begins to contemplate revenge. Even though the family situation improves under his leadership, he harbors within him a desire to see Valérie punished for manipulating his father and father-in-law. Again, it is Bette who unwittingly provokes him to act. Once too often she brings Victorin news of the progress of Valérie's schemes, and he resolves to rid himself of "the demonic woman to whom his mother and his family owed so much unhappiness" (103:384). Victorin hopes at first to seek his vengeance through legal channels, but when the malevolent Mme Nourrisson arrives, offering to kill Valérie for forty thousand francs, she explains that "the police should not appear at all in an affair of this nature" (107:397). Victorin has no illusions about the evil that Mme Nourrisson represents—she is, in his own words, "the criminal side of Paris personified" (108:399)—but he tries to bargain with her, arguing that he wants nothing to do with any kind of criminal act.

Mme Nourrisson points out how untenable Victorin's position is here: "You would like to remain upright in your own eyes, but at the same time you wish for your enemy to die. . . . You are not logical. You call for combat, but you don't want any injuries" (107:398–399). Victorin cannot play the game of revenge, she suggests, without accepting the consequences. If he wants to use the means she offers him, he cannot remain immune to its evil. What Victorin is not willing to do before Valérie's marriage, he finds the will to do when the new Mme Crevel sends an ominous message to Adeline via Bette. "I have had enough of scruples," he declares. "If I had the power I would crush this woman like a viper. . . . She who attacks the life and honor of my mother!" (112:413). Like Adeline, Victorin can justify almost anything in the name of preserving the family. When Victorin finally engages the talents of Mme Nourrisson, he helps to complete the project of revenge that Montès has masterminded. And in doing so, he compromises his own virtue, bringing himself to the level of those he seeks to punish.

In the "Avant-Propos" to *La Comédie humaine,* Balzac argues that although his work describes much evil, on the whole, the portraits of virtue outnumber those of vice: "In the picture that I have created, one will find more virtuous characters than reprehensible characters. The guilty actions, the errors, the crimes, from the less severe to the more serious, always find their punishment, human or divine, public or secret."[25] Balzac suggests here that portraying vice punished makes his point as clearly as portraying virtue rewarded, since after all, society is, for the most part, more evil than good. But however valid this assertion that he shows more virtue than vice in his earlier novels, it does not apply to the world he describes in *La Cousine Bette*. True, Crevel and Valérie are punished for their part in the events of the novel, and Bette dies a painful death shortly thereafter, having lost everything. On her deathbed, Valérie repents her life of sin, recognizing in her affliction not the revenge of Montès but the hand of God. But just as in *Les Liaisons dangereuses,* virtue is scarcely rewarded; there is little compensation

Dreadful Games

for those who might be called victims. There are no winners in the games that play themselves out in this novel, and even those who survive and flourish, like Victorin Hulot, lose something of their own integrity and self-worth in the process of playing.

In *La Cousine Bette,* what remains at the end is not a character's fiction, but Balzac's own fiction of the world—a world in Maurice Beebe's words, "at once better (more logically controlled) and worse (more evil and distorted) than the real world."[26] Balzac seems to imply that Valérie's death is a just punishment, that it represents the triumph of virtue over vice, yet Bette states what seems closer to the truth, as the novel portrays it: " 'I have seen vengeance everywhere in nature; insects perish in order to satisfy their desire for vengeance when they are attacked. And these men,' she said pointing to the priest, 'don't they tell us that God avenges himself and that his vengeance endures for eternity?' " (122:448). The cycle of betrayal and vengeance, and the evil it produces in human life, is an inescapable fact, whether one takes a rational, scientific view of life, or turns to religion for consolation. Ultimately, the vengeance of God cannot be distinguished from the acts of revenge that insects instinctively pursue. In a moment of self-awareness, Victorin secretly admits, but never openly acknowledges, his own part in the deaths of Crevel and Valérie; he continues to believe it was a necessary evil. Bette dies, the secret of her hatred locked in her heart. Balzac portrays a world in which the act of avenging oneself becomes, like a game, an end in itself, neither good nor evil, neither condoned nor condemned. The images of game playing in *La Cousine Bette* emphasize not only the futility of competition but the blind destructiveness of the acts of revenge that competition often inspires.

5

The Play of Fate

Dostoevsky's *Crime and Punishment* and Hardy's *Jude the Obscure*

■ The fatalist, as Mikhail Lermontov illustrates at the end of his novel *A Hero of Our Time* (1840), is the person who believes in "a man's fate being written in heaven."[1] Lermontov's narrator, Pechorin, tells of an encounter he has with another officer, Lieutenant Vulich, whose one passion, one vice, in life is gambling: "Once seated at the green table, he forgot everything, and usually lost" (183). One night when the discussion among their fellow officers turns to the question of "whether a man may dispose of his life at will or a fateful minute is assigned to each" (184), Vulich risks his life in a wager. Pechorin offers him twenty gold pieces to prove that the moment of a man's death is predestined. As he observes Vulich closely, Pechorin detects "the imprint of death upon his pale face" (185). To prove that the moment of his death has not yet come, Vulich chooses a weapon at random, raises it to his forehead, and pulls the trigger. The pistol misfires, and Vulich, lucky for once, collects his winnings, leaving Pechorin to wonder what had made him think that Vulich's death was imminent.

This experience heightens Pechorin's conviction that life is without order, that luck and misfortune occur randomly. As he contemplates what has just occurred, Pechorin compares himself to his distant, primitive ancestors, envying the "strength of will they derived from the certitude that the entire sky with its countless inhabitants was looking upon them with mute but permanent sympathy." In contrast to these ancient men who "rushed from one delusion to another," Pechorin believes that men like himself "roam the earth without convictions or pride," while they "pass with indifference from doubt to doubt" (188).[2] "Doubt" has replaced "delusion" as the principle that explains human existence. But even as Pechorin considers the hopelessness of life without belief or meaning, his vague premonition of Vulich's death is confirmed. Vulich's luck has run out: he is murdered by a drunken Cossack in a dark street. Later that same night, Pechorin finds and subdues the drunken Cossack, risking his own life in a courageous but foolhardy gesture. Like the wager Vulich makes, Pechorin's act is fatalistic. If a man acts as if he has nothing to lose, as if no risk were too great, he implies by his actions a belief that the episodes in his life are "assigned to him at his birth" (194).

As the narrator of this story, Pechorin denies that his experience has made him a fatalist like Vulich—such a belief demands more faith than he possesses. Doubt, he argues, makes a man more "resolute"; as he says, "I always advance with greater courage, when I do not know what awaits me" (194). Pechorin seeks to prove he is a man of will and action, a man of freedom and power, when he confronts the Cossack murderer. But Pechorin is one of those fictional narrators whose egotism and insincerity make them peculiarly blind to the significance of their own words and actions. Pechorin has not actually denied the role of fate in his life; he has merely tested his fate in a different way than Vulich tested his. Like the fatalist, the skeptic finds himself willing to take almost any risk. What Lermontov calls "the gaming passion" (183) infects both the man who believes that his fate is sealed at birth and the man who believes in nothing.

Lermontov's story, of course, neither proves nor disproves that a person's life is governed by fate, but *A Hero of Our Time* does describe the fatalism and hopelessness that motivate many nineteenth-century heroes to pursue what seem like wasted lives. Many heroes in the literature of the European Romantic tradition find themselves overwhelmed by solipsism—by the formidable and engrossing task of self-fulfillment. But in the special environment of nineteenth-century Russia, this Romantic hero develops in a unique way. Pechorin belongs to a long tradition of "superfluous men" in Russian literature, a tradition that includes such alienated and inauthentic heroes as Pushkin's Eugene Onegin and Turgenev's Bazarov in *Fathers and Sons*.[3] Dostoevsky's own novelistic heroes emerge from this tradition. They find themselves no less driven to risk everything than the doomed and secretive Vulich or the "bored and disgusted" (by his own admission)

Pechorin, and sometimes, as in Raskolnikov's case, a character emerges who is both Vulich and Pechorin—both fatalist and skeptic at once. Dostoevsky's hero is often an actual gambler, someone who spends his life at roulette or cards, but more often he is someone who risks not money but other things that have special value for him. The narrator of Dostoevsky's *The Gambler* tries to explain the attraction of risk, when he wagers all that he has won: "I ought to have left at that point, but a strange sort of feeling came over me, a kind of desire to challenge fate."[4] A game of chance moves almost inevitably toward defeat, even as victory remains strangely unsatisfying. Risk becomes an uncontrollable obsession, and fate a kind of competitor, to be subdued and manipulated as the pattern of the game repeats itself.

Unlike the "superfluous men" of Pushkin, Lermontov, or Turgenev, the "gamblers" who populate Dostoevsky's novels are not pampered aristocrats or dissipated officers, who take risks because nothing really matters to them, but men for whom risk is a means to an end—a way to avert humiliation or subjection, a way to rise above circumstances perceived as degrading. Dostoevsky's characters gamble not out of boredom or pleasure but because they have some need for the particular prize they hope to win. Very often, the gambler finds himself pursuing an idea or concept, seeking to prove something to himself or others. The risks that gamblers take reflect a desire to accomplish great things or to control others, as well as a fear that they might fail under ordinary circumstances. A character like Raskolnikov can be distinguished from a character like Julien Sorel by his refusal even to consider such projects as tutoring students or working in Luzhin's law practice, even as a temporary expedient—an attitude that makes him both less foolish and more dangerous than Stendhal's character. Games of chance differ from other forms of competition in that players often stand to lose more and to gain more when they gamble. If they lose, they must risk even more to regain what they have lost; and if they win, they invariably continue playing on the premise that they can win even more. As Roger Caillois explains in his study of games, "To gamble is to renounce work, patience, and thrift in favor of a sudden lucky stroke of fortune which will bring one what a life of exhausting labor and privation has not."[5] In this way, gamblers demonstrate an ambition rooted in pride, in feelings of superiority, and at the same time, a rejection of the more traditional forms of social competition. In a world that values work and accomplishment, gamblers refuse to work, preferring instead to play at their own advancement.

Dreadful Games

Stendhal's Julien Sorel, Dostoevsky's Raskolnikov, and Hardy's Jude Fawley typify the circumstances of three distinct generations of young men—in the 1830s, 1860s, and 1890s—who seek to rise from modest beginnings and to give their lives an almost heroic significance.[6] Needless to say, such a comparison cuts across those distinctive national considerations that provide part of the context for each novel—the fall of Napoleon in France, the rise of radical politics in Russia, and the demise of an agrarian community in England, just as examples—and addresses instead the problems of individual desire that each novel explores and the pattern of success and failure that structures each novel. In *Le Rouge et le noir* Julien's efforts are shaped by the play of competing historical and cultural factions, which provide the character with specific opportunities for advancement. Although Julien remains an outsider to the power plays from which he benefits, something more than pure chance—as either luck or misfortune—governs the ultimately circular progression of both his "career" and the plot of the novel. Stendhal never underestimates Julien's ability to seize and manipulate opportunities, and always undercuts the character's attempts to deny his ability to shape his own destiny. Julien's eventual failures are less the result of bad luck than of poor judgment.

In contrast to *Le Rouge et le noir,* both *Crime and Punishment* and *Jude the Obscure* are shaped by the play of fate—by a recurring cycle of luck and misfortune. In both novels, individual effort is pitted against the impersonal forces of culture and history, thus undermining the significance of individual merit and making both success and failure seem random, incomprehensible, and inexorable. In a world governed by such impenetrable forces, individual accomplishment can be negated at any moment; hours of study and hard work may never pay off. Although Dostoevsky proposes, most clearly in the controversial Epilogue to *Crime and Punishment,* a way—through faith in God and in human love—to avoid the debilitating fatalism that comes to characterize a life governed by such forces, Hardy rejects the possibility of transcending fatalism through the kind of faith Dostoevsky describes. Hardy's characters are ultimately crushed by the weight of coincidence and superstition, not to mention the forces of society and biology. Ironically, of the three characters, it is Jude whose aspirations seem the most modest and reasonable, yet the obstacles in the way of his realizing any happiness prove the most insurmountable. What emerges from a comparison of these three novels is the image of a world with in-

The Play of Fate

creasingly diminished opportunities, a world where failure seems more and more inevitable.

Just as Julien Sorel seeks both comfort and identity in the myth of Napoleon, the central characters of *Crime and Punishment* and *Jude the Obscure* rely on "fictions" to sustain them. In this sense, Raskolnikov's theory of the extraordinary man is analogous to Jude's perception of Christminster as "a city of light." Both of these fictions arise from the characters' desire for a world that recognizes and rewards individual merit. Both fictions provide a kind of wish-fulfillment, compensating for what seems missing in the characters' everyday lives. Just as Don Quixote sought, by playing at knight-errantry, to make his world more ordered and honorable than he found it, both Raskolnikov and Jude play out their dreams of a world of wider opportunities; all three characters share a vision of a better world. The dreams are no less noble, no less utopian even, for being essentially compensatory. But these texts are about role playing as well—about the creation and performance of self. In much the same way that Julien plays at being Napoleon, Raskolnikov plays at being the extraordinary man of his theory (another interpretation of the Napoleonic myth), and Jude plays at being the Christminster scholar of his imagination. In each case, the "fiction" finds itself opposed to some conception of "reality."

As Raskolnikov considers his plan to murder the old pawnbroker, he tells himself, "I am just amusing myself with fancies, children's games . . . perhaps I am only playing a game [*igruški*]."[7] In this way, Raskolnikov assures himself that his theory is only a child's game, without serious consequences. In a reversal of this logic, Jude himself takes his Christminster dream seriously, opposing it in his own mind to the "bit of fun" that someone like Arabella offers him. Just as the psychologist Piaget linked play and dreams in the psychic lives of the children he observed, *Jude the Obscure* links the individual's aspirations—his "dreams" of self-fulfillment—with playing. Everyone in the novel sees Jude as playing at the expense of work: the neighborhood discusses "his method of combining work and play," and people argue that he "should not be allowed to read while driving" his aunt's bakery wagon.[8] All of Jude's creative effort, albeit misguided or poorly directed, is, somewhat unfairly, characterized as mere idleness. Thus, while Raskolnikov's theory inspires horror, Jude's dream invites derision. Yet despite this difference, each of these fictions represents the character's attempt, however misguided or illusory, to formulate a co-

Dreadful Games

herent system of belief, to give meaning and purpose to what appears to be an otherwise futile life.

The conflicts in both novels arise when the boundaries between "fiction" and actual experience, between belief and action, between theory and execution, between dream and duty, begin to dissolve. The metaphor of the game serves in both novels to signal this moment when belief and action collide. In *Jude the Obscure* this boundary dissolves slowly, over time, but in *Crime and Punishment* it ruptures more suddenly, often with violence. For Raskolnikov the boundary is "transgressed"—the word *prestuplenie* in the Russian title of the novel might best be translated as "transgression"[9]—the moment he steps across the threshold of the old pawnbroker's flat, the moment he commits himself to giving his fiction a life of its own.[10] Raskolnikov himself often denies that he has commited a crime; he has merely tested a theory, or killed a "principle." The threshold he crosses is more than just a legal or moral boundary: in "playing out" his theory Raskolnikov violates the boundary that separates the artificial, closed world of theoretical speculation, where ideas have no direct or immediate consequences, from the world of actual experience, where an individual must be prepared to take responsibility for his actions.

Even after he "rehearses" the murder, Raskolnikov fails to see where his actions are leading him: "his recent *rehearsal* had been no more than a *test,* and far from a serious one" (60). That his game escalates from "theoretical" murder to actual murder follows from the fact that he must take greater and greater risks in order to keep his theory viable in his own mind. In other words, he must escalate the "game" or cease playing it. Furthermore, when this first attempt to validate his theory proves inconclusive—when he recognizes that "the successful perpetration of the murder owes less to his physical and mental powers than to chance"[11]—Raskolnikov must raise the stakes of the game he plays. He risks more in order to gain more, and in order to make up for what he has already lost. As a result, he eventually finds himself unavoidably drawn into the riskier, more complex game that he plays with Porfiry Petrovich.

In place of the conspiratorial forces that structure events in Stendhal's *Le Rouge et le noir* or the revenge "plots" that structure Balzac's *La Cousine Bette, Crime and Punishment* relies on the play of conflicting ideologies to generate events. Events occur because characters seek through word or action to affirm their own cherished theories. Rather than act against one another, Dostoevsky's principal characters argue

The Play of Fate

with one another; they defend their ideologies. As a result, almost every conversation becomes a kind of "game," a strategic transaction where points are scored or lost. Although the most significant events of the novel can be traced to Raskolnikov's act of murder, other characters play out their own desires at the same time. Some of these "games," like the name-calling matches between Katerina Ivanovna and her German landlady, have comic overtones, even while they suggest fundamental conflicts. But the games that Luzhin and Svidrigaylov involve themselves in are more "serious"—they have more significant consequences—and, therefore, they are more clearly indicative of deeply rooted conflicts in Dostoevsky's novelistic world.

Luzhin, who has commercially contracted, with debts and obligations, to make Raskolnikov's sister Dunya his wife, uses this situation to affirm his own rather twisted and arrogant theories about what makes for happiness in marriage: he seeks to marry a woman "who had known a great many misfortunes . . . one who would all her life think of him as her saviour, reverence him, obey him, admire him" (260). Just as Raskolnikov seeks to test his extraordinary man theory, Luzhin has searched for a woman on whom to test his theory. This "playful theme" [*igrivuju temu*] has sustained him for years before he finds Dunya. Luzhin believes he has taken a calculated risk in contracting this marriage—"scorning public opinion"—and he waits impatiently to see his investment pay off. As he tells Dunya directly, "I was certainly completely and absolutely entitled to count on being recompensed and even to demand your gratitude" (259). But the more desperately he acts out his role of benevolent despot, the more decisively he fails. He reveals himself to Dunya and to everyone else as an imposter, a man who comprehends the forms but not the essence of human relationships.

When Dunya turns him away, Luzhin refuses to believe that his theory has been invalidated and that satisfaction of his desires has been put at risk: "He still imagined that the game was not utterly lost" (259).[12] His hope here indicates not only that he has completely misjudged Dunya but, more importantly, that he understands the demands and rewards of successful game playing but not the value of love or respect. He prefers winning at any cost to retaining his dignity, even to being happy. If Luzhin "values" Dunya, as he tells her, he does so precisely because she is the prize he seeks to attain. His belief that this prize remains within reach prompts him to play out the charade of giving Sonya the one hundred-rouble note at the Marmeladovs' funeral

93

dinner. Lacking the strength of will to confront Raskolnikov—whom he blames for all his troubles—Luzhin chooses an opponent, Sonya, whom he perceives as completely powerless and vulnerable, an easy mark. By choosing such an unequal opponent, he seeks to neutralize the risk he takes to win Dunya. In making Sonya appear guilty of theft, Luzhin seeks to prove his "theory" about Sonya's moral character and to discredit Raskolnikov, thus regaining his position of favor with Dunya.

But Luzhin's attempt to manipulate others in this way is foiled first by Lebezyatnikov and then more conclusively by Raskolnikov. Guided by poorly understood socialist principles, Lebezyatnikov attacks every problem with a logic that leaves him exhausted. He considers the possible reasons why Luzhin might have slipped Sonya the note: to conceal an act of charity from Lebezyatnikov, who believes that charity "accomplishes no radical cure" (337), to "surprise" Sonya, to test her gratitude, or to avoid her gratitude all together. His reasoning leads him in circles. When he calls Luzhin a "traducer" [*klevetnik*] in accusing Sonya, he acknowledges in the same breath, "I still don't quite see the logic of it" (336). He is looking for the light of human reason in a situation where only the desires of the individual will and the logic of rational game playing are in question.

Lebezyatnikov's ideas about human nature lead him to imagine a world where, if left to their own devices, people act rationally, without prejudice or superstition—a world where insanity can be cured "by the use of nothing but logical persuasion" (358). But Lebezyatnikov's ideas are foolish, and his understanding of them superficial, as the text suggests through his speech and manner. Dostoevsky strives to repudiate this view of human nature in his fiction and his essays; the events of his novels seem based on the premise that, with few exceptions, people will act *irrationally*, if left to their own devices. The experience of his characters confirms that individual desire cannot be regulated or reasoned away. Consequently, a Lebezyatnikov can never be expected to understand a Luzhin. But for Raskolnikov, who not only knows what has already happened, but also understands Luzhin's moral character in a way that Lebezyatnikov never could, Luzhin's motives are transparent: he seeks to grasp power, to shape people and events to his own will. Ironically, Luzhin's attempt to injure Sonya is not unlike Raskolnikov's murder of the old woman. Both characters seek to affirm their own theories and both must injure others to do so—and neither succeeds in securing the power he desires.

Luzhin and Svidrigaylov function in the novel as indicators of the extent to which a gambler will pursue the prize. The risks that Luzhin takes in the novel are cautious and calculated; he is a self-conscious player and an uneasy gambler. It is not just his language or his arrogance that makes him so often look foolish, but his inability to commit himself unequivocally to his own projects, the way that he always seeks to diminish the risk he faces. In making the arrangements for his marriage to Dunya, he spends money frugally, since "more than anything in the world he loved and prized his money" (259). The value he places on money, and the power he attributes to it, can be discerned in the way he uses it to injure Sonya. From the beginning, Luzhin finds himself in the awkward position of wanting Dunya very much, but not wanting to spend too much to obtain her. He is tentative, always ready to pull back if the risk becomes too great. In contrast, Svidrigaylov, like Lermontov's Vulich or the narrator of Dostoevsky's *The Gambler,* is the player who never knows when to leave the table.

Like Luzhin, Svidrigaylov has decided that Dunya is the object he wants most to possess, but he is willing to go further than Luzhin is in his efforts to accomplish this goal. And unlike Luzhin, Svidrigaylov is completely unencumbered by philosophy and self-image; his only "theory" is that of the will to power.[13] Svidrigaylov tries to impose his will on Dunya in many ways—as he explains to Raskolnikov at the end of the novel, he has tried seducing her with flattery, offering her all his money, and threatening to murder his wife—and he remains undaunted when each plan of attack fails. When he learns through eavesdropping at the door to Sonya's room that Raskolnikov has murdered the pawnbroker, he lures Dunya to his room, tells her what he knows, and offers to take Raskolnikov safely away if she will submit to him. Svidrigaylov's blackmail scheme might be compared with Luzhin's scheme to discredit Raskolnikov through Sonya. But Svidrigaylov is both more formidable and more threatening than Luzhin. The truth he learns about Raskolnikov's crime proves to be a more powerful and dangerous weapon than the "fiction" Luzhin devises of Sonya's guilt.

And perhaps because Svidrigaylov is *not* foolish or pompous or humorless—Dostoevsky never makes fun of him the way he does Luzhin—Svidrigaylov comes closer to "winning" his game than Luzhin ever does. When he dares Dunya to shoot him to escape from his room, he risks his life in order to possess her. Dunya realizes "that he would rather die than let her go," but she cannot bring herself to kill him. When she lays the revolver down, he thinks to himself, "She has given up!" (420). But he cannot endure the hollowness of his victory; the aversion she demonstrates when he touches her transforms his desire into despair. This moment offers him only the grimmest kind of satisfaction. All of his efforts to possess Dunya have been rendered meaningless by her refusal to submit to his will and by her denial that he could ever make her love him. Svidrigaylov has nothing left to risk and nothing more to gain. Just as Lermontov's Vulich escapes death at the card table only to face it a half hour later in a dark street, Svidrigaylov escapes death at Dunya's hands only to suffer it at his own. He does, as Dunya intuits, choose death over letting her go. In the end, Svidrigaylov fails, because Dunya refuses to grant him the kind of victory he has anticipated. The characters of Luzhin and Svidrigaylov show the ultimate futility of actions pursued on the premise that obstacles can be surmounted by the sheer force of individual will. They are both gamblers who lose what they value.

By using the language and attitudes of game playing, the novel also shows how pure logic fails to address the problems that individuals face. In several instances, characters in the novel are described by others as having a limited number of options open to them, an observation that often falls short of accuracy. In the episode where Raskolnikov taunts Sonya with the argument that "you have abandoned and destroyed yourself *in vain*" (272), he thinks to himself that there are only three options open to her: "to throw herself into the canal, to end in a madhouse, or . . . or, finally, to abandon herself to debauchery that will numb her mind and turn her heart to stone" (273). Later, with the same kind of logic, Svidrigaylov tells Sonya that Raskolnikov is left with only two options—suicide or Siberia. In both these cases, the character is perceived by others as a game player, whose "moves" are prescribed and limited by circumstances and by the choices, or moves, he or she has already made.

Perhaps simply because they are both "game players," Svidrigaylov is essentially correct in his evaluation of Raskolnikov's position. Raskolnikov can either end his life, as Svidrigaylov himself does, or confess and be exiled to Siberia, as he eventually does. He can *postpone* making this choice, as he does for most of the novel, but he cannot defer resolution forever unless he can continue to play the kinds of games he plays with Porfiry. His position is like that of Scheherazade in *The Thousand and One Nights,* who must keep making up stories in order to avert death. The game playing only postpones the inevitable. But, regardless of how correct he is about his own options, Raskolnikov is not at all correct about the limits to Sonya's options, as the ending of the novel seeks to prove. Sonya refuses to play the games of logic in which Raskolnikov indulges—refuses even to look for an answer to the kinds of questions he asks her: "Suppose you were allowed to decide . . . either that Luzhin should live and go on doing evil, or that Katerina Ivanovna should die. How would you decide." Raskolnikov asks her to resort to the same "utilitarian arithmetic" expressed in the conversation he overhears before he commits the murder: What will result in the greatest good for the greatest number?[14] Sonya's response to his question indicates how foreign his logic is to her way of thinking: "Why do you ask questions that have no answer? Where is the point of such empty questions?" (344). In Sonya's mind, nothing can reveal "God's intentions," not even the most carefully formulated, most logically sound human reasoning.

When Sonya calls Raskolnikov's questions "empty," she implies that they are unresolvable, that they can be pursued endlessly and without resolution, just as the "game" Raskolnikov commences in the beginning of the novel can be played as long as he can will himself to play it. Far from resolving Raskolnikov's inner conflicts, the murder itself only encourages him to keep pursuing risks; afterward he roams the streets, unconsciously looking for a way to continue his game. When summoned to the police station because of his landlady's complaint, Raskolnikov feels he must find some role to play in order to prevent the discovery of his crime. That he does not know how to act in this situation, that he cannot strike the right balance between truth and deception, leads to his highly unpredictable and seemingly irrational behavior. Afterward he realizes, with some disgust, that he has not managed the situation very skillfully: "How loathsomely I fawned on that filthy Ilya Petrovich and played up to him [*zaigryval*]" (92). He expresses here contempt not only for his own poor performance but also for "the Squib's" apparent inability to recognize its mediocrity. After each of the gamelike encounters that he enters—especially the complex games he plays later with Porfiry—Raskolnikov critiques his performance, brooding about how he has played and going over each "move" and "countermove" in his mind.

Raskolnikov seeks in other ways to continue the game he has begun, always taking more risks. He returns to the murdered woman's flat, drawn there by what the narrator calls "an irresistible and inexplicable desire" (146). Pretending he is interested in renting the flat, he annoys the workmen and the porters with questions about blood stains left

Dreadful Games

from the murder, finally prompting one of the porters to exclaim, "You're up to some game or other all right" (149),[15] as he throws him out of the building. Raskolnikov deliberately draws attention toward himself. When he meets Zamyotov, in the Crystal Palace tavern,[16] he "rehearses" his confession, much as he rehearses the murder before he commits it. He begins by teasing the police clerk, assuring him "I am not talking like this from spite, 'but in pure affection, playfully [*igra-juču*],' as that workman of yours said, when he was punching Mitka, in that case of the old woman" (136). Raskolnikov does several things in this one statement: he "frames" his encounter with Zamyotov as play, where anything can be said without being taken seriously; he raises the issue of the pawnbroker's murder; and he places Zamyotov on the defensive by suggesting that he knows as much about the murder as the police clerk himself. Raskolnikov enters into his own game so completely that only after he says, "And what if it was I who killed the old woman and Lizaveta?" does he realize what a risk he has taken. But Zamyotov, who is, after all, no Porfiry, finds himself more confused than suspicious as a result of Raskolnikov's "confession." Raskolnikov leaves the tavern, "shaking all over, with a feeling of wild hysteria mingled with almost unendurable pleasure" (141). He finds the danger of his actions exhilarating, as well as a little fatiguing, and significantly, he does not find the release of tension that should come from play.

The ambivalence of Raskolnikov's attitudes toward himself and his actions emerges even with those who pose no threat of discovery. When he goes to visit Razumikhin, ostensibly to inquire about doing translations, his irratic behavior prompts Razumikhin to demand, "What sort of game do you think you are playing?" (95).[17] What makes Razumikhin a crucial character in this context is that even though he plays no "game" of his own in the novel,[18] he often perceives that others are playing games, and even admires, sometimes grudgingly, the skills they demonstrate. For example, Razumikhin tells Raskolnikov that compared with Zamyotov, "You're a master, I swear it; that's just what they need" (164). In this way, Razumikhin comments on Raskolnikov's skill in analytical thinking, acknowledging that intellectual discussions and theoretical arguments can be stimulating and pleasurable. Of course, when he makes this statement, Razumikhin has no way of knowing where Raskolnikov's theoretical arguments have already taken him.

Razumikhin also highlights the game metaphors that contribute to the tone and texture of Raskolnikov's encounters with Porfiry. He warns Raskolnikov, during his first encounter with Porfiry, that the police

The Play of Fate

examiner is capable of making those with whom he spends time look like "fools," referring to earlier situations where Porfiry has exercised his skills of "mystification"; Razumikhin claims that "he's quite capable of keeping this up for a couple of weeks" (218). During the conversation, Razumikhin comments not only on the content of Raskolnikov's article, which he finds not only unoriginal but "terrible," but also on the tone of the conversation itself, when he says to Porfiry and Raskolnikov, "You are amusing yourselves at one another's expense, aren't you? Sitting there and poking fun at one another!" (223). Razumikhin's presence here makes it clear that Porfiry and Raskolnikov are using the structure of games to address issues that are anything but "amusing." But afterward, Razumikhin refuses to agree with Raskolnikov that Porfiry has tried to manipulate Raskolnikov in this encounter. When Raskolnikov suggests that Porfiry has tried to trap him with a question about the workmen, Razumikhin insists that Raskolnikov has made a mistake: "What sort of a trap was it? . . . Work it out! If you had done *that*, would you have let it out that you had seen the flat was being painted?" (228). Even though he recognizes the gamelike quality of this encounter, Razumikhin, like many readers of the novel, is reluctant to believe that Porfiry has ulterior motives, that he uses the techniques of interrogation to trap Raskolnikov.

Raskolnikov matches wits with Porfiry on three separate occasions in the novel, and on each occasion the characters speak in riddles and questions, without ever saying what they think or mean. Porfiry, in particular, as Bakhtin argues, "speaks in hints, addressing himself to Raskolnikov's hidden voice."[19] There are, in effect, two games being played in each of these episodes: the verbal game between Porfiry and Raskolnikov and another game that the text plays with the reader, a game of concealment. The text delineates the contradictions between what Raskolnikov says and what he really thinks; in other words, it shows the game of concealment that Raskolnikov plays with Porfiry. And yet the text conceals from the reader what Porfiry really thinks. It is implied, but never actually confirmed, that Porfiry conceals just as much from Raskolnikov as Raskolnikov does from him. Without this missing information, without some sense of Porfiry's true thoughts, the reader can never know his motives. As a consequence, all of his words, all of the ideas he pursues in Raskolnikov's presence, remain somehow suspect.[20]

The question of what Porfiry means is further clouded by the way each encounter is framed as game; neither the reader nor Raskolnikov can rely on Porfiry's carefully revealed bits of information and casual, rambling arguments, any more than Zamyotov can trust Raskolnikov's Crystal Palace confession. Significantly, Porfiry never summons Raskolnikov to him in any official way, thus emphasizing the supposedly spontaneous, inconsequential nature of their meetings. In the beginning, he merely expresses an interest in meeting Raskolnikov, having heard about him from Razumikhin. He lures Raskolnikov to him, placing him in an awkward position, much as Raskolnikov himself does to Zamyotov when he meets him in the Crystal Palace. Raskolnikov is thrown off balance and put on the defensive by the tone and context of their meeting. In the first interview, he even has difficulty understanding what Porfiry wants from him. Angered by the way that Porfiry has compromised him, he silently demands that Porfiry "go straight to the point, don't play with me like a cat with a mouse" (215).[21] The image of cat-and-mouse can be traced throughout Raskolnikov's encounters with Porfiry, and it sets the tone for everything that takes place between them.

What seems to frighten Raskolnikov the most in his second encounter with Porfiry is that the examiner neither accuses him of anything nor admits he is free from suspicion. Toward the end of their meeting, Raskolnikov begs Porfiry to make the rules of their game clearer: "Arrest me, search me, but be good enough to act in the proper form, and don't play with me [*ne igrat' so mnoj-s*]" (295). But Porfiry has begun by telling him that "the average case, the case for which all the legal forms and rules are devised, which they are calculated to deal with . . . does not exist at all" (287). Porfiry is a master at creating new games as his investigations demand them, and he seems to take pride in this creativity. After their first encounter, where Porfiry tries to manipulate Raskolnikov with questions,[22] the examiner apparently senses that his opponent may just defeat himself, and that the key to success in this game lies in letting Raskolnikov reveal his own guilt.

Raskolnikov does not always find it easy to follow Porfiry's lead, but he does recognize that Porfiry's approach has changed since their first meeting. He thinks to himself, "It is no longer a case of cat and mouse. . . . He is not showing me his strength" (288). Raskolnikov finds himself "straining all his powers of judgment to fathom Porfiry's game" (292).[23] Finally he accuses Porfiry of either trying to frighten him or laughing at him. Porfiry is, in fact, probably doing both at the same time. Even though Porfiry maintains a confident attitude and cheerfully relaxed manner throughout their conversation, Raskolnikov is driven foolishly to accuse his adversary of manipulation: "You want to prove to me again that you know my game [*igru moju*], that you know all my answers beforehand" (293). If Porfiry does suspect Raskolnikov of the crime—and that is, after all, the only way to explain his interest in him—he is clearly using these conversations to test this theory and to solve the crime. He seeks to determine Raskolnikov's guilt as well as to uncover some "scientific fact" about the criminal mind.

In contrast to Raskolnikov, who becomes more convinced and at the same time more visibly outraged that Porfiry is "teasing" him to "betray himself" (295), Porfiry remains poised and collected, asking Raskolnikov what he has to fear. What upsets this balance of power is something that neither Porfiry nor Raskolnikov could have expected, the painter Nikolay's confession. Raskolnikov sees the hand of fate in this development—"he felt that there was something astonishing and mysterious in Nikolay's confession that he was quite incapable of understanding" (300)—coming, as it does, at the very moment in which Porfiry suggests to Raskolnikov that he has some "surprise." Raskolnikov also realizes that Porfiry has suffered a setback, a realization that he underscores with a gambling metaphor: "Porfiry had shown almost all his cards; of course, he was taking a risk, but he had shown them and (so it seemed to Raskolnikov) if he had really anything more, he would have shown it" (300). Logic alone suggests to Raskolnikov, "that for today at least he could almost certainly consider himself out of danger" (301). Porfiry has begun to dominate Raskolnikov, using as a weapon some unmentioned, secret knowledge he supposedly possesses, but he loses this advantage when the painter confesses.

Their third and final encounter shows that Porfiry has had to revise his strategy to account for this contingency; he can act expediently when he must. Raskolnikov is not surprised to see Porfiry, but wonders how he "approached so quietly, like a cat," and he wonders if Porfiry is "going to play the same old game again" (378).[24] But as the narrator says, giving a brief glimpse into Porfiry's mind, the examiner acts "as if he now scorned to use his earlier tricks and stratagems" (379). The "as if [*kak*]" that the narrator uses here is a clue to the fact that Porfiry is no more genuine here than he has been before, but rather that he wishes to create the *illusion* of open and honest communication. Porfiry says that he has not come to ask questions or to debate Raskolnikov's ideas, but to apologize to Raskolnikov for what occurred at the previous meeting, and to prove to Raskolnikov that he is "a man with a heart and a conscience" (380). In this way, he creates the impression in

Dreadful Games

Raskolnikov's mind that he might now consider him innocent—a thought that Raskolnikov finds suddenly frightening.

Having created the impression that Raskolnikov is no longer suspected, Porfiry uses it to his own advantage. He provides some details about the painter who confesses, offering an explanation of why he confesses. But then he twists his own argument, suggesting that Mikolka could not have committed the crime, despite his confession and the evidence that supports it. Porfiry argues that the crime is not that of a man, like Mikolka, "who believes his own inventions" (383), but "the work of a man carried along into crime, as it were, by some outside force" (385). Of course, Porfiry's analysis only captures part of the truth. Coincidences—"fate"—in part one encourage Raskolnikov to commit the crime he has already planned. He is, in fact, "carried along into" the crime, *in order* to affirm his own inventions; he is after all, both the fatalist and the skeptic. By making this statement in the aftermath of what Raskolnikov believes is a "recantation" of his earlier suspicions, Porfiry forces Raskolnikov to ask the question, If not Mikolka, who is the murderer? to which Porfiry replies, "But it was *you*, Rodion Romanovich." Porfiry makes an accusation, without having to take the posture of an accuser.

Porfiry's technique is particularly effective. The narrator compares the stunned Raskolnikov to "a frightened small child caught red-handed in some misdeed" (385). Even so, Porfiry's manipulation does not stop there. Having confronted Raskolnikov with his "conviction," Porfiry adopts the pose that he does not care whether Raskolnikov admits to the crime: "Confess or don't confess—it's all the same to me now, I am convinced in my own mind, without that" (386). Porfiry's apparent lack of interest in the precise outcome of his investigation recalls the Underground Man's description of man as a "fickle and disreputable creature," who, "like a chess player is interested in the process of attaining his goal rather than the goal itself."[25] Porfiry's comment about confession suggests that the rational and intuitive process of determining Raskolnikov's guilt has been more satisfying than seeing him punished for his crime.

Once again, Porfiry's strategy shifts slightly as the conversation continues. Having now established that he has no *personal* interest, no stake, in Raskolnikov's confession, Porfiry "invites" Raskolnikov to confess, with the argument that "it will be infinitely better for you, and it will be better for me too—because it will be a weight off my mind" (387). The benefit to Porfiry himself is, of course, only secondary, since,

The Play of Fate

as he says, he has no doubts about Raskolnikov's guilt. He emphasizes the advantages to Raskolnikov of a confession, even suggesting that his sentence might be reduced. Porfiry once again mentions that he has "proof," that "perhaps" he is still concealing his knowledge from Raskolnikov. He promises that the details of Raskolnikov's "theory" will be suppressed, that his crime "will seem to have resulted from a clouding of your faculties" (387), if only he confesses. He promises to leave Raskolnikov at liberty for a day or two, at which time he will be forced to arrest Raskolnikov and produce his "proof." Oddly, Porfiry's strategy here links him to the voices of foolishness and radicalism in the novel: just as Lebezyatnikov believes that sanity can be achieved by logical persuasion, Porfiry seems to believe that Raskolnikov can be logically persuaded to confess.

Throughout this "last trial of strength" (378), Porfiry's motives remain suspect—despite the references to his concern for Raskolinikov's mental and spiritual well-being—for several reasons. Too much remains concealed, once again, from both Raskolnikov and the reader. The mysterious "proof" Porfiry mentions may exist or it may not; either way, mentioning it remains little more than a way to tease and to manipulate his opponent and secure a victory. In practical terms, Porfiry must now not only prove Raskolnikov guilty—if he does not confess—but also discredit the painter's confession. There is even something a little bit desperate about what Porfiry does here: he has truly "shown all his cards" this time around. He has conveyed to Raskolnikov at different moments in the encounter the attitudes of humility, sincerity, conviction, admiration, disinterest, and compromise. As he departs, he even suggests that Raskolnikov may want to commit suicide, and asks him to provide a "short circumstantial note," just out of generosity (390). Porfiry has adopted too many poses, offered too many conflicting and contradictory explanations. It may be that the only time he speaks the truth is when he tells Raskolnikov, "Perhaps you should never believe me completely" (389). No true self emerges from Porfiry's performance, only a play of possible selves, each designed to manipulate Raskolnikov in a different way; as a consequence, no real truth emerges from his discourse. What Porfiry ultimately offers Raskolnikov is not a moral solution to his inner conflict, but a legal, rational, psychologically sound explanation of it. Significantly, when Raskolnikov does confess, he refuses to confess to Porfiry; he refuses to allow his opponent this victory. He returns instead almost to the point where he began, giving his confession to Ilya Petrovich, "the

103

Squib"—the most incompetent game player of them all—having first parodied public confession and repentance by kneeling in the public square.

Without the Epilogue, the plot of *Crime and Punishment* resembles the plot of *Le Rouge et le noir;* without the spiritual regeneration described in those last few pages, Raskolnikov's career becomes like that of Julien Sorel, circular and oddly nonproductive. As one critic has explained the problem, "the novel up to its last three pages chronicles the failure of Raskolnikov's gamble in the lottery of selfhood."[26] Just as Julien fails to "create himself," succeeding only in destroying himself, Raskolnikov almost never manages to escape the self-doubt that leads him to murder in the first place. At the end of part six, the novel remains unresolved, except in a purely formal way. Raskolnikov brings an end to the game he has played, but he is not a different character—the "schism" in his soul remains as wide as ever. Many readers, however, perhaps having grown accustomed to the gamelike strategies of the novel, see the "logical" ending of the story at the end of part six and find the Epilogue somehow superfluous.

But the Epilogue is important precisely because it evades logic—what Dostoevsky must see as the logic of pointless circularity. What happens to Raskolnikov in the Epilogue of *Crime and Punishment* is of a completely different order of narrative experience than his experiences in the first six parts of the novel. This difference is reflected in both the manner of narration and in the metaphorical texture of the Epilogue. Game metaphors are conspicuously absent, signaling that Raskolnikov has moved out of the world that can be described by that kind of language, as is any real sense of that "dialogic" dimension that makes Dostoevsky's fiction so distinctive. Whereas prior to the Epilogue the text has consisted almost exclusively of gamelike dialogues—Raskolnikov's inner dialogues as well as dialogues between characters—the reader finds little conversation in the Epilogue, and much of what is said or thought is reported indirectly by the narrator. There is a nonverbal quality to the Epilogue that distinguishes it from the rest of the novel.[27] The reader is not permitted by the text to *analyze* what happens to Raskolnikov in the Epilogue, but rather encouraged to *believe* what happens and to accept as true the character's "regeneration."

As a result of these textual and metaphorical differences, the Epilogue undercuts the impression of circularity that emerges from the first six parts of the novel and emphasizes instead the novel's antithetical, or dualistic, structure. The novel symmetrically juxtaposes each of Raskolnikov's encounters with Porfiry to his meetings with Sonya, where Raskolnikov ironically takes Porfiry's role, insisting that Sonya justify and explain her beliefs. Dostoevsky's world is based on a fundamentally dualistic relationship between legality, represented by Porfiry, and morality, represented by Sonya. The "text," or "fiction," that governs Sonya's life—what might be compared with Raskolnikov's extraordinary man theory—is the narrative from the Gospel of John that tells of the raising of Lazarus, the story of belief and of resurrection. That Sonya repays her stepmother's debts—when, as Svidrigaylov argues, she has no *legal* obligation to do so—is emblematic of her moral "logic," which, as Dostoevsky suggests, is not logic at all, but faith.

Even though civil justice is served by Raskolnikov's confession, the novel suggests that there is a "higher," more essential justice, which cannot be served until he comprehends the evil of his crime. The Epilogue illustrates the "failure" of the legal system, by detailing the "fiction" it devises to explain Raskolnikov's crime, but significantly, also by denying representatives of that legal system the opportunity to speak in their own voices. In the courtroom, to declare remorse is sufficient; the system cannot judge the crminal's heart and does not try to. The novel makes it clear that Raskolnikov has committed a horrible crime in murdering the old woman and her pregnant sister, but what ultimately appears more horrible is the shallowness of his thinking, the deceit of logic, which leads him to commit the crime. Raskolnikov must do more than make a *legal* confession; he must recognize, accept, and atone for his *moral* transgression—something he cannot do, the novel suggests, in a Petersburg governed by the logic of games.

The logic that governs the fictional world of *Jude the Obscure* is an even more brutal and dehumanizing logic than that which governs the play of characters in Dostoevsky's Petersburg, and the possibility of transcending it is never suggested. The ending of Hardy's novel—in other words, Jude's death—provides not a resolution but simply an end to the conflicts that have structured Jude's "career," much as Julien Sorel's execution effectively puts an end to his ambitions. In Hardy's novel, just as in *Crime and Punishment,* law and individual morality

Dreadful Games

come into conflict, with the Epilogue giving the last word to intrinsic moral values, but in *Jude the Obscure* the legal argument always prevails, even when it seems most arbitrary and meaningless. The novel upholds legal forms that crush the individual spirit, and most especially, crush the spirit of play inherent in Jude's dreams and aspirations.

There is something almost inevitable about what happens to Jude, an inevitablity underscored by the way the text narrates his story. J. Hillis Miller argues that Hardy's narrators "speak as though the events and characters were historical happenings, as if they had taken place before the eyes of a spectator who records what he has seen with the fidelity of an objective witness."[28] This objectivity reinforces the impression that the characters are dominated by impersonal forces, that some external system shapes their destinies. The text manipulates the characters mercilessly. Furthermore, the text virtually forces the reader to participate in this process of manipulation, a fact that perhaps explains why so few readers "enjoy" reading Hardy, even as they appreciate the power of the novels. Hardy's text concerns itself little with the details of contemporary society and historical events—the kinds of details found in abundance in a Balzac text, or even in a Dostoevsky novel. History and culture become impersonal forces with a mysterious power over human life. At the same time, Hardy's text conceals little from the reader; instead, the use of classic dramatic irony allows the reader to see what Jude, like Oedipus, is too blind to see. The "game" that Hardy's text plays is not a game with the reader but one with the characters themselves, and it is a game that the characters always seem to lose.

The language and attitudes of game playing are less explicit in Hardy's text than in *Le Rouge et le noir, La Cousine Bette,* or *Crime and Punishment*. Human play seems so absent from Hardy's fictional world—as it does from the world described in so much Naturalist fiction—as to be almost a meaningless or irrelevant issue. For one thing, what Huizinga calls the "play element in culture" is feebly represented in the character of Jude, a man of little pleasure and less self-knowledge. But throughout the novel, Jude's ambitions are characterized as "dreams," which are consistently opposed to "work," and his dreams are about learning and self-fulfillment—the subjects of play. This clear opposition—especially since Jude must always "work" to support and sustain his "dream"—places all his efforts into the same category as those of Julien or Raskolnikov. And even more vigorously than these other characters, Jude pursues his "dream" at the expense of what

The Play of Fate

everyone else calls his "work"; the play of ambition becomes almost embarassingly marginal. Jude finds himself much at odds with a world governed by a mechanistic view of human effort and accomplishment. What is significant in Hardy's novel are the number of "tricks" played on Jude, not only by other characters but by the impersonal forces of fate. Both the "dream game" of studying at Christminster, which is debased by events of the novel, and the "trick games" played against him show the corruption of games in Hardy's fictional world.

Coincidence is a useful technique in most fictional plotting. Coincidences abound in *Crime and Punishment,* for example, almost straining the credibility of the narrative at moments. It is coincidence that Raskolnikov overhears that Lizaveta will be gone at a certain time, that he meets Marmeladov and hears Sonya's story, that Sonya and Lizaveta were friends, and that Svidrigaylov's lodgings are next door to Sonya's. Raskolnikov interprets many of these events as something more than simple coincidence; he sees them as the work of some mysterious force that compels him to act in certain ways, a notion that the text strives to repudiate, showing that Raskolnikov uses "fate" to rationalize acts that he has already planned, choices he has already made. Hardy similarly uses the motif of the "fateful incident"[29] to emphasize the contingencies that arise in Jude's life, and in the context of the novel, these events become more significant than mere chance occurrences. It appears to be the work of fate that he meets Arabella at a particular moment, that he meets Sue accidently in Christminster, or that he meets Arabella again on his way to meet Sue. The contingencies a character faces either propel him toward some act or prevent him from accomplishing his goal. Hardy's character reminds himself, in the beginning of the novel, that "people said that if you prayed things sometimes came to you, even though sometimes they did not" (19). For Jude, even faith seems no more reliable or predictable than a game of chance. More clearly than in Raskolnikov's case, contingencies always work against Jude, preventing him from ever realizing any happiness.

In his efforts to realize his dream of studying at Christminster, Jude faces many unexpected obstacles, moving in the novel from one moment of frustration and disillusionment to another. The game metaphors in the text highlight these moments when the demands of reality intrude on his dream. Like Julien Sorel, Jude determines that he must first learn the language of the world he seeks to enter, and he contrives to purchase some used grammar books of the ancient languages. His dismay when he receives these books arises from his recognition that

Dreadful Games

the books contain "no law of transmutation," no "clew of the nature of a secret cipher." He realizes instead that Greek and Latin can only be learned "at the cost of years of plodding" (31). Significantly though, he does not renounce the effort, but accepts it as an immutable fact. In no time at all, "Jude had grown callous to the shabby trick played on him by the dead languages" (32). Jude looks for magic, for a lucky charm, and finds instead only a prescription for hard work.

Although the dead languages represent only the first of many "shabby tricks" played on Jude, he refuses to abandon his dream. He even develops an interim skill, stonecutting, as a way in which "he could subsist while carrying out an intellectual labor which might spread over many years" (37). In this novel, work and play are always pursued at the expense of one another. Jude never sees his talent as a stonecutter as anything other than a means to an end, a way to make the money he needs to pursue his true desire. Despite his dedication, though, Jude is not prepared to overcome the obstacle that Arabella presents. Others are amazed that Jude has "descended so low as to keep company with Arabella" (51). But he thinks to himself that there is nothing serious about the time he spends with Arabella; he tells himself that she poses no risk, even though a part of him recognizes "something in her quite antipathetic to that side of him which had been occupied with literary study and the magnificent Christminster dream" (45). Not unlike Raskolnikov, Jude fails to perceive the dangers of game playing; he fails to anticipate where this particular kind of "amusement" might eventually lead him.

Even though Jude and Arabella belong to the same community, they inhabit distinctive and essentially incompatible mental worlds. They demonstrate different moral codes and different values. Jude rarely sees himself as a member of a community, while Arabella derives her sense of identity from her family and friends. As a result, Jude fails to comprehend how and why he is becoming the object of her desires. Arabella directs her desire toward Jude not because she admires or respects him, but because she wants to possess him. Arabella's pride is injured and her confidence in her own "skills" shaken when others suggest that he cannot be deterred from the course he has set for himself. Arabella feels challenged by the suggestion that he would choose Christminster over her, and she sets out to prove this notion wrong. Jude becomes more attractive to her because he seems so unmovable. Her lack of genuine feeling for him and of respect for his ideas is reflected in the narrator's description of her laugh as "the low

The Play of Fate

and triumphant laugh of a careless woman who sees she is winning her game" (51). Arabella learns to manipulate Jude's sexual desire—what he will later, after it spells his downfall, think of as "a new and transitory instinct which had nothing in it of the nature of vice, and could be only at the most called a weakness" (71). The illusion of spiritual intimacy and emotional commitment that Arabella creates, primarily by encouraging physical intimacy, forces Jude to ask himself whether "it was better to love a woman than to be a graduate" (54); the two options are, in his mind, mutually exclusive. But as the text demonstrates, Jude's question is essentially meaningless, since his "love" for Arabella is as much a fiction as his Christminster dream.

Arabella takes a number of calculated risks in her game with Jude. Arabella's friends warn her that Jude is "to be had, and as a husband, if you set about catching him in the right way." Arabella innocently presumes that this means "taking care he don't go too far." But to the contrary, Arabella's friends suggest that with "a romancing, straightfor'ard, honest chap" like Jude, another method is more effective. In a rare moment of concealment, the text suppresses the advice that Arabella's friend whispers to her, but the essence of it is clear. Arabella responds that if the man proves less than honorable, "a woman had better not have tried it" (56). More like true gamblers than Arabella is, her companions envy her opportunity, arguing that the risk is worth the potential reward: "Nothing venture nothing have!" they exclaim (57). In the end, Arabella agrees that she might have more to gain by drawing Jude closer to her than keeping him at a distance.

The wager pays off, primarily because Arabella is a reasonably clever strategist, when she tells Jude that she is pregnant: Jude is willing to "take the consequences" of his actions, even though it means a "complete smashing up" of his Christminster dream (65). Jude remains blind to those things that the text reveals about Arabella, the clues it provides about her. To make the marriage more palatable, he even creates an imaginary image of Arabella, as an antidote to what he knows in "the secret centre of his brain, that Arabella was not worth a great deal" (65). This fiction seeks to resolve the contradiction between what Jude believes he must do and what he wishes he could do, and makes him willingly substitute life with this image of Arabella for the dream of Christminster. Yet after Arabella has secured Jude through marriage, she loses interest in him, having attained her goal. She does almost everything she can to shatter Jude's useful fictions about her: she hangs her false tail of hair on the looking glass, she reveals her past as a

Dreadful Games

barmaid in town, and she persists in practicing dimple making, much to Jude's disgust. But Arabella's revelation that she is not pregnant after all—which the text has suggested is certainly not an honest mistake but a deliberate subterfuge—deprives Jude of all remaining consolation for the loss of Christminster. Jude is "inclined to inquire what he had done, or she lost, for that matter, that he deserved to be caught in a gin which would cripple him, if not her also, for the rest of a lifetime" (71). Jude reveals himself as a man, like Job of the Old Testament, invoked several times in the course of the novel, for whom the misfortunes of life seem inexorable.

Jude attributes the pain of his situation to neither Arabella nor himself but to "a social ritual which made necessary a cancellation of well-formed schemes" (71). Jude is willing enough to marry Arabella when he believes that he has necessitated such action by his own moments of pleasure, but he resents being bound to her by virtue of a "mistake." Jude's aunt explains his resentment as a kind of genetic curse: "There's sommat in our blood that won't take kindly to the notion of being bound to do what we do readily enough if not bound" (81). For Jude, the problem is not one of human weakness but of the social system that regulates human desire. Jude sees himself not as a victim of Arabella's "cruelty and cunning,"[30] but of a system that has proved itself devoid of meaning. Even so, Jude remains bound to Arabella until fate, in the form of Arabella's parents, intervenes to save him from her. Arabella has told Jude, "What's done can't be undone" (71), but when the opportunity arises to emigrate to Australia, she seizes it. For his part, he can pursue his dream again, returning to the place he had been "before he had been diverted from his purposes by an unsuitable woman" (86), much like starting over again in a conventional game that has gone badly. By mutual agreement the marriage ceases to bind them to one another, and what had seemed to shatter Jude's Christminster dream proves to be no more than a temporary postponement of it.

Like *Le Rouge et le noir*, Hardy's text repeatedly defers closure; resolution of conflict is always somehow out of reach. The irony of Jude's situation at this point in the novel is that having overcome what seemed like an insurmountable obstacle—his marriage to Arabella—Jude has little luck in pursuing his ambition to be a Christminster scholar. Once in Christminster, Jude devotes much of his thought and energy to locating his cousin Sue, whose picture he has seen on his aunt's mantle. He is almost inexplicably drawn to her, but at the same

The Play of Fate

time afraid of making himself known to her. When he finally does meet her, she casts a doubt over his scheme of becoming a scholar by telling him that Phillotson, the schoolmaster from whom Jude had gotten the idea of going to Christminster, had failed in his attempt to become a theologian. He finds this disheartening, "for how could he succeed in an enterprise wherein the great Phillotson had failed" (118), but feels that this sadness is tempered by the pleasure of having met Sue. Jude now seeks not only the intellectual advantages of academic life, but also the sexual and emotional fulfillment that a relationship with a woman offers. Jude cannot become the man he was before he met Arabella. He cannot, as he had hoped, simply begin again.

Jude's disillusionment also compares to Julien Sorel's sense of frustration with the life he leads in the Hôtel de La Mole. Living in Christminster, watching others lead the life he wants to lead, Jude feels further away than ever from achieving his goal: "Only a wall divided him from those happy young contemporaries of his with whom he shared a common mental life. . . . Only a wall—but what a wall!" (99). Like the threshold in *Crime and Punishment,* the wall separates the theory from its realization and represents the obstacle that the individual must overcome. Jude decides to write to the heads of various colleges, seeking advice as to how he might become a student. Only one of the masters replies, and his advice is terse and unencouraging: "I venture to think that you will have a much better chance of success in life by remaining in your own sphere and sticking to your trade" (139). All of Jude's hours of study are rendered meaningless by the suggestion that he never should have attempted to move from one "sphere" of life to another. The system again proves itself immutable. Jude does not understand why he has been brought to this moment, any more than he has understood why he should have been forced to marry Arabella: in an impulsive moment, he scribbles a verse from the third chapter of The Book of Job on the college walls. Yet even though he cannot make sense of his misfortune, this brief letter forces Jude to see "himself as a fool indeed" (141), and in this moment, Jude abandons the dream that has sustained him for ten years.

By deferring resolution, the novel relentlessly devalues both the character and the "dream game" he has played. Not only success, but failure as well, are postponed; in short order Jude is able to replace the Christminster dream with another goal that makes his life seem less futile. A fateful incident serves to give Jude new direction. Returning to his aunt's house, he meets a curate, in whom he confides his dreams and

Dreadful Games

failures. Despite the collapse of his Christminster dream, Jude still harbors the desire "to do some good thing" and regrets "the loss of my chance" to be an ordained minister (149). The curate suggests that if his call to the ministry is genuine, he might consider entering the Church as a licentiate: "It was a new idea—the ecclesiastical and altruistic life as distinct from the intellectual and emulative life." Suddenly, Jude sees the shallowness of his "mundane ambition masquerading in a surplice" and seeks to pursue "nobler instincts" (151). Jude's new plan offers the added advantage of allowing him to follow Sue to Melchester, where she has gone to a teachers' training school. But just as Arabella forces Jude to abandon his Christminster plans, Sue prevents Jude from realizing this new plan to become a licentiate, something Jude himself will recognize only much later: "Strange that his first aspiration—towards academical proficiency—had been checked by a woman, and that his second aspiration—toward apostleship—had also been checked by a woman." Significantly, Jude blames neither himself nor the women, but asks if it is not "the artificial system of things, under which the normal sex-impulses are turned into devilish domestic gins and springs to noose and hold back those who want to progress" (262). Once again, not people, but the system under which they live explains individual failure.

One critic has called Jude's relationship with Sue an example of "cat-and-mouse playing with love."[31] Their relationship conveys this impression because they never seem able to commit themselves to one another. They are never truly alone with one another: the presence of Arabella and of Phillotson remains with them always, intruding upon any happiness they manage to achieve. From the first moment Jude begins to think of Sue, he knows that their relationship can never lead anywhere; his prior marriage to Arabella, still legal despite their separation, precludes his ever joining his life to Sue's, but he pursues her nonetheless. Inasmuch as Jude never commits himself to her, Sue becomes more committed to a relationship with Phillotson. Yet even as she moves in this direction, she never relinquishes her hold over Jude.

The language of games helps to emphasize the futility and destructiveness of Jude's relationships with Sue and Arabella. From the time Sue arrives at the Melchester Normal School, she causes the other girls to wonder "what games she had carried on in London and in Christminster before she came here" (167). When things at the school go badly for her, Sue runs not to Phillotson but to Jude, thus making her situation even worse. Sue commits herself to marriage with Phillotson, only when Jude finally tells her about his marriage. Even though she has made this decision, she seems reluctant to break away from Jude. She asks him to give her away in marriage, "being the only married relation I have" (203). Jude cannot determine whether Sue refers to him in this manner "in satire" or "in suffering" (204). But in either case, Jude finds himself forced to give the woman he loves to another man. Just before her wedding, Sue takes Jude to the church, to stand with him on the spot where she is soon to marry Phillotson; the narrator describes this strange rehearsal as part "of the curious trick in Sue's nature of tempting Providence at critical times" (206). Sue seems unsure of her resolve in marrying Phillotson, but at the same time, she seems compelled to go through with it. Sue's inability to decipher her own desires, to commit herself to her own actions, leads to nothing but unhappiness for them both.

Fate as well continues to play tricks on Jude. Once again a fateful meeting intrudes upon the life to which Jude has resolved himself, and he begins to doubt whether the sacrifice of Sue to Phillotson has been necessary. Sue's and Jude's aunt falls ill, and they agree to return to Marygreen to sit with her, a journey that takes him once more through Christminster, where he finds Arabella working as a barmaid, and presenting herself as a married woman. This chance meeting with Arabella forces him to postpone his meeting with Sue. He believes that he has no choice but to meet with her, because he believes that she is legally his wife: "there was only one thing now to be done, and that was to play a straightforward part, the law being the law" (218). It is not until they have spent the night together that Arabella tells Jude she has married another man in Australia. Jude is aghast at her "crime," but she argues that in the colony it is not considered a crime: "Crime! Pooh. They don't think much of such as that over there! Lot's of 'em do it" (222). Arabella is a master at interpreting social conventions to serve her own needs—at twisting the rules of the game of life to suit her own purposes. Arabella no longer thinks of Jude as her husband—no longer demands the rights and duties of a wife—but Jude is still not free; the woman he loves is already married to another man.

If Jude feels trapped between his legal obligations to Arabella and his love for Sue, Sue herself expresses a similar kind of ambivalence—an ambivalence that is not resolved for either Sue or Jude by the legal process of divorce. As Jude argues to Sue at one point, "What those legal fellows have been playing at in London makes no difference in my real relationship to her" (323). Divorce, like marriage, is a formality with

Dreadful Games

little significance to those who reject its meaning. Sue's feelings for Jude make her marriage with Phillotson intolerable. Her affection for Jude intensifies the physical aversion she feels for her husband, an aversion that even Phillotson himself recognizes when she sleeps in a closet filled with spiders rather than in his bed. Phillotson gives Sue her freedom, even though he risks his own reputation: most of his neighbors assume "that she had played him false" (299), but when it is discovered that he let her go freely, he is blamed for encouraging domestic disintegration. When Phillotson falls ill, Sue returns to him, but finding that he is in no danger of death she returns again to Jude, having, in Phillotson's words, "played the thoughtful nurse for half an hour" (301). Sue is no more able to commit herself completely to Jude than she is able to abandon Phillotson completely. Not only does she postpone physical intimacy with Jude, but as he argues, she even fails to give him an honest declaration of love. He warns her that such lack of candor can destroy a relationship: "A Nemesis attends the woman who plays the game of elusiveness too often, in the utter contempt for her that sooner or later, her old admirers feel" (316). Jude perceives Sue's attitude toward him as gamelike, and this perception threatens the love that he has nurtured for her. Sue never masters her conflicting impulses. Even though she eventually offers herself physically to Jude, she can never bring herself to marry him.

The narrative goal of *Jude the Obscure* seems to be the return of Sue and Jude to the spouses they have married without love, parted from, and divorced, but whose influence they have never escaped. Their situation suggests that the legal bond of marriage holds a person against his will. Sue and Jude live as man and wife and raise children together— including Father Time, a mysterious child that Arabella claims is Jude's—but they never legally marry, despite several attempts to do so. The Widow Edlin believes that Sue and Jude have overestimated the significance of marriage; as she says, "when I and my poor man were married we thought no more o't than of a game o'dibs" (351). In this sense, Sue and Jude and guilty not of too much desire for one another, but of too much intellectualizing about the desire.[32] They refuse to see marriage as little more than a social game. Marriage is, the Widow Edlin says, a convention, a mere formality between two people, but it is nevertheless a formality that Sue and Jude cannot accept for themselves. This passage suggests that, rather than taking their commitment to one another too lightly, Sue and Jude have taken it too seriously, made too much of it. They are, ironically, guilty of *not* seeing marriage as a "mere" game.

The Play of Fate

Jude, in effect, loses control of his own destiny as the novel moves toward its ultimate resolution of his problems. The social and legal irregularity of his relationship with Sue becomes widely known wherever they live, eventually making it impossible for Jude to work as a stonecutter. In the end, he turns to making cakes shaped like the buildings at Christminster—an ironic debasement of the dream with which he began. Each move the family makes is to smaller and poorer lodgings; they have long since sold their household goods. They face their misfortunes with determination, but without comprehension. When Father Time asks Jude why the family must move, he tells the child, "Because of a cloud that has gathered over us; though 'we have wronged no man, corrupted no man, defrauded no man!' Though perhaps we have done that which was right in our own eyes" (377). Jude still blames the system for his troubles—a system that defines as immoral an act that in his own eyes injures no one. He makes no more sense of what has happened to himself and his family than he does of his other misfortunes.

The novel returns Jude not to the point at which his story begins, to the antiquated village of Marygreen, but to that place which has been all along for him a magical dream world. But in these final episodes, this dream world turns nightmarish. What little happiness Sue and Jude have been able to create for themselves is destroyed by their return to Christminster. An unfortunate comment by Sue to Father Time prompts this old man masquerading as a child to kill himself and the other children. Sue sees this event as a punishment against them, lamenting that she had once taken joy from "what instincts [Nature] afforded us." She sees it as a cruel trick that this joy should be turned against them: "Now Fate has given us this stab in the back for being such fools as to take Nature at her word" (414). What "Nature" gives, "Fate" takes away. Unlike the faith that characterizes Sonya's life in *Crime and Punishment,* the faith that Sue discovers in her grief is more fatalistic than hopeful, and verges on madness. Sue becomes the "religious fanatic" that Raskolnikov erroneously believes Sonya to be. In the spirit of duty, Sue returns to Phillotson, leaving Jude with nothing, shattering all his illusions about what they have meant to one another. She even tells him that however their relationship has ended, "it began in the selfish and cruel wish to make your heart ache for me without letting mine ache for you" (434). Sue condemns herself to life with a man whose touch repels her, preparing the circumstances for Jude's remarriage to Arabella. Now a widow, and like Sue, having discovered piety, Arabella thinks that just as Sue belongs to Phillotson, she belongs to Jude "in heaven's eye, and to nobody else, till death do us part" (461)—a platitude that serves her present interests. She plies Jude with liquor and leads him off to a clergyman, who congratulates them for righting past wrongs. It is Arabella, then, who nurses Jude in his final illness and Arabella who slips off to the Christminster Remembrance Games as Jude slips into death, reciting from the Book of Job.

It is significant that Jude's references to The Book of Job all come from the third chapter, well before God speaks from the whirlwind to address Job's lament. Unlike Job, Jude's heart is never changed, and he never makes any sense out of the misfortunes that have structured his life. His lamentations become more and more meaningless. The questions that Jude asks of life are never answered, and all the fictions that have sustained him are mercilessly revealed as fantasies, without foundation in reality. It is also significant that Arabella has gone to amuse herself as Jude dies. She has tricked him into marriage, and once again lost interest in him afterward. Her feelings for Jude and her responses to him have never been more than a way of providing herself with the pleasure of possession. Her final actions toward Jude demonstrate clearly her self-interest and heartlessness.

Throughout Hardy's novel, images of games and play mark the degradation of the human heart and imagination. The novel chronicles the triumph of social convention—a convention that both Jude's and Sue's experiences prove tawdry. Jude is twice married to Arabella and both times deceived and abandoned. The legal system prevails, and the value of morality based on the individual conscience is undermined. Jude refuses to admit that he and Sue have been immoral; they are merely living ahead of their times: "Our minds were clear, and our love of truth fearless. . . . Our ideas were fifty years too soon to be any good to us" (492). They have tried to affirm their theory about human love, which the novel suggests is superior to the view of love promulgated by those like Arabella, but the system that regulates sexual desire places insurmountable obstacles in their way.

Like moths to a candle—an analogy that Porfiry uses with Raskolnikov (287)—both Raskolnikov and Jude are drawn to the obsessions that promise to destroy them. Both characters gamble with their own destinies, with disastrous results. But while the individual can escape the trap of his own logic, he cannot escape his own heredity. Raskolnikov almost becomes a victim of his own games of logic, but Jude succumbs completely to the "fascinating but ruinous game"[33] of sexual relationships. Society and biology conspire in Hardy's novel to

The Play of Fate

stifle ambition, to render the individual incapable of meaningful action. If the game of life takes place on the "threshold" of experience in Dostoevsky's novel, in Hardy's world it takes place outside the walls that divide the individual from his objects of desire. In *Crime and Punishment,* Raskolnikov rises above the forces that would subvert his innate goodness, but Jude finds no such consolation; he never escapes from the play of fate that crushes all his hopes.

6

Playing by the Rules

Henry James's *The American* and *The Portrait of a Lady*

■ In *Jude the Obscure,* Hardy suggests that much of Jude's unhappiness and misfortune stems from his persistent inability to choose between observing social conventions and dedicating himself to a radical style of nonconformity. As a result, Jude can neither reject his formal commitment to Arabella nor accept unequivocally the spiritual commitment he makes to Sue. The language of games helps to show how, trapped between society's expectations and his own notions of morality, Jude can neither play by the rules as he finds them nor reject them in favor of rules he formulates himself.

Many of Henry James's fictional characters, especially in his early novels, share aspects of Jude's dilemma; like Hardy's character, they find themselves forced to choose between conventional behavior and the demands of the individual conscience—between the rules of society and their individual moral codes. And like *Crime and Punishment,* many of James's novels are concerned with the conflict that sometimes arises in human experience between "law" and "morality." James recognizes that different social groups accept different conventions, governing themselves according to different codes of behavior. This fascination with the rules that regulate groups makes the comparison between James and French novelists like Laclos and Balzac almost unavoidable. William W. Stowe argues persuasively that both Balzac and James practice a variety of "systematic" realism: both novelists "describe and analyze systems of behavior, communication, exploitation, and so on that structure the world," at the same time that they rely on these systems to "structure their texts and to provide them with figurative language."[1] But while this approach to the problems of realist fiction underscores an important similarity between Balzac and James, it obscures a key difference between them: Balzac seeks to define and to illustrate how these systems of behavior and communication work; James, on the other hand, explores what happens in the hearts and minds of those individuals who participate in such systems. As James himself says of Balzac, he carried his characters "about in his pocket," like "a tolerably befingered pack of cards, to deal them about with a flourish of the highest authority whenever there was the chance of a game."[2] The game, not the players, engages Balzac's interest. But the metaphor James chooses for himself in his early novels is that of the "biographer,"[3] whose job it is to select and present those events that highlight his subject's unique character. The individual's response, whether spoken or unspoken, to the systems that structure experience thus becomes the subject of two of Henry James's early novels—*The American* (1877) and *The Portrait of a Lady* (1881).

An early reviewer of *The American* calls it "a very modern novel." The "power" of the novel, in the reviewer's mind, depends on the success with which James represents both character and environment.[4] Though in retrospect this novel is not quite as "modern" in subject or technique as the novels that would follow it in James's career—especially the novels of his "major phase"—the way in which James portrays Christopher Newman's fictional experience distinguishes *The American* from other nineteenth-century novels it resembles. In a general sense, the subject matter of the novel resembles that of a novel like *La Cousine Bette,* inasmuch as it raises the issues of ambition, betrayal, and revenge. The novel's representation of characters like the Bellegardes is probably derived as much from James's reading of French fiction and drama as it is from the author's own experience of life.[5] Just as in Balzac's novel, the language of games highlights the play of ambition and revenge within the narrative pattern of the novel. But in *The American,* and again in *The Portrait of a Lady,* the language of games indicates how the cycle of betrayal and revenge is broken: the acts of revenge contemplated by those characters who find themselves betrayed are planned but never realized. In these two novels, James reformulates the narrative strategy that governs a novel like *La Cousine*

Dreadful Games

Bette.[6] Rather than prove the inevitability of revenge, as Balzac does, James uses game metaphors to show that revenge may offer only the hollowest kind of satisfaction.

Even before he had finished *The American,* James had already contemplated the novel that would become *The Portrait of a Lady.* In a letter to William Dean Howells, who serialized the earlier novel in *The Atlantic,* James announced that his next novel would recount "the adventures in Europe of a female Newman, who of course equally triumphs over the insolent foreigner."[7] While this comment begs the question of whether, in fact, either Christopher Newman or Isabel Archer "triumphs"—something that James leaves open to interpretation at the end of both novels—it nonetheless shows that James saw both these novels as a conflict of values, or in other words, a contest where one set of values emerges dominant, and furthermore, that the themes and events of the two novels were linked in James's imagination. Both novels describe what happens to the individual who enters a new social world; they are novels of education and social initiation, not unlike *Les Liaisons dangereuses* or *Le Rouge et le noir.* James raises the question not of an individual's social mobility but of his or her citizenship in a particular cultural and political group, and yet he is not particularly interested in conveying a historically accurate account of either Europe or America. In both novels, but most clearly in *The American,* "Europe" and "America" are little more than "theories," or more precisely, textual constructs, which enable James to explore the contradictions between different sets of rules. The construct labeled by the text as "America" consists almost exclusively, in *The American,* of Christopher Newman's evaluation of his own world—what he believes America and its people to be; the construct "Europe" is, in turn, constituted by Newman's interpretations—both accurate and inaccurate, both precise and willfully imprecise—of the European society he encounters.

As Americans who have come to Europe in order to learn more about themselves and about life, both Christopher Newman and Isabel Archer prove to be eager students, anxious to learn the customs and conventions of the world in which they find themselves. Newman employs M. Nioche to help him practice French conversation and urges his guests to interpret their jokes for him. When he reveals to Valentin de Bellegarde his ambition to marry Claire de Cintré, he implores the Frenchman to teach him the proper forms: "I want to do what is customary over here. If there is anything particular to be done, let me know and I will do it. I wouldn't for the world approach Madame de Cintré without all the proper forms."[8] By professing his willingness "to do what is customary," Newman demonstrates his respect for the rules of social interaction, as well as a naive confidence in his ability to master those rules and to realize his ambitions. Isabel Archer similarly urges Mrs. Touchett to instruct her in the proper forms: "I always want to know the things one shouldn't do."[9] But unlike Newman, Isabel does not promise to follow the rules she learns. She tells Mrs. Touchett, who suspects that Isabel wants to learn the rules simply in order to violate them, that she intends "to choose" whether to obey them. Although Isabel embraces these new rules more equivocally than Newman—he, after all, has a clearly defined goal in submitting to the rules—both characters emphasize their lack of obligation to submit themselves. They assert that they are not irrevocably bound by those social forms that distinguish social life in Europe from that of America; rather, for the sake of their own advantage and convenience, they agree to learn a particular set of rules.

In the Epilogue to *Crime and Punishment* Dostoevsky suggests that through faith individuals can transcend the evil and destruction that action governed by the logic of the game so often produces. In *The American,* James is similarly concerned with the problem of avoiding the temptations of evil or the possibility of corruption, but significantly, he does not oppose "America" to "Europe," the way Dostoevsky opposes "Siberia" to "Petersburg." America is not portrayed by James as inherently more innocent—or less "gamelike"—than Europe.[10] As in Dostoevsky's novel, both the narrator and the characters of *The American* use the language of games to describe human experience, but in James's novel, such metaphors characterize both the world of Europe and the world of America. Of Newman, the narrator states: "Life had been for him an open game, and he had played for high stakes" (32). The world of business has been for him a sheltered game world, in which he has pursued money for its own sake, by means of calculated wagers and carefully formulated schemes. But when he realizes that these wagers and schemes constitute the sum total of his experience, he is drawn up short. When he meets his American friend Tristram, Newman explains how an aborted plan of revenge has inspired his European holiday: He has plotted to take revenge on a business competitor, who "had once played him a very mean trick" (34), but when an opportunity arrives to repay this trick, he finds himself unable to exploit it. The feeling of disgust that comes over him, just at the thought of what he almost does, forces him to abandon his business: "As soon as I could get out of the game I sailed for Europe" (35). In this way, James shows that even before Newman reaches "Europe," he has been indoctrinated in the gamelike encounters of life; he is not an innocent. He is "sophisticated" enough to have plotted revenge, even though he has chosen to renounce it.

But despite this degree of sophistication, Newman's perception of the world is solipsistic; he is his own source of moral judgment and his own arbiter of taste. He responds to art—for example, to the rather unskillful copies that Mlle Nioche produces at the Louvre—in a spontaneous, purely personal way: he knows what pleases him, and he does not try to analyze this feeling. When Noémie rather contemptuously rejects his offer to buy half a dozen of her copies, he puzzles over the motives of what he calls her "game": "What was it she expected to win? The stakes were high and the risk great; the prize therefore must have been commensurate" (63). Newman is always baffled by actions that violate his own sense of reason and good manners, or in the language the text uses, by games he cannot fathom. Despite his eagerness to observe the "proper forms," he constantly questions the rationale of the rules and values that others attempt to explain to him, most of which remain incomprehensible to him. Mrs. Tristram tries to explain Claire's obligations to her family—"In France you must never say Nay to your mother, whatever she requires of you" (79)—just as Valentin tries to warn him that "you cannot marry a woman like Madame de Cintré for the asking" (105), but neither of his counselors succeeds in making him understand the values expressed by these injunctions.

Newman even insists on defining words according to his own logic; he quibbles with Valentin over the notion of nobility, asserting that by his own definition he is "noble": "it's a fine word and a fine idea; I put in a claim to it" (105). Valentin looks to the past to understand the meaning of the word—Newman has, he says, manufactured washtubs—but for his definitions, Newman looks only at the present and future: "Tell me something I have *not* done—something I cannot do" (105). Newman, in fact, does not believe that there is anything he cannot do, if he only works hard enough. In contrast to Stendhal's *ambitieux,* who exploits the play of imitated selves as a means to advance his cause, Newman adamantly refuses to imitate anyone—except, of course, the man he believes he has already become. He assures Claire that "I shouldn't like to resemble anyone. It's hard enough work resembling oneself" (158). In this rather odd turn of phrase, Newman offers his own definition of "integrity": to resemble oneself. In the way he formulates Newman's character, James is not so much promoting Newman's specific moral standards as he is dramatizing Newman's unwavering consistency in applying those standards to all of his own decisions and actions. Newman's words and actions in the novel all reflect a belief in his own unflinching honesty and what can be called at different moments either self-esteem or self-righteousness.

His confidence in his own ability to judge correctly influences the way Newman makes decisions. He evaluates his choices in terms of the amount of time and effort to be expended in pursuing a goal and the potential benefits of achieving it. He is methodical and not the least bit impatient: "No man seemed less in a hurry, and yet no man achieved more in brief periods" (65). Newman conveys the impression of someone who allows very little to elude his grasp. His actions furthermore demonstrate his belief that experience can be acquired, warehoused, and inventoried—he buys a certain number of paintings at a certain price, and visits a certain number of cathedrals, cataloguing all the vital statistics. That he often seems unable to make sense of his own amusements is explained by his previous devotion to work; he tells Mme de Bellegarde, "after all, that was my amusement" (87). And having left his business behind, he now puts the same amount of energy and effort into amusing himself. As he tells Mrs. Tristram, he has "a sort of a mighty hankering, a desire to stretch out and haul in" (42). Newman has attained as much satisfaction as he can in the "game" of making "the largest possible fortune in the shortest possible time" (124); having acquired money, his thoughts turn to how he might spend it, and how he might, in the process, satisfy heretofore unrealized desires.

Newman articulates all his intentions without ambivalence, including his desire to "marry well": "I not only want to make no mistakes, but I want to make a great hit. I want to take my pick. My wife must be a magnificent woman" (44). He describes the ideal wife in precise, if sweeping, terms: "Goodness, beauty, intelligence, a fine education, personal elegance" (106). The kind of extravagant ambition that another kind of character might publicly conceal or even deny, the way Julien Sorel hides his portrait of Napoleon in his mattress, Newman voices without embarrassment or false modesty. His ability to articulate his desires and to pursue them without hypocrisy is both his charm— Valentin tells him, "You make me feel as if I had missed something" (94)—and what makes him vulnerable, by allowing others to manipulate those desires with ease. At the same time that Newman interprets the actions and values he finds in the world around him, others are just as actively engaged in interpreting him.[11] Newman's most critical mistake lies in believing that all of the other characters will express their desires as clearly as he does, and pursue them as openly. If Newman leaves behind a life that has been for him an "open game"—one of unlimited possibilities and opportunities for success—he finds in the Europe of his experience what ultimately reveals itself as a "closed game"—one that he can win only by not playing.

Perhaps to emphasize how much his experiences have changed him by the time he reaches Europe, Newman never uses the language of games to describe his pursuit of Claire. Only at the end, when she obeys her mother and turns away from him, does he resort to a game metaphor: "I see your game," he tells her, "You are blackening yourself to whiten others" (241). But before this moment, Newman's desire for Claire seems opposed in his mind to the "game" he has abandoned in order to see something more of life. In his mind, marriage to Claire offers the possibility of a new and richer form of experience. As the narrator explains his state of mind, "He had spent his years in the unremitting effort to add thousands to thousands, and now that he stood well outside of it, the business of money-getting appeared extremely dry and sterile" (79). The pursuit of money has become an empty experience for him; it has become too much of a game, without purpose or resolution. Newman comes to Europe hoping to find something more "real." But ironically, his attempt to escape the logic of games, in other words, to transcend the life of game playing that he renounces in a cab on Wall Street, fails rather miserably; instead of transcending the logic of games, he merely finds himself engaged in a different style of game playing.

Although Newman does not use the metaphor of the game to describe his attempts to make Claire his wife, his project is nevertheless implicitly framed within the text as a game. Mrs. Tristram is, after all, the one who gives him the idea—who praises Claire's virtues and suggests that she might measure up to his exacting standards. The narrator describes Mrs. Tristram as "without personal ambitions" (38), but nonetheless ready to offer unsolicited advice or to share her "abundant gossip" (39). When she first meets Newman, Mrs. Tristram seeks to "appropriate" him, though her purposes are, at first, undefined: "She wished to do something with him—she hardly knew what" (39). Newman's deisre to find a wife becomes her own project, as she helps him further his cause. Her game is not, however, entirely vicarious; she has hoped not so much to savor Newman's success, as to "put [him] in a difficult place" (42). She is only "half-pleased" with his various successes; as the narrator explains, "she had succeeded too well; she had played her game too cleverly, and she wished to mix up the cards" (117). Having once praised Claire, she now takes "a purely critical view" (117) of her friend. The narrator mentions, so as to reject, the possibility that Mrs. Tristram is jealous, or that she has overestimated her own disinterest. To the contrary, Mrs. Tristram is merely perverse: "she was capable, at certain times, of imagining the direct reverse of her most cherished beliefs" (117). She is disappointed in the end, when Newman destroys the evidence he has obtained of the Bellegardes' evil; she had hoped to experience his revenge vicariously; she believes that the secret he discovers "would have served for my revenge as well" (308). That she functions so clearly as a "spectator"—as someone who derives pleasure from the events she observes, safely, at a distance—implies that Newman's project might be appropriately described as a game played for another's pleasure, even though Newman never quite recognizes this characteristic for himself.

James also uses the character of Valentin de Bellegarde to show implicitly that Newman's project assumes the structure and attitudes of a particularly dangerous game. Like Mrs. Tristram, Valentin observes Newman and derives pleasure from his progress. When Newman presents his plan to Valentin, although Valentin has no doubt of Newman's seriousness, he nevertheless finds Newman both "amusing" and "inspiring" (108). He wishes Newman well, and even agrees to help him—yet not without a degree of self-interest: No matter what happens, Valentin says, laughing, "I shall get my own fun out of it" (109). At the same time, Valentin suggests the possibility of some more ominous result, when he warns Newman that in championing his project, "you don't know just what I am doing" (108). What he alludes to here is open to a number of interpretations. He may simply be noting that Newman fails to comprehend the implications of his project. Or he may be referring to the risk he takes himself in opposing his family, in undermining the standards by which his family has lived for centuries. But his comment may also reflect a fear that he may be encouraging Newman to unleash destructive forces. As the novel reveals much later, Valentin believes that his mother and brother are more than capable of "foul play" (234). What Newman "just doesn't know" here is that the Bellegardes are capable of subverting Newman's plan in order to serve their own interests. By finding amusement in Newman's project, and by

Dreadful Games

foreshadowing the possible outcome, Valentin helps to define Newman's pursuit of Claire as a game that has dreadful consequences.

But Valentin does more than simply interpret and define Newman's ambitions, as Mrs. Tristram does; his own experience in the novel serves as a kind of commentary on Newman's experience. The relationship that develops between the two characters seems most notable in the lack of insight it produces; neither ever gains significant insight into the other's inner life. Newman remains a kind of enigma in Valentin's mind, and Newman willfully misinterprets the nature of Valentin's malaise, seriously offering to find him a job in a bank in America. Their experiences in the novel are nevertheless remarkably similar. Valentin's pursuit of Noémie is as extravagant, as quixotic, as Newman's pursuit of Claire—and even more clearly ill-fated. Just as Valentin brings Newman and Claire together against his better judgment, Newman regrets having introduced Noémie to Valentin. Newman cautions Valentin, calling his "infatuation" with Noémie "child's play" (205). Valentin is, however, more fully cognizant than Newman of what his actions mean. If Newman fails to see the romantic nature of his ambition to marry Claire,[12] Valentin has no illusions about Noémie's value or his feelings for her.

The narrator reveals, early in the novel, what motivates Valentin and what determines how he will act: "His rule of life, so far as it was definite, was to play the part of a *gentilhomme*" (92). The quarrel that Noémie inspires, and the duel that costs Valentin his life, are not about love but pride and self-image—what passes, in his vocabulary, as "honour."[13] Valentin explains to Newman that "I simply wish to make a point that a gentleman must" (205). Although he believes that Noémie is "a bore," he also believes that "a man can't back down before a woman" (209). Valentin considers the duel a formal obligation, his duty as a *gentilhomme:* having been offended by the impudence of a brewer's son, Valentin must avenge himself, even if he has to die to do so. Newman is no more than a spectator to the events that lead to Valentin's death, but the experience educates him in the forms of vengeance: it is not coincidental that as he watches over the dying Valentin, he reads *Les Liaisons dangereuses*. On his deathbed, Valentin offers Newman the key to his own revenge.

A subtle and almost ironic narrative symmetry links the circumstances of Valentin's duel to Newman's final series of negotiations with the Bellegardes: Newman's position parallels Valentin's, and the Bellegardes respond to Newman in much the same manner as the brewer's son from Strasbourg responds to Valentin. Just as the "deplorably heavy-handed" (226) M. Kapp insists on fatally wounding Valentin, even after Valentin good-naturedly fires off to the side, the Bellegardes depend on Newman's good nature to protect them from any threat he might represent. When the Bellegardes withdraw their permission to marry Claire, Newman's pride, like Valentin's honor, is offended, although the narrator articulates the nature of his feelings more clearly than he does himself: "To lose Madame de Cintré after he had taken such jubilant and triumphant possession of her was as great an affront to his pride as it was an injury to his happiness" (220). Thus his injured pride, perhaps even more than his love for Claire, justifies the act of revenge that he contemplates in the remaining episodes of the novel.

Newman's dispute with the Bellegardes is characterized from the beginning by the conflict of what might best be called "two kinds of self-complacency,"[14] each incomprehensible to the other. The Marquis de Bellegarde is unshakably confident of his own superiority; even when Newman threatens to expose his act of parricide, Bellegarde adopts the pose of "a man who believed that his mere personal presence had an argumentative value" (288). Even though the text compares Mme de Bellegarde and her son to the petty, insignificant M. Kapp from Strasbourg, the Bellegardes themselves "pretend," in the words James uses in the preface to the New York edition, "to represent the highest possible civilisation."[15] Newman himself recognizes that Mme de Bellegarde "is a woman of conventions and proprieties" and that her world "is the world of things immutably decreed" (120). But even though the Bellegardes seem to worship "propriety," they are capable of secretly committing acts that violate the most basic notions of decency. They are tempted by Newman's money, but, so they say, they are unable to accept his "commercial" background; they are willing to forfeit the money to avoid undermining a position of superiority that money cannot buy. Mrs. Tristram explains their dilemma succinctly: "They wanted your money, but they have given you up for an idea" (221). And yet, this explanation, though perhaps the most convenient, is not the only one. It is perhaps equally possible that the Bellegardes turn Newman away because Lord Deepmere offers himself instead, forcing them to question both the advantage and the necessity of their earlier arrangement. Newman makes the mistake of thinking that because the Bellegardes are, by their own definition, "very proud," they will keep their word, but as he tells them at the moment they betray him, "You are not proud enough" (218). He has relied too heavily on his own definition of pride.

From the moment Claire enters the convent, the novel moves slowly

Dreadful Games

but inevitably toward the consummation of Newman's revenge. At first, he wants Claire more than he wants revenge—ambition is still the stronger desire—and he sees the knowledge that Valentin has given him as a bargaining chip, not as an instrument of revenge. At the same time, vengeance animates his thoughts. He considers himself "a good fellow wronged" (245), and the thought that the Bellegardes "should go scot-free" (246) deeply distresses him. And yet he does not want to pursue his revenge until after he gives them "another chance . . . he would appeal once more directly to their sense of fairness, and not to their fear" (247). The confrontation between them is structured as a series of negotiations, where Newman appeals to reason and the Bellegardes refuse to concede anything. He outlines what he calls "easy terms" (250): if they withdraw their opposition to his marriage, he will free Claire from the convent. When they reject this proposal, claiming that Claire's becoming a nun is the lesser of two evils, Newman tries to shame them by telling them that on his deathbed Valentin "apologized to me for your conduct" (251)—an assertion they simply refuse to believe. It is only when these other efforts have failed that Newman threatens to expose "a skeleton in the closet" (252). Despite his initial reluctance to force this issue, he is exhilarated by the power he suddenly holds over them.

No matter how exciting the game has been, Newman has been doing little more than pretending he knows a damaging secret; like the poker player his friend Tristram remembers, he is merely bluffing. He has nothing on which to base his accusations, other than Valentin's deathbed allusion to "foul play" and a conviction that the humble Mrs. Bread is hiding some terrible secret. Although he shows genuine affection for Mrs. Bread, Newman's dealings with her represent a financial investment in his vengeance. By promising her a life of security, Newman purchases the story of the secret crime, even obtaining evidence in the dead man's handwriting. But what makes the knowledge he gains even more valuable to him is that he has begun to crack the Bellegardes' ethical code. He no longer willfully misinterprets them, and he defers to their definitions of key concepts, in effect, playing by the rules they have established in their dealings with him, and attempting to use those rules against them.

Newman has become someone the Bellegardes must take seriously, someone with whom they must play as equals. M. de Bellegarde admits that he thinks the document genuine, but he is not willing to offer Claire in return for it. Instead, he offers Newman what he calls "a chance that a gentleman should appreciate" (287), the opportunity to abstain from injuring a man who had done him no harm. Calling the offer "nonsense," Newman concludes immediately that since the Bellegardes have previously refused to consider him an equal, their appeal to his honor as a "gentleman" is "a poor rule that won't work both ways" (287). Bellegarde as much as dares Newman to expose him, arguing that Newman will injure himself as much as he injures his adversaries. When he assures Newman that exposure will be no more than "very disagreeable," Newman responds that as he had come to understand the Bellegardes, "that will be quite enough" (288). Newman calls on the Bellegardes' friend, the duchess, planning through her to make the secret public. But the duchess's manner toward him causes him to abandon the plan: "had he come to that—that he was asking favours of conceited people, and appealing for sympathy where he had no sympathy to give?" (291). Newman shows that there are limits to how much he is willing to become like the Bellegardes in order to defeat them.

Although Newman refuses to use the duchess as an agent of his vengeance, he does not completely reject the possibility of avenging himself until the last pages of the novel. He travels aimlessly, but having dreamed of possessing Claire, he can no longer find any pleasure in the world of business: whereas he had once visited factories and mills, now "he would not have given the smallest sum for the privilege of talking over the details of the most 'splendid' business with the shrewdest of overseers" (295). He returns to America and travels from New York to San Francisco, but "nothing that he observed by the way contributed to mitigate his sense of being a good fellow wronged" (303). He tells no one of "the trick that had been played him" (303) by the Bellegardes. His satisfaction in the "commercial life," his pride in the virtues of his native land, and his unshakable self-confidence have been diminished: "He had nothing to do" (304). He attributes his discomfort directly to those who betrayed him: "A hopeless, helpless loafer, useful to no one and detestable to himself—this was what the treachery of the Bellegardes had made him" (303). Convinced that he must still settle the score, he returns to Paris, where Mrs. Tristram recognizes how much he has changed: "You look wicked—you look dangerous" (305), she tells him. Self-righteous anger brings him closer to committing an act of pure vengeance.

In returning to Paris, though, Newman demonstrates that he has not yet reconciled himself to the loss of Claire, who by this point in time has already taken her vows as a Carmelite. Just as Jude Fawley stands outside the walls of the colleges at Christminster, Newman stands outside the convent walls, finally accepting the death of his ambitions and his love.[16] But knowing that he can never have Claire, he does not seek to compensate for his loss by injuring those he holds responsible. Unlike other nineteenth-century fictional heroes who contemplate acts of revenge, Newman's thoughts of vengeance last only as long as he has even the most distant hope of realizing his goal. He does not consider revenge as a direct response to frustrated ambition. Only moments after he stands outside the convent wall, he comes to the conclusion that his desire for revenge is shameful: "They had hurt him, but such things were really not his game" (306). He recognizes the essential truth of revenge, that he can gain little from it. Newman chooses to play his own game, rather than the game into which the Bellegardes—Valentin included—have drawn him; he will not violate his own rules simply to defeat the Bellegardes at their game.

Newman's decision at the end of the novel to abandon his project of revenge recalls the episode that brings him to Europe in the first place. But although they share some structural similarities, these two events are essentially different, reflecting the way in which the novel has depicted the closing off of Newman's possibilities and opportunities.[17] When Newman sacrifices sixty thousand dollars and the opportunity to pay back a grudge, he gives up something of minimal value to him—he already has more money than he knows how to spend, and he suddenly recognizes how litle he cares about his adversary. Furthermore, the kind of "revenge" he plots then is entirely justified by the code of the business world to which he belongs. Newman does not ever question the ethics of the business world, nor does he seem to feel that his own business practices have been at all amiss—business is not the kind of "dreadful" game that his affair with the Bellegardes becomes. He sacrifices the sixty thousand dollars simply because he is tired of playing the game, not because the game itself is corrupt. He leaves the game of business, knowing he can always return to it later.

But while Newman renounces the sixty thousand dollars along with his revenge, he gives up nothing more measurable than a vague emotional satisfaction when he burns up the piece of paper that reveals the truth about the Bellegardes. He does not "renounce" Claire, as some readers have suggested: he can *resign* himself to her loss, but he cannot *renounce* what he has already lost. Just as he had tired of business affairs, he tires of the game of revenge he has struggled so hard to learn. When he permits the Bellegardes, in their own terms, to win—when he denies himself the psychological compensation offered by revenge—he demonstrates his weariness with the satisfaction offered by game playing. For perhaps the first time, he recognizes and accepts how antipathetic to his own nature the Bellegardes' whole way of life is. It is one thing to make the affairs of business a game, but quite another to make the affairs of life one, and this difference distinguishes Newman from his adversaries. The essence of what Newman learns in the novel is expressed aphoristically by Valentin de Bellegarde: "You can't go mountaineering in a flat country" (178). To defeat the Bellegardes, he would have to become one of them.

Despite Newman's conscious decision to forsake vengeance, the ending of the novel is persistently ambiguous—an ambiguity that arises from the sense in which Newman fails to understand whether he has "won," by choosing to play according to his own rules, or "lost," by becoming, in effect, a pawn in the games of others. He has taken a kind of comfort in the thought that he has had the "revenge" he wanted by seeing the Bellegardes frightened of him. But Mrs. Tristram robs him of this comfort when she explains that the Bellegardes have counted not on "their talent for bluffing things off" to secure their victory, but rather on his own "remarkable good nature" (309). This appraisal of the conflict diminishes the value of Newman's characteristic good nature. In their dealings with him, the Bellegardes have translated a strength of character into a strategic weakness. That Newman is aware of this irony is suggested in the text when he "instinctively" turns to see if his evidence has yet been destroyed—either to make sure that he has succeeded in destroying it, freeing him from the Bellegardes, or to see if he cannot still retrieve it from the fire. In either sense, the Bellegardes have the last word in the novel; they have made Newman respond in certain ways, just as they have made him see his own world as narrower and less open to possibilities. At best, he will be forced to create an entirely new set of possibilities for himself; at worst, he faces a life of bitterness and regret.

In *The Portrait of a Lady,* Isabel Archer shares Newman's experience of a world of diminishing possibilities, but in this novel James makes the distinction between kinds of playing even more precise. By opposing the language of games to what might be called the more general

Dreadful Games

language of play, James makes the essential differences between clusters of characters even clearer than they are in *The American*. The opposition of "Europe" and "America" is less significant in *The Portrait of a Lady,* despite Henrietta Stackpole's comic obsession with the topic: it is hard to imagine that Osmond and Mme Merle would have posed a lesser evil if they had lived in America. The discussion of specific rules is also less important in *The Portrait of a Lady* than in *The American,* and James is also less concerned with the structure of specific games. But the question of whether to submit to the will of others, as that will is expressed in the rules by which they live, becomes even more critical for Isabel than it is for Newman; she does not vacillate between acts of revenge and renunciation, the way he does, but rather between the forms of bondage and the possibilities of freedom. While Newman takes the "open game" of life more or less for granted—he is, after all, a man with money and the advantages that combination of circumstances confers—Isabel must be given the means to play such an "open game." For James, as for virtually all nineteenth-century novelists, money provides a character with "means." Money is what promises to make Isabel's life as open to possibility as Newman believes his to be. But what freedom the novel gives Isabel, it proceeds to take away from her. The irony of Isabel's experience is that what is intended to set her free leads her instead toward enslavement. In the process, the novel links the idea of freedom to the nature and effects of play.

There are, in fact, two "portraits" of Isabel Archer: the one presented in the London edition of 1881 and the one that emerges from the revisions made for the New York edition of 1908. Some readers prefer the earlier version, arguing, as Nina Baym does, that in the revisions the character's "intellectual agility is greatly extended at the expense of her emotional nature."[18] But the changes James made in this novel—unlike some of the more substantive changes he made in the 1908 edition of *The American*[19]—do not fundamentally alter Isabel's character; the distinction between her intellectual and emotional responses to life are not that clear-cut in either case. Many of the changes, while they do not alter the meaning of the novel, do affect the way readers constitute that meaning. The metaphorical changes, in particular, require the reader to make difficult kinds of connections, to interpret rather than simply to read, and for this reason, the revised version of the novel is closer to the complicated style of the later novels. But despite these stylistic changes, James does nothing to alter the basic structural and thematic architecture of the novel: like *The Amer-*

ican—and numerous other European novels of the century—*The Portrait of a Lady* is a novel of ambition and betrayal, which chronicles the diminution of human possibilities and the temptations of revenge.

Some of the changes James made in the later edition of *The Portrait of a Lady* actually clarify his intentions with regard to his character, as for example, when he substitutes the phrase "free play of intelligence" (88) for the earlier reference to Isabel's "fine freedom of composition" (504). Both phrases are metaphorical, and both describe the methods of Isabel's imagination, but the revision links the description to the language of play and games used elsewhere in the novel. It also connects the issue of the freedom that Isabel values so highly to the idea of play.[20] Perhaps only coincidentally, James frequently uses figures of speech like "play of intelligence" in his essays on novelists, particularly when he writes about women novelists or female characters. Writing about George Sand in 1899, James refers to "the play of perception"[21] in fiction, as well as to the novelist's "play of mind."[22] In his 1902 essay on Flaubert, he argues that in *Madame Bovary* "Emma interests us by the nature of her consciousness and the play of her mind."[23]

In all of these expressions, James tries to describe a variety of imagination that cannot be confined within the rigid forms that are often characterized by the language of games. In both versions of the novel, the narrator describes Isabel's thoughts as "a tangle of vague outlines which had never been corrected by the judgment of people speaking with authority" (53), implying that she does not easily accept conventional standards. Isabel's vagueness and her imprecision in the beginning of the novel make her a much different character than Newman, whose desires are clearly articulated and whose "game" is clearly defined. At the same time, Isabel clearly reserves the right, as Newman does, to dispute the authority of conventions and to play the "open game" of life according to her own rules. The language associated with the idea of play helps to emphasize the freedom and creativity of Isabel's imagination.

Like Christopher Newman, Isabel is enormously self-complacent, especially about her ability to judge. The narrator suggests that Isabel is "probably very liable to the sin of self-esteem" (53). Even when she discovers an error she has made, she indulges in "a week of passionate humility," but preserves "an unquenchable desire to think well of herself" (53). Much as Mrs. Tristram imagines what Newman might be like in a difficult position, Isabel herself wishes "that she might find herself some day in a difficult position, so that she should have the pleasure of being as heroic as the occasion demanded" (54)—a fantasy that ironically foreshadows what actually happens to her in the novel. Isabel's rule of life is that one "should move in a realm of light, of natural wisdom, of happy impulse, of inspiration gracefully chronic" (54). Even more clearly than Christopher Newman, who has devoted so much time to the rigidly formalized "game" of business, Isabel sees life as a kind of pure, unstructured play of both intellect and emotion; she might, in this sense, be described as a "ludic" personality. But the only way Isabel has of translating this attitude toward life into everyday experience is by means of an imprecisely defined notion of independence.

Isabel values her independence, but in the beginning it is only an imaginary, theoretical version of independence, the appearance of which Mrs. Touchett agrees to preserve when she brings Isabel to Gardencourt. But when Isabel refuses to marry Lord Warburton, that, in Mrs. Touchett's mind, is taking the theory too far: as she says to her niece, "One would think you were awfully pleased with yourself and had carried off a prize!" (122). In a way, of course, Mrs. Touchett's assessment is accurate; Isabel has reason to feel pleased at having so successfully defended her freedom. Her cousin Ralph Touchett, whose illness, like Mrs. Tristram's lack of charm and beauty, makes him a spectator to life, is himself pleased that Isabel has "kept the game in [her] own hands" (133), and he urges her to make use of her advantage. But Isabel is asserting her independence in purely negative terms; the right to choose is, in fact, little more than the right to reject. In this sense, when she exercises her right to reject potential husbands, Isabel merely postpones an inevitability. It is Ralph who decides to make Isabel's freedom more than theoretical, by asking his father to leave her enough money "to meet the requirements of [her] imagination" (160). He wants to prevent her from reaching that moment when, for the sake of money, she can defer marriage no longer. By diverting half his own inheritance to Isabel, Ralph hopes to find pleasure in the unimpeded play of her imagination.

By contrasting Isabel with Ralph, James emphasizes those qualities that make Isabel a more playful personality than other characters in the novel. Where Isabel is lively and active, Ralph is bored and idle. Poor health has come to be the principle of his life. James makes a revision in the New York edition that helps to distinguish, even more clearly than in the original version, Ralph's perception of life from that of Isabel. In the original version Ralph is described as having "a certain fund of indolence" that "came to his aid and helped to reconcile him to doing nothing; for at the best he was too ill for anything but a passive life" (499). In the New York edition, Ralph's "certain fund of indolence" becomes "a secret hoard of indifference," his "doing nothing" is defined as "sacrifice," and his "passive life" is described as "that arduous game": "A secret hoard of indifference—like a thick cake a fond old nurse might have slipped into his first school outfit—came to his aide and helped reconcile him to sacrifice; since at the best he was too ill for aught but that arduous game" (45). Though certainly less straightforward, the revised version of the description more fully emphasizes how Ralph seeks to compensate for the circumstances of his life: he plays the game of indifference in order to impose meaning on the sacrifices that life has demanded of him. Ralph is not truly indifferent to anything in life, but the attitudes of indifference protect him from suffering from the limitations of his life. Ralph's "arduous game" is thus opposed metaphorically to Isabel's "free play of intelligence"—perhaps to suggest the ways in which they will find themselves "playing somehow at cross-purposes" (189)—an expression that Isabel uses in her own mind to describe Henrietta Stackpole's relationship with Mr. Bantling, but which just as clearly describes Ralph's relationship with Isabel.

From the beginning, Ralph frames his interaction with his cousin as a harmless kind of amusement; he establishes "a reputation for treating everything as a joke" (61).[24] The joking attitude helps him to conceal his emotions from her and from others. He transforms his secret affection for her into what must be seen as a game of power and possession, even though he never means to harm her. By manufacturing the circumstances that will make her free, he seeks to participate in determining her destiny. The freedom he bestows on her is not, paradoxically, bestowed freely, since in his own mind he demands that she measure up to the standards he has set for her. He makes her play the game that he has devised for her. He even finds himself disappointed when she fails his test, by surrendering so quickly to the resolution of marriage, and with someone, in Ralph's mind, so clearly unworthy. When he forces her to defend her reasons for marrying Osmond, she echoes his own reasons for giving her the money: "I've only one ambition—to be free to follow out a good feeling" (293). She marries for no other reason than to "please herself" (294). He has, after all, expressed the desire to let her follow her own imagination. But Osmond becomes for Ralph, in the narrator's words, "the husband of the woman he loved" (332). In his objections to her marriage, Ralph does more than predict Isabel's

Dreadful Games

disillusionment; he also reveals that in his heart he had hoped that the money would prevent her from marrying at all.

Ralph devotes himself to following Isabel's progress; it becomes his only purpose. When Lord Warburton accompanies him to Rome several years after Isabel's marriage, Ralph remarks, "I suspect we've each been playing our little game" (334). The irony of Ralph's game is that while trying to free Isabel from acting expediently, he has made her vulnerable to those who do not hesitate to commit acts of expediency. Without the money Ralph imposes on his cousin, Mme Merle would have had no reason to introduce her to Gilbert Osmond; Isabel would have avoided the dangers inherent in that meeting. Before he acquiesces in Ralph's plan, Daniel Touchett asks if giving Isabel the money is not somewhat "immoral": as he prophetically says to his son, "Doesn't it occur to you that a young lady with sixty thousand pounds may fall a victim to the fortune-hunters" (162). Ralph has considered this possibility, but having "calculated" the "risk," he decides that "I am prepared to take it" (162)—in other words, he is willing to gamble with his cousin's future and her happiness.

Oddly enough, given that Isabel clearly values the freedom of her imagination more than she does money, Ralph's exploitation of her imagination is not nearly as sinister in the context of the novel as Osmond's exploitation of her money. This difficulty can be resolved by contrasting the way in which Ralph plays his game with the way in which Osmond and Mme Merle play theirs. Perhaps because Ralph's "betrayal" of her, if it can be called that, is unintentional, resulting from his errors in judgment and from his lack of self-knowledge—and perhaps too, because he has been duped by Mme Merle—Isabel vindicates him in the end, when she fully comprehends her own errors of judgment. In contrast, Osmond and Mme Merle deliberately deceive Isabel, precisely in order to exploit her. If Ralph injures her through foolishness and ignorance, they injure her through cunning and greed. The ulteriority that Mme Merle and Osmond demonstrate makes their game more corrupted than Ralph's could ever be.

That Mme Merle mentions her "friend" Mr. Osmond very early in her acquaintance with Isabel suggests that the plan she forms to make Isabel Osmond's wife occurs to her almost as soon as Isabel becomes an heiress. In Isabel, she finds someone who, as she assures Osmond, "fills all your requirements" (206)—beauty, cleverness, wealth, intelligence, and virtue—aware that only on those conditions would Osmond be drawn into her scheme. In this conversation between Osmond and Mme Merle (chapter 22), James uses dramatic irony to reveal to the reader the side of Mme Merle that she reveals to none of the characters except Osmond and the Countess Gemini. Mme Merle has mastered the game of concealment. By all of the other characters, she is considered simply a woman of many talents and mysterious means, hardly a threat to anyone. When Ralph surrenders Isabel to the influence of Mme Merle he believes that the risk of her being hurt is minimal. Knowing that Isabel has "a great deal to learn," he decides that she "would doubtless learn it better from Mme Merle than from some other instructors of the young"; he concludes that "it was not probable that Isabel would be injured" (217), and that Isabel might improve herself through the friendship. Once again, Ralph has unfortunately, for Isabel's sake, miscalculated the risk involved. As the narrator says, he has not been left "wholly unbeguiled by such a mistress of the social art" (216).[25] The character of Mme Merle indicates that James, like his character Christopher Newman, had read *Les Liaisons dangereuses*, since Mme Merle's actions are comparable with those of Laclos's Mme de Merteuil. Just as Merteuil seeks to avenge her wounded pride and frustrated ambition in the person of Cécile de Volanges, Mme Merle seeks Isabel's marriage to Osmond as a rather vengeful form of compensation for her many disappointments in life.

The novel proposes more than one reason for Mme Merle to bring about this marriage and to practice so many deceptions to promote it. The first reason proposed is the one she insists upon in Osmond's presence, "My ambitions are principally for you" (205)—a statement she makes with "nobleness of expression" (526), in the London edition, a phrase that James changed simply to "courage," perhaps to emphasize the extent to which she is playing a carefully calculated game with Osmond here.[26] Isabel's money permits Osmond to live his life of "indolence" more comfortably. Once it becomes known, however, that Mme Merle is Pansy's natural mother, another motive suggests itself, the one that the Countess Gemini gives to Isabel: "She has failed so dreadfully that she's determined her daughter shall make it up" (454). Making Isabel Pansy's stepmother offers Mme Merle two possible ways of securing her daughter's success: not only might Isabel provide for Pansy directly, but she might also direct Lord Warburton's affections toward Pansy. Then too, having long since lost Osmond's love, Mme Merle may hope to experience it again vicariously, through her intimacy with Isabel, much as Merteuil makes love to Valmont indirectly, through her correspondence with Cécile. But whatever the case, it is Mme Merle's methods rather than her motives that the novel seeks to expose; the various interpretations of her motives help the reader and the other characters to recognize more fully the nature of her methods.

Mrs. Touchett is the first to suspect Mme Merle of deception; she believes that her friend has "deceived" her by not preventing Isabel's marriage, and she refuses to accept Isabel's argument that Mme Merle could not have influenced it. Mrs. Touchett knows that Mme Merle is capable of manipulating appearances, of fostering certain illusions to advance her own causes, but Mrs. Touchett makes her own distinction between this useful talent and the art of willful duplicity: "I knew that she could play any part; but I understood that she played them one by one. I didn't understand that she would play two at the same time" (283). As Mrs. Touchett sees the situation, Mme Merle has promised her to prevent the marriage at the same time she has undoubtedly promised Osmond to promote it. But in fact, Mme Merle's methods are even more subtle than Mrs. Touchett suspects.[27] She has not merely promoted, but actually initiated Osmond's interest in Isabel. But much more sinister, of course, than the way in which she "deceives" Mrs. Touchett, is the way Mme Merle violates Isabel's trust. In speaking to Isabel about Osmond, she makes it clear that "he was a person not to miss" (210), especially for an American visiting Italy, yet she never indicates that she has any special or unusual interest in him: "she hinted at nothing but a long-established calm friendship" (211). After Osmond's first visit, Mme Merle extends herself too far when she tells Isabel "you were just as one would have wished you"; when Isabel shows resentment at these words, Mme Merle quickly revises: "it matters little whether he likes you or not! But I thought you liked *him*" (213). She helps to foster the illusion that Isabel is choosing, rather than being chosen. Especially when compared with Ralph's and Mrs. Touchett's loudly voiced disapproval of her marriage to Osmond, Mme Merle's appearance of disinterest helps to further her carefully conceived scheme. Her attitude helps to convince Isabel that the idea of marrying Osmond is her own.

Mme Merle's plan to marry Isabel to Osmond succeeds as well as it does partly because Osmond is to all appearances so unlike the "fortune-hunters" that Daniel Touchett imagines when he fears for Isabel's safety. Osmond's motives are virtually unfathomable. His smooth, impenetrable external self makes it easy for Isabel to imagine anything she wants to about him; when at their first meeting he gives "a rather dry account" of his life, Isabel manages to embellish it: "her imagination supplied the human element which she was sure had not been wanting" (228). It is somewhat ironic that the one fault Osmond finds in Isabel is that she has "too many ideas" (244), since had she not had them, he might not have been able to win her. Osmond gives the impression of a man who has transcended the more ordinary forms of ambition. Isabel assures Ralph that part of her attraction to Osmond comes from the fact that he "has never scrambled nor struggled—he's cared for no worldly prize" (293). What Isabel likes most about Osmond is her inability to place him in a category: "Her mind contained no class offering a place to Mr. Osmond—he was a specimen apart" (224). She tells Caspar Goodwood, almost with pride, that Osmond is "not known for anything in particular" (278). Having already rejected both Goodwood and Warburton, Isabel takes delight in an "alliance" that in Mrs. Touchett's words has "an air of almost morbid perversity" (234). But Isabel's choice is more than perverse; even after she has begun to suspect that she might have "married on a factitious theory," she refuses to admit that she had been "mistaken about the beauty of his mind" (358). Isabel marries Osmond because she believes they share the same vision of the ideal life.

The text distinguishes, in the second half of the novel, between Isabel Archer, and "Mrs. Osmond," the woman she becomes. Isabel Archer might have argued, along with Christopher Newman, the advantages of resembling oneself, but Mrs. Osmond has modeled herself on Mme Merle and has begun to imagine the "advantage" of being like her, "of having made one's self a firm surface, a sort of corselet of silver" (337). Without knowing precisely how or why her marriage has changed her, Ralph notes that "whereas of old she had a great delight in good-humoured argument, in intellectual play," she comes to demonstrate a conviction that "there was nothing worth people's either differing about or agreeing upon" (330). Her life with Osmond offers few opportunities for "good-humoured argument," when all differences of opinion lead to strife. What Ralph notices here is a diminution of the spirit of play that has characterized Isabel's personality from the beginning of the novel. She is less free and spontaneous than Ralph remembers her as being.

Much of Isabel's "education" in the novel consists of her growing awareness of how different her own values are from those of her husband and Mme Merle. Only after her marriage does Isabel learn that although she and Osmond share the same respect for "the aristocratic life," they define this ideal in different ways. This moment echoes an earlier moment when Isabel comes to realize that Mme Merle "was the product of a different moral or social clime from her own" (275); Isabel comes to acknowledge that Mme Merle possesses a different sense of morality.[28] When she makes this distinction, Isabel not only opens up the possibility, to be realized much later, that Mme Merle conceals some past transgression, but also explains why she begins to draw away from Mme Merle's influence, in order to preserve her own sense of values.

In much the same way that she perceives the differences between herself and Mme Merle, Isabel admits to herself that she and Osmond "attached such different ideas, such different associations and desires to the same formulas" (361). If for Isabel "the aristocratic life" is "the union of great knowledge with great liberty," for Osmond it is "altogether a thing of forms, a conscious calculated attitude" (361). Osmond is like Mme Merle in his feelings about tradition and propriety; the Countess Gemini tells Isabel that Mme Merle's "great idea has been to be tremendously irreprochable" (454), despite the many ways in which she has secretly violated the essence of "propriety." Isabel believes that both she and her husband respect "the old, the consecrated, and the transmitted," but unlike Osmond, Isabel insists that she can do what she chooses with it (361). Isabel reserves the right of picking and choosing from that group of ideas labeled "tradition." But pleading "the cause of freedom" (361) in this way, she incurs her husband's scorn.

In becoming Mrs. Osmond, Isabel has unwittingly opened herself up to playing the kinds of games that Mme Merle plays. If Osmond is a man who values form over essence, he reveals his true nature when he insists that Isabel use her "influence" (354) with Lord Warburton to arrange a marriage with Pansy. Isabel wants to be able to perform this act; she wants to "play the part of the good wife" (348), but she cannot. To do so, to "make" Pansy's marriage, Isabel would have to become like Mme Merle, who has "made" Osmond's own marriage. And like Mme Merle, she would be doing it to regain Osmond's affections. She would have to exploit Lord Warburton's affection for her, much as Mme Merle has exploited Isabel's friendship. Isabel is also unwilling to take the risk that Warburton's interest in Pansy arises from a lingering desire for Isabel herself—she is not willing to gamble with Pansy's happiness as others have gambled with hers, especially since she knows that Pansy does not love Lord Warburton. Isabel chooses not to influence

Playing by the Rules

Warburton in Pansy's favor—although for the sake of form she encourages him to ask Osmond for Pansy's hand—simply because she can think of no good, but much evil, that might come of it. By following her own conscience here, she incurs more than her husband's scorn. He accuses her of betraying his interest. Judging her according to his own style of action, he tells her with the bitterness of a man defeated by an unscrupulous opponent, "You've played a very deep game; you've managed it beautifully" (401). He calls her "game" "deep" because he believes that she has deceived him about what she intended to do, and because in his mind, her logic is unfathomable. He believes that Isabel has deliberately frustrated his desire to see his daughter married to a lord, and he fails to see "why you wanted this particular satisfaction" (402). That Osmond is so quick to find the logic of game playing in Isabel's actions helps to clarify for Isabel the nature of his own.

The language of games highlights Isabel's opportunities for revenge. The Countess Gemini provides Isabel with the last bit of information she needs to understand the true nature and circumstances of her marriage. Like Valentin de Bellegarde, who gives Christopher Newman the key to revenge only when his own life is finished, the Countess Gemini reveals what she has known from the beginning about Osmond and Mme Merle only when she recognizes that her own "game was almost played out" (448). Knowing that "she had already overstayed her invitation" (448) in her brother's home, she tells Isabel the secret of Osmond's past relationship with Mme Merle and the truth of Pansy's parentage. The Countess Gemini has been a rather amused observer of events, held silent by Mme Merle's threat of exposure: "She let me know then [the first time the countess met Isabel] that if I should tell tales two could play at that game" (454). But she has reached that point in her "game" where her silence buys her less satisfaction than speaking does. The Countess's revelation permits Isabel to make sense out of past events, and inspires her to compare her life with Osmond to "an attempt to play whist with an imperfect pack of cards" (465). This metaphor—where for the first time the text uses the logic and language of games to describe Isabel's situation—suggests that she herself may now act to exploit another's weakness. The choice of words here associates Isabel with those other characters—Ralph, Mme Merle, Osmond, the Countess Gemini—who have been guided by the logic of games. Having perfected her pack of cards, Isabel finds herself in a position to play as the others have played.

Isabel's opportunities for vengeance—and for resisting the temptation of it—are somewhat less easily defined than those of Christopher Newman, whose means of avenging himself are inscribed on a small piece of paper. The two characters nevertheless face similar kinds of choices. Just as Newman takes satisfaction in the Bellegarde's discomfort, Isabel exacts a kind of revenge in forcing Mme Merle into the "unprecedented situation" (459) of having nothing clever to say, when she realizes that Isabel knows the truth. In this instance, Isabel chooses the power of silence over that of words: "Isabel would never accuse her, never reproach her; perhaps because she would never give her the opportunity to defend herself" (459). After seeing Pansy, however, Isabel does seize the grim satisfaction of telling Mme Merle, "I think I should like never to see you again" (464). And yet this moment is neither a victory for Isabel, nor a moment of revenge. Mme Merle, in effect, banishes herself primarily because Osmond has shattered her hope of playing a role in Pansy's life (436), not because of anything that Isabel says to her.

Isabel also considers her opportunities to exact revenge from her husband. She defies Osmond by traveling to Ralph's deathbed, but it is hardly an act of pure defiance. She does so not to defy her husband, to injure him as he has injured her, but to affirm her feelings for Ralph. She seeks to assert here, by returning to Gardencourt, her own ability to take positive action. Isabel also successfully resists what might be called her ultimate revenge—leaving Osmond forever. She forsakes this mode of vengeance not despite Caspar Goodwood's offer, but because of it. He offers her not freedom, but merely a different form of bondage, to the kind of compromised life lived by other wives who have chosen the same means of exacting vengeance from their dreadful husbands.

Isabel has learned how others play and, like Christopher Newman, has ultimately insisted on playing by her own rules. What makes *The Portrait of a Lady* somewhat different in tone from *The American* is the way James has distinguished the attitudes of Isabel's play from the attitudes of those who reveal themselves as her adversaries. She resists the temptation to become like those who have betrayed her, but rather than leaving them behind as Newman does, she must continue to live among them. Isabel submits herself to a life with Osmond, to what one critic has called "the hopeless, unfree world of the sick soul,"[29] but it is a form of bondage she herself chooses. She chooses to allow Osmond the last word, just as Christopher Newman's actions confer that privilege on the Bellegardes. When Ralph predicts that by marrying Osmond she is "going to be put into a cage," she retorts, "If I like my cage, that needn't trouble you" (288). Although at the end she likes this cage a great deal less, she chooses it in preference to an alternative that in her mind has already proven itself—in the lives of Mme Merle and the Countess Gemini—even less satisfying and far more ugly than the life she looks forward to with Osmond.

As at the end of *The American* a certain ambiguity surrounds the issues of victory and defeat. Like Christopher Newman, Isabel has chosen to avoid the emptiness of revenge, but at the same time she faces a world of narrower possibilities than the one she faces at the beginning of her "career." The novel chronicles the suppression of Isabel Archer's "playful" attitude toward life, an attitude reflected most clearly in her love of freedom and in her belief that life is always open to possibility. She learns that the play of choices is sometimes nothing more than a choice between different forms of bondage, sometimes even a choice between two evils. The question of whether Isabel will try to create a new life for herself, perhaps by devoting herself to Pansy, creating for Osmond's daughter a happier life than her own,[30] remains well outside the scope of the novel, just as the reader can only guess about Christopher Newman's future. More important in these novels than the suggestion of future possibilities is the way in which the characters' illusions about life are shattered, without making them vengeful. In his later novels, James would explore the ways in which fictional characters might create new possibilities for themselves, but in *The American* and *The Portrait of a Lady,* he shows instead how they might avoid the instinctual responses of the past. In this sense, both novels are "modern," as the early critic of *The American* had defined it: they have only the subtlest "flavor of the past" and the vaguest "prophecy of the future."

7

Games as Rituals

The Wings of the Dove and *The Golden Bowl*

■ Competitive games are structures, as Claude Lévi-Strauss illustrates in *The Savage Mind,* that distinguish between winners and losers, that establish a relationship of inequality between participants. By this definition, the logic of competitive game playing prevails in the endings of both *The American* and *The Portrait of a Lady,* even though James has tried to reformulate the narrative strategies of other nineteenth-century novels of ambition and revenge. Despite the sense of dignity that both Christopher Newman and Isabel Archer acquire by resisting the temptations of revenge, their circumstances remain almost grimly deterministic. Even if they have "won" a moral victory over those who have betrayed them, they have "lost," in the process, their sense of life as an infinite play of possibilities. Both novels define the notion of choice according to the logic of games: the characters "choose" between mutually exclusive options, which offer them fewer and fewer opportunities for individual satisfaction.

In his last two major novels, however, James demonstrates a different kind of structural logic, not unlike the logic that governs ritual structures. Like games, rituals are "played"—they integrate participants into a common fiction that governs specific events. But unlike competitive games, rituals propose to erase, rather than to underscore, distinctions of status and talent among participants. As Lévi-Strauss says, in rituals there are no losers: "All participants pass to the winning side by means of events."[1] Rituals are also distinguished from games by the message that frames such encounters. The message "this is play," which frames a game encounter, is replaced in ritual by the message "let us believe."[2] It is this "belief" in the intrinsic power and value of the actions that take place within the middle ground of ritual that helps to create the "equilibrium," or harmony, characteristic of ritual. Rituals seek to mediate opposition—the kind of opposition that in *The Wings of the Dove* and *The Golden Bowl* exists between those who know and those who do not know, those who conceal the truth from others and those who are deceived by such deceptions, and those who desire and those who offer the means of fulfilling such desires.

That Henry James's later novels differ remarkably from his early novels reveals itself in several ways: in differences of style, language, narration, and characterization. Despite these unmistakable changes in method, many of the conflicts in the later novels involve characters and narrative situations that parallel those James explores in the earlier novels: wealthy Americans, worldly Europeans, ambitious marriages, unwitting victims, heartless deceptions. Nevertheless, the ultimate resolutions of conflict in the later novels can be distinguished from the resolutions of the earlier novels not only by the author's style and tone, but even by the way the texts define and illustrate such elusive notions as good and evil, truth and falsehood. For instance, it is simply not as easy in the later novels to sympathize with the circumstances and sufferings of one particular character, as it is in novels like *The American* and *The Portrait of a Lady*. In *The Wings of the Dove* and *The Golden Bowl*, isolated, individual actions are not definitively good or evil in themselves, and can be interpreted only within the pattern of events that either restrict or fulfill the human potential represented by the characters' fictional lives.[3] The issue in these novels is no longer what characters do, but how and why they make such decisions.

In *The American* and *The Portrait of a Lady* James concerns himself with the victims of games of ambition, and the movement in both novels is from a world of infinite possibilities to a much more circumscribed world of fewer, more compromised choices. Those who initiate the "plots" of the earlier novels—the Bellegardes, Mme Merle, Gilbert Osmond—are motivated by an obsessive ambition for love or fortune, by feelings of superiority, and sometimes even by a desire to avenge themselves by injuring those who have attained fortune or love. Christopher Newman and Isabel Archer find themselves hopelessly trapped in a web of manipulatory games, perpetrated by worldly and cunning characters. The division of characters into such clearly delineated categories helps direct the reader's sympathy toward the subject of each of these "biographies." The text affirms and justifies the reader's sympathy when these "victims" refuse to become like those who have betrayed them.

In contrast, *The Wings of the Dove* and *The Golden Bowl* provide no such useful categories by which to interpret the endings. Those who would become victims of games of ambition, betrayal, and revenge, become players in their own right, who transform through their actions and choices the pattern of entrapment and victimization. The endings of these novels—unlike the ending of *Crime and Punishment,* for example—promise neither a mystical redemption for the would-be victims of manipulative schemes, nor a legally appropriate punishment for the perpetrators; they do not describe a safe place where the logic of game playing is magically transcended. Rather, the events of both *The Wings of the Dove* and *The Golden Bowl* suggest, somewhat paradoxically, that the game of hidden being—particularly in the sense of pretending to a common fiction or of refusing to expose someone else's lies—provides an alternative to that hard choice faced by Christopher Newman and Isabel Archer: to become like one's betrayers or to accept having been duped and betrayed. As in earlier examples of drama or fiction, deception leads to self-knowledge and enlightenment. In the process, deception opens up possibilities for all characters, rather than, as so many other deceptions do, systematically limiting alternatives.

Just as these novels attest to the power of human play to mediate and resolve conflicts, the style James uses to convey this notion suggests the possibilities inherent in the play of language. In both *The Wings of the Dove* and *The Golden Bowl* language becomes an event; characters are more likely to speak than to act. What is said, or not said, and the particular form those utterances or silences assume, define narrative situations. In contrast to the Realist novel, as defined by a critic like Leo Bersani, where "society" is "either beyond or prior to the work,"[4] nothing exists beyond or prior to the play of language in James's later novels. Language does not represent "reality," but rather, constitutes it; language defines, distorts, and transforms relationships between characters. Through language, a relationship can be denied—as is the love shared by Kate Croy and Merton Densher in *The Wings of the Dove*. Or it can be distorted, even concealed—as when the Prince refers to Charlotte as his "mother-in-law" in *The Golden Bowl*. The private means of communication that Charlotte and the Prince share, by speaking to one another in Italian, not only heightens the sense of their intimacy, but also underscores their differences from the Ververs. Events do not merely "occur" in either novel, they are "discussed." A résumé or evaluation of events, provided by either the characters or the narrator, often replaces the dramatic presentation of events, as for example, in *The Wings of the Dove,* where the reader is not permitted to participate in Lord Mark's and Densher's last visits with Milly Theale. Furthermore, objects in the later James do not serve to reveal something about character or environment, as they do in Balzac's fictional world, but rather exist to be discussed by the characters, and in the process to become significant to them—whether paintings, palaces, latch keys, or golden bowls. The language of the text alone gives people, events, and even objects their special significance.

James breaks the typical Realist formula even in the way he begins *The Wings of the Dove* and *The Golden Bowl.* Almost without exception, Realist novels begin by invoking the material reality on which the text depends, often, by naming the date, the place, and the other circumstances that establish the context for the characters' actions. *Le Rouge et le noir* begins with a long description of the town of Verrières. Both *La Cousine Bette* and *Crime and Punishment* begin with sentences that place an as yet unnamed character in a particular place at a particular time: in Dostoevsky's text, "Towards the end of a sultry afternoon in July a young man came out of his little room . . . ," in Balzac's text, "Towards the middle of July, in the year 1838, one of those new vehicles called *milords* was travelling on the Rue de l'Université." Balzac often provides an even larger context: *Les Illusions perdues* begins not with the circumstances of Lucien de Rubempré's or David Séchard's careers, but with a discussion of the development of the Standhope printing press. The opening sentences of both *The American* and *The Portrait of a Lady* link these novels to this same narrative tradition. *The American* begins with a sentence that places the unnamed Christopher Newman on a divan in the Louvre in May of 1868. *The Portrait of a Lady* begins with a long, generalized description of Gardencourt, and then marks the beginning of the second half with precise details about Edward Rosier's visit to Mme Merle three years after Isabel's marriage: "One afternoon of the autumn of 1876, toward dusk . . ." (chapter 36). Each of these novels delineates a precise geography, and often a chronology as well, which provides the context for the events that follow.

In contrast, *The Wings of the Dove* and *The Golden Bowl* provide what might be called a "psychological" context. Both beginnings grant the reader access to a particular character's consciousness as a way of suggesting some of the human conflicts that will emerge in each novel. *The Wings of the Dove* begins with Kate Croy's thoughts as she waits impatiently for her father. The scene emphasizes the shabbiness and vulgarity of her father's life, as well as her own impatience with finding herself there—two circumstances that indirectly inspire the game of ambition she plays with her Aunt Maud. The material reality of the room in which Kate stands is constituted almost entirely by her thoughts about her life and family. The author uses Kate's thoughts about the room, not the room itself, to define her character. *The Golden Bowl* begins, similarly, with the Prince's thoughts as he window-shops in Bond Street in London. Not what he does, but the way he does it, reveals something about his character: his imagination confronts the assortment of objects collected, somewhat haphazardly, in the shop windows, but his interest is not long sustained by anything, including the women who pass him on the street. In this way, James notes the Prince's lack of direction and, more importantly, his half-hearted attempts to make sense of a world that values objects for their collectibility. And significantly, the issue of collectibility, of purchase and possession, becomes a source of conflict in the novel, since both the Prince and Charlotte are destined to become items in the Ververs' "collection." James does something more in both of these opening passages than simply violate the Realist formula; he violates the reader's expectation of how to constitute meaning. These opening passages do not provide the reader with "background information," and in fact, the reader most likely to make sense out of these passages is the one who already knows what will happen, who has already read the rest of the novel.

Thus, these novels refute the notion that language is merely the instrument of meaning, that words can reproduce reality. The difficulty, the abstraction, and the intangibility of the style and syntax of these novels reinforce this idea.[5] The complex sentences must often be broken apart and reorganized in order to be comprehended, and the abstract, often inanimate subjects and metaphorized verbs remain open to a variety of possible interpretations. James deliberately selects "words which draw attention to themselves as language."[6] Words that suggest a wide range of possible meanings are repeated over and over in these novels—words like "prodigious," which can mean "wonderful," "amazing," "powerful," or even "ominous," in different contexts. Using words in this way opens the text up to a number of possible meanings. James deliberately exploits these possibilities of meaning, risking ambiguity of interpretation, but simultaneously demanding the reader's conscientious attention to the way in which words are used.

The reader penetrates the fictional world of these novels, not because enough details and facts have been collected in the opening pages to give the illusion of the material world, but because the reader must participate in the process of discovery, the process of uncovering the desires and deceptions that structure the novel. In other words, the reader participates in the play of events. In addition to demanding the reader's attention to language, James permits and encourages the reader to participate in the discovery of facts, by shifting the point of view in both novels between the deceivers and the deceived. The narrative structure depends on both the suppression of material facts and the discovery of long-suspected truths. Elizabeth Stevenson describes the relationship that the text establishes with the reader as a "game": "As long as the spell lasts, [the reader] is thinking the thoughts of the characters and feeling their emotions. . . . Once everybody has agreed to pretend . . . the rest comes easily."[7] The style, syntax, and diction of these novels, along with the manipulation of narrative perspectives, make these novels special kinds of literary games.

Even though the "game" that these texts play with the reader is a different kind of game than that played by other nineteenth-century Realist novels, both *The Wings of the Dove* and *The Golden Bowl* describe events that resemble the games of ambition and revenge that structure those other novels—games where players seek to coerce or to dominate other individuals in an attempt to satisfy their own desires. Just as he does in *The American* and *The Portrait of a Lady,* James uses, in the later novels, the language of games to describe these narrative events. Both literal and figurative games take place in these novels, but the distinction between literal and figurative often remains blurred. For example, in *The Golden Bowl,* the bridge game at Fawns in chapter 36 (Book Fifth:II) functions not only as an actual event in the narrative, but also as a symbolic representation of the play of relationships between the characters. The episode serves to link the actual event to other card game metaphors that Maggie's consciousness fashions before and after this point.[8] Thus, the bridge game at Fawns functions as both an actual and a "metaphorical" event, which links Maggie's initial blindness to what becomes her keen perception of things.

More often, though, the games in James's novels are purely figurative:

Dreadful Games

common or unusual expressions used to describe people or events. The language of games, frequently in the form of an extended simile, compares characters' actions to specific children's or adults' games. Children's games, for instance, are used to describe Milly Theale and Maggie and Adam Verver. Frequent also, are ironic or cynical references by the characters to their own and others' actions as a "game," references that are more like clichés than true metaphors, but which, by being repeated so many times in the text, give the actions they describe a special significance.[9] Many critics have examined the kinds of imagery that recur in James's fiction. In his extensive compilation of these categories of imagery, Alexander Holder-Barell identifies the general function of game imagery. According to Holder-Barell, such images indicate the risks, or the luck or difficulty, or the triumph or loss, inherent in a given situation; such images also note oppositions between characters or groups, and stress such character qualities as "secrecy" or "wickedness."[10] This interpretation identifies the most common ways in which James, just like Stendhal, Laclos, Balzac, Dostoevsky, and Hardy, uses game imagery to emphasize opposition, secrecy, and danger.

James uses the idea of play in the language of the text in still other, less immediately perceptible ways. Clearly, his thoughts about the nature of play evolved over a period of time, as the revisions to *The Portrait of a Lady* suggest. In the later novels, just as in the revisions to that earlier novel, language that defines the nature of play contrasts with other figures of speech that refer to games. In addition, other large categories of images, such as drama or acting images, as well as images of warfare and aggression, share much of the same vocabulary as game images and function in much the same way. These "indirect" game images also stress qualities inherent in characters or events.[11]

Perhaps the most interesting use, in the later novels, of the idea of play is James's frequent use of "play" as a noun or verb in unusual and often abstract metaphorical constructions similar to more common figures like "the play of light" or "a play on words." Many of these figures are similar to those used to describe Isabel Archer in *A Portrait of a Lady,* but they are used to describe a much broader range of characters in the later novels. In *The Wings of the Dove,* for example, Densher finds a kind of "beauty" in Aunt Maud, "in the play of so big and bold a temperament" (19:77).[12] Milly finds that the Englishmen she meets "concealed their play of mind so much more than they advertised it" (19:151). In *The Golden Bowl,* the Prince catches in Maggie "the

Games as Rituals

mere play of her joy" as she speaks about her father (23:8), and notes in Charlotte "the play of her extremely personal, her always amusing taste" (23:45). These two figures are especially important, since in this way the text opposes Maggie's often rather childlike, spontaneous "joy" with life to Charlotte's drier, more formalistic concern with matters of "taste."

Such figures of speech do more than attribute certain qualities to characters, however; they also help to underscore the importance of special moments in the text. The house at Matcham, where Charlotte and the Prince find themselves the host and hostess, is filled with "the quickened play of possible propinquity" (23:30): the nature of their relationship has already been affirmed before the act of adultery takes place, and the play of their desire fills the house. In the second volume of *The Golden Bowl,* several figures are used to describe the patterns of Maggie's awakening consciousness, as she formulates her own deception. As she contemplates her discussion with her father, "her own passionate prudence played over the possibilities of danger" (24:84); thoughts of the gathering at Fawns "played all duskily in her mind" (24:97); and when Fanny Assingham smashes the golden bowl, a "rapid play of suppressed appeal and disguised response" (23:180) passes between Maggie and the Prince when he enters the room. In each of these passages, play describes the activity of the imagination; as he had begun to do in the revisions to *The Portrait of a Lady,* James uses play in this context as a metaphor for the characters' intellectual and emotional responses. These figures also suggest the mediating power of play as interpretation; the process of producing meaning is described metaphorically as play. The unusual quality of these expressions also contrasts vividly with the triteness of so many other game images in both novels.

An elaborate pattern of games of ambition establishes itself in the first two books of *The Wings of the Dove,* long before the "heroine," as James describes Milly Theale in the preface, enters this fictional society in the novel's fourth book. The "plottedness" of early portions of the text recalls the many subplots of a novel like *La Cousine Bette*. At least four distinct, but interrelated schemes unfold as the novel proceeds, each representing the interests of a different character: Kate, Maud, Densher, and Lord Mark. First, Kate's Aunt Maud has offered to "adopt" her, but only on the explicit condition that Kate renounce her family—a degenerate father and an impoverished, widowed sister—and with a tacit understanding that Maud will find Kate a husband accept-

151

Dreadful Games

able to Maud herself. Kate's vague fear of Maud—a wariness that drives her first to her father and then to her sister, hoping in vain that they can decide her fate for her—issues, no doubt, from the manipulative, exploitative nature of their relationship. Not only are the conditions of Maud's arrangement with Kate ungenerous and arbitrary, but they testify to Maud's penchant for making sure that the risk she faces in any social "game" is minimal. Maud has nothing to lose and everything to gain from the choice she offers Kate. Maud plans to use Kate to serve the interests of her own social maneuvers, and she need not give Kate anything unless she agrees to marry Lord Mark, Maud's own choice for Kate's husband. And even Lord Mark stands to gain more than Kate does: Maud's financial support and the possession of a lovely wife. Under these circumstances, faced with the selfish and ambitious desires of others, Kate not surprisingly thinks that "there were always people to snatch at you. . . . [T]he more you gave yourself the less of you was left" (19:33).

But while she resents these circumstances and the uncompromisingly hard choice that Maud asks her to make, she does not refuse to play Maud's game. She ostensibly accepts the premises that govern this fictional society. Although she proves herself willing to cheat, or at least to bend the rules until they are ready to snap, she acknowledges her aunt's power over her. Kate's initial discussion with her father—whom the narrator describes as dealing out "lies as he might the cards from the greasy old pack for the game of diplomacy to which you were to sit down with him" (19:7)—helps to frame what both Kate and Maud do in the novel as part of the logic of game playing. Kate also uses her meeting with her father to justify her subsequent actions. To reject Maud's offer in favor of a relationship with Lionel never really seems a credible option, given Kate's character as it emerges by the end of the novel. This gesture nevertheless provides her with the comforting illusion that she is a victim, rather than a manipulator, that she has no choice but to play Maud's game. When her father assures her that "the only way to play the game *is* to play it (19:9), he assumes that she will recognize the good sense, the "logic," of following her aunt's wishes—or at least of making the *appearance* of compliance as convincing as she can. The one option that Kate never seems to consider is the one that Christopher Newman and Isabel Archer choose: she never confronts Maud with the refusal to play by her rules. She could, but does not, call Maud's bluff, thus calling into question the premises that govern her game.[13]

The illusion that she has no choice, that she has been victimized by her family's lack of will and her aunt's exploitative tendencies, provides Kate with a rationale for the game of deception that she and Densher play with Maud. In the preface, James describes Kate and Densher as "a pair of natures well-nigh consumed by . . . the reciprocity of their desire," and explains that they use "intelligence" to support them in their "game" (19:xiv). The narrator uses the language of ritual to describe the moment when Kate and Densher agree to be secretly engaged to one another: "They had exchanged vows and tokens, sealed their rich compact, solemnized . . . their agreement to belong only . . . to each other" (19:25). But although they unite themselves in this secret ritual, the logic of game playing characterizes their actions. In the beginning, this game belongs more to Kate than to Densher. Even if Kate is willing to dissociate herself from her father and sister in order to fulfill the terms of her arrangement with Maud, she is not willing to relinquish Densher. Kate submits herself to the logic of the choices Maud gives her, secretly believing that ultimately she can have both Maud's money and Densher. In other words, she submits herself to these choices even as she believes that she will not have to make them.

Like Kate, Densher takes an almost fatalistic approach to his own participation in this scheme. Although he agrees to the actions that Kate suggests, he remains little more than a pawn in the power struggle that develops between these strong-willed, egocentric women. He nevertheless demonstrates an increasing awareness of not only the risks they take but also the futility of it all. As the plan progresses, he begins to resent his participation, questioning himself about "the oddity, after all, of their game" (20:21). He cannot imagine what success they will be able to achieve; as he tries to explain to Kate, "remember that she can play with us quite as much as we play with her" (20:23). He also begins to consider what effect their actions will have on their feelings for one another; he begins to wonder if he is showing a lack of respect for her. He is disconcerted to think that " 'respect' in their game seemed somehow . . . a fifth wheel to the coach," when it should have been "a thing to make love greater, not to make happiness less" (20:5). Clearly, self-respect is at issue for him as well. When Kate urges him to be "charming" to Aunt Maud, he argues that he can only be "charming" if he deceives her about his feelings for Kate. He argues that to be nice to Maud would be "a game"; Kate replies, "Of course it's a game" (20:24), arguing once again that they have no other means of achieving their goal.

Dreadful Games

Densher does not initiate his own game until that moment when he exchanges his continued participation in Kate's game for a sexual commitment from her. But he thinks about making this demand long before the moment of confrontation between them. He has begged her to end their deception of Maud, to "have done with it all and face the music as we are" (20:198), but she refuses, arguing "we've gone too far" (20:199) to end their game now. When Kate urges him to propose marriage to Milly, he threatens to leave Venice the next day, unless she comes to his rooms; in what is a moment of triumph for him, he finds himself "fairly playing with her pride" (20:231). Kate chooses to submit to Densher's terms in order to ensure his continued involvement, just as she agrees to "sacrifice" her father. Thus, "the game of social concealment," in Kenneth Graham's words, "provokes the most ancient game of all, the sexual power game."[14] Densher shows himself willing to bargain his own honor in order to possess her. Both characters consistently find ways to rationalize and to justify the actions they take, just as Raskolnikov seeks to rationalize his actions in *Crime and Punishment*. And just as in Dostoevsky's novel, such efforts demonstrate the logic of competitive game playing.

But as long as Maud, Kate, and Densher are satisfied with manipulating one another, the game they play remains essentially sheltered, and the consequences of it limited to themselves. It remains a closed game, its energy controlled. Kate's and Densher's games of deception and power—of ambition and revenge—become "dreadful" to use Densher's own word, not because they deceive Aunt Maud—whom, after all, they never really convince with their efforts at concealment—nor even because they are so willing to manipulate each other. This kind of "evil" is a given in the social relationship to which they have committed themselves. Their moves are legitimate; they constitute "fair play," as Kate herself says at the end of the novel.[15] What makes the actions of all three characters reprehensible, and on the same order as the schemes of the Bellegardes, Mme Merle, and Osmond, has less to do with the way in which they exploit one another, than with the way that they exploit Milly, however reluctantly or cautiously, to serve their own ends. Just like Christopher Newman and Isabel Archer, Milly at first fails to perceive that she is a pawn in the games of others.

Milly values much the same kind of freedom that Isabel Archer does in the beginning of *The Portrait of a Lady:* James describes his heroine as having "a strong and special implication of liberty, of liberty of action, of choice, of appreciation, of contact" (19:ix). Maud, Kate, and

Games as Rituals

Lord Mark, each value Milly for those qualities that make her special, and for what she can help each of them to accomplish. She is both magically, incredibly wealthy and an outsider to their world, someone from whom they can hide the darkest, most manipulative aspects of their society. Lord Mark first and foremost sees Milly's money, though it is clear that she eventually engages his affections as well. Maud perceives Milly first as a threat to her own plans for Kate and Lord Mark and then as a way of separating Kate and Densher. Kate sees in Milly an opportunity to have both money and Densher without having to honor Aunt Maud's terms. The game of ambition that Kate has planned before Milly enters her world not only finds an outlet in Milly's circumstances, but becomes a form of revenge as well. Kate sees in Milly the wealth that she herself lacks but urgently desires; by exploiting Milly, she seeks to compensate for her own unjustifiable poverty. Kate's relationship with Milly consequently always remains an ambivalent mixture of affection and envy, the two emotions never reconciled, even after Milly's death.

The "dove" image, which Kate confers on Milly in chapter 15 (Book Fifth:VI), like so many of the characterizing images in James's fiction, both reveals and obscures certain truths about the character. The image is faithful to the mildness and innocence of Milly's character, her essential generosity, and the value she places on freedom. Doves, after all, spread their wings to fly. But Milly is not as easily duped as Kate's image suggests. Kate, of course, sees Milly's money as easier to be had than Aunt Maud's. But the impression created by the image of the dove obscures the degree to which Milly possesses both self-knowledge and knowledge of others—a shrewdness that the reference to the pigeonlike dove undermines. Even if she believes herself to be more perceptive than a dove, Milly accepts this image for herself, recognizing "the measure of success she could have as a dove" (19:284). In this way, Milly demonstrates her willingness to play the part that others have assigned to her.

The extent of Milly's knowledge about herself and others reveals itself in her almost intuitive responses to those who would implicate her in their schemes. In this regard, Milly is far more alert to the dangers that Kate and Densher represent than Isabel Archer is to the potential threat posed by the partnership of Mme Merle and Osmond. When Maud attempts to enlist her in the game of surveillance she wants to play with Kate and Densher, Milly first agrees, and then later, in her own mind, refuses to participate. Kate's initial silence about her rela-

Dreadful Games

tionship with Densher proves more revealing to Milly than almost anything that Kate could say about him: "the quantity her new friend had told her might have figured as small, or smallest, beside the quantity she hadn't" (19:187). Milly perceives that "there were clearly more dangers roundabout Lancaster Gate than one suspected in New York or could dream about in Boston" (19:182). She notes in Kate something "brutal" (19:192)—a word that, like "prodigious," opens itself to several possible interpretations. It may suggest either cruel and unfeeling actions, or simply plain and direct expression. But whatever the word actually means to Milly, it demonstrates how astutely she judges other people; unlike Isabel Archer, who succumbs to the self-image that Mme Merle portrays, Milly is not taken in by the illusions Kate tries to foster. Milly demonstrates powers of judgment that others often fail to perceive.

Despite all of her knowledge and self-knowledge, however, Milly finds the most critical facts hopelessly concealed from her: that Kate has suggested to Densher that she could provide them with a cover for their affair, that Maud has encouraged Densher to cultivate his acquaintance with her, or ultimately, that Kate plans for Densher to marry her so that he can inherit her money when she dies. But Maud, Kate, and Densher are not the only ones to manipulate Milly to serve their own ends. Perhaps the cruelest exploitation of Milly comes at the hands of Lord Mark, who finds Milly's money just as attractive as any of the others do. By telling Milly that Kate and Densher are secretly engaged—something he has only surmised by observing their behavior—he indulges in what Densher himself later calls "mere base revenge" (20:290). Having failed to win either Milly or Kate, he has nothing to gain from his revelation to Milly other than to make her suffer as he believes he has suffered, and to ruin Kate's and Densher's chances of achieving what he assumes to be their goals. But unlike Isabel Archer, who often willfully misinterprets people or circumstances, Milly cannot be expected to know all of the critical facts; she has looked for the truth, but others have concealed themselves from her.

The suspicions that Milly does have lead her to play a game of her own, by pretending that she believes what everyone else has led her to believe. This game allows her to control the balance of power among the characters and to create a new kind of equilibrium for them. By trusting the others in this way, she eludes her own victimization, simply by refusing to recognize the possibility of it. Her pretense begins most actively after she sees Kate and Densher at the National Gallery, a situation that can accurately be called "a precarious 'golden bowl' in the making."[16] Like Maggie Verver, her counterpart in *The Golden Bowl,* Milly plays the role that others have assigned to her, permitting things to happen that would never happen if she were not to keep up the pretense of trust. By the time the novel is resolved, the relationships that have been falsely asserted suddenly seem more true than the relationships that these "fictions" were intended to mask. Densher comes to love Milly's memory in a way that makes it impossible for Kate to marry him, and they part, fulfilling the lie they have insisted that others believe. Milly remains in Kate's and Densher's lives in a way that alters them permanently, "by bequeathing an opportunity for them to decide their own destiny."[17] Milly's gesture helps to redefine the ideas of winning and losing; Kate, in particular, comes to understand that to win by her own standards is at once both a victory and a defeat. Milly's game of concealment even opens up possibilities for Lord Mark, by convincing him that Densher loved her, not Kate; as a result, he can still pursue Kate, provided that he still wants her as his wife.

Milly's final gesture and Densher's response to it, like so many issues in James's later novels, have been interpreted in an almost staggering number of different ways.[18] What seems unmistakable, however, is that Milly's almost sacrificial bequest to Densher is made possible only because she believes, or pretends to believe, that Densher really loves her. Her gesture becomes for her the "counter-move to fate" (20:142) that her aged Venetian retainer Eugenio had urged her to find with her money; it allows her to maintain the illusion of having been loved. Although the text never conclusively reveals Milly's motives or the manner in which she presents the gift, Densher's response to it, and especially the difference between his response and Kate's, is explored in detail. Even before the bequest has been made, Densher reveals how much he has been transformed by his experience with Milly. In his last meeting with Susan Stringham, he renders a performance, purely for her benefit, worthy of Milly's finest performance. He and Susan try to determine how Lord Mark could have thought that Densher had been up "to some 'game' as they say." Without denying what Lord Mark has already said, he carefully allows Susan to believe that all of this is "a monstrous supposition," that Lord Mark has been indisputably mistaken (20:291). In this episode, Densher shows his willingness not only to protect Milly from any humiliation, but also to put on a performance in order to keep a private fiction intact.

Densher's final actions, the choices he asks Kate to make in the novel's final chapters, can, like all games, be explored both through their structure and through the desires that motivate them. The structure, the form his actions take, seems in some ways as ambitious and manipulatory as the actions that have come before. But significantly, Densher has nothing material to gain from the choices he offers Kate, except to enhance both his self-knowledge and his understanding of Kate's basic motives. Milly's bequest allows Densher to find a new basis for his commitment to Kate—a basis that will free them both from the "dreadful game" (20:347) that they have, in Densher's words, played and lost, even while seeming to win. He gives her several opportunities to take some action that will confirm her willingness to find this basis: he asks her to marry him immediately, before they learn about Milly's bequest, but she begs him to wait a little longer; he offers to let her open and read Milly's last letter to him, which he considers "sacred," and which Kate flings, unopened into the fire; he sends her the unopened packet from Milly's lawyers in New York, and she breaks the seal and reads it, making it impossible for Densher to decline Milly's gift by returning it. Each of these events permits Kate to formulate her own course of action, and in each case she responds in a way that convinces Densher that she is committed not to preserving her own integrity, but to the logic of winning and losing as defined by the game. Kate reveals through the choices she makes that she has inherited her father's weakness: as with him, "the inconvenience . . . was not that you minded what was false, but that you missed what was true" (19:7).

The choices Kate makes reveal the widening gap between hers and Densher's sense of how ethical decisions are made. The choices that Kate makes are not "wrong," but in comparison to actions she could have taken in all three instances, her decisions are selfish and egotistical—testimony to the gamelike, superficial logic that governs all her decisions, from the moment she decides to deceive Aunt Maud. Although Densher clearly never intends to take Milly's money for himself—willing, at the most, to make the money over to Kate if she refuses to marry him without it—the gift allows him to play a game, which while seemingly cold and calculating, permits him to discover the differences between himself and Kate that the lie they have shared has obscured. The game Densher plays with Kate at the end of the novel is based on a desire for self-knowledge and the desire to have Kate share his own perceptions, and not on self-interest and the desire to subordinate her will to his own. He seeks to set them both free of the schemes that Kate's desire for both love and money have set into motion.

Games as Rituals

In spite of the great differences that exist between Kate and Densher at the end of the novel, Densher offers to fulfill his commitment to marry her. But he refuses to play the waiting game—"the game of dupes" (20:2), as he has called it—that she has forced him to play all along. He will fulfill his commitment only if together they renounce the profits of their dreadful game. In the end, the money for which she has fought so viciously, becomes less important than the way in which their dreadful game has transformed their relationship. Kate refuses to marry him because of what she perceives as Densher's love for Milly's memory, arguing in the last sentence of the novel, "We shall never be again as we were!" (20:405). The one renunciation that Kate does not utter in these closing pages is that of Milly's money, an omission that continues to highlight the differences that now exist between herself and Densher as a result of Milly's game. Densher makes Kate choose in the end between having Milly's money or having him on the only basis that seems honorable to him any more.

The schemes that Kate, Densher, Maud, and Lord Mark have pursued become increasingly sinister as the novel progresses. Without Milly's attempt to transform this process, the novel resembles *The Portrait of a Lady,* with Milly in Isabel's position of the character who is deceived and betrayed. But like *The Golden Bowl, The Wings of the Dove* leads through a dreadful game, finally achieving an equilibrium, a structure of choices, that offers a different kind of conclusion than most nineteenth-century novels prescribe. Milly gains Densher's admiration not by revealing her power and knowledge or by confronting him with her sense of betrayal, but by preferring to believe that he has not betrayed her. What Densher himself does in the last few episodes of the novel is less a renunciation of Kate or a refusal to play her game any longer, than it is an attempt to "right everything that's wrong" (20:347). He asks her to share in his own transformation.

In *The Wings of the Dove,* James's interest remains focused on game playing; the energy of it still fascinates him, and his fullest portraits are of those manipulators who play games of ambition or revenge. Even with Densher, James is more successful in showing his weaknesses than in making it seem as if the character has been fundamentally transformed. What distinguishes an act of renunciation, like that at the end

Dreadful Games

of *The American* or *The Portrait of a Lady,* from one that demonstrates an individual's transformation is not always clear. In *The Wings of the Dove,* unlike *The Golden Bowl,* much of the transformation process remains cloaked in narrative secrecy. Milly's most important, and undoubtedly most significant, "performances" are never revealed to the reader: her response to Kate's explanation of why Densher stays in Venice, her last visits with Lord Mark and with Densher, and even her last letter to Densher, which Kate regrettably incinerates. Because the novel moves further and further away from Milly's consciousness as it moves toward a resolution, the distinction between what Milly believes and what she merely pretends to believe remains intentionally ambiguous. In contrast, in *The Golden Bowl,* the process of transformation, the way in which Maggie strives to formulate a fiction that will allow her to preserve her marriage, is explored more fully than the game of adultery that requires such a fiction to counter it.

The game of adultery toward which the events of the first book of *The Golden Bowl* move is, in effect, a game that violates the "rules" of the "game" of marriage. By using the theme of adultery, James links *The Golden Bowl* to a number of other nineteenth-century novels, including Flaubert's *Madame Bovary,* Fontane's *Effi Briest,* and Tolstoy's *Anna Karenina.* As Tony Tanner's study of fictional adultery suggests, the issue of adultery points to the general problem of social equilibrium: through the institution of marriage "society attempts to bring into harmonious alignment patterns of passion and patterns of property."[19] The theme of adultery also suggests the more general problems of legislating and enforcing society's rules. By committing adultery, Charlotte and the Prince call into question the authority of "society" to govern human passion according to its own legal and economic logic. The Prince and Charlotte "pledge" their love for one another (23:312) in a secret ritual that echoes in language and tone the moment in *The Wings of the Dove* where Kate and Densher agree to a secret engagement, except that the characters in *The Golden Bowl* are already "pledged" to others, and their "ritual" necessarily echoes and embraces those other commitments. The conspiracy of Charlotte and the Prince is somehow not as sinister or as blatantly manipulative as the games that begin with Kate and Maud in *The Wings of the Dove.* In this sense, *The Golden Bowl* differs from nineteenth-century "novels of adultery," especially Tolstoy's *Anna Karenina,* where the text directs, almost unwillingly, the reader's sympathy toward the circumstances of those who violate one of society's sacred laws.

Games as Rituals

Although Charlotte and the Prince betray their spouses, no one is manipulated and exploited in quite the way that Milly is exploited. The Ververs, in fact, are even implicated in their own betrayal, because they fail to recognize the strangeness that their own intimacy confers on both marriages. F. O. Matthiessen suggests that adultery seemed ugliest to James in those societies where marriages were contracted with the greatest freedom of choice.[20] Both Charlotte and the Prince choose freely to make their marriages, and neither of them is manipulated to do so by external pressures. Committing themselves to the Ververs in marriage is not a question of survival but of greater security and more personal comfort than they might otherwise expect. Unhappiness in their marriages, even the neglect they both experience, explains but never justifies their actions, any more than Kate and Densher can justify their actions by pointing to their relative poverty. Like Densher, the Prince seems eventually to renounce the "utilitarian ethics" that justify his intimacy with Charlotte.[21] But while the text hardly excuses the actions of Charlotte and the Prince, neither does it make them seem like "villains," in the way that James's early novels distinguish so clearly between villains and victims.

Significantly, James points to the moral complexity and ambiguity of Charlotte's and the Prince's actions—an ambiguity that contrasts with the more clearly exploitative treatment by Kate and Densher of Milly. One way in which the author stresses this difference between the characters of the two novels is by avoiding the more clichéd game metaphors that characters in *The Wings of the Dove* use so frequently to describe their actions. The metaphors used to describe Charlotte and Amerigo's affair are as mysterious and unusual as the circumstances of the affair itself. An example of this use of language can be found in the episode describing the visit to Matcham. Charlotte maneuvers to send the Assinghams home, making the Prince aware that she has arranged for them to be alone. The recognition of what Charlotte has done is for the Prince "an image that flashed like a mirror played at the face of the sun" (23:346). Like so much of the figurative language that characterizes James's later style, this simile suggests several things about what occurs here between these two characters: the words "flash" and "sun" allude to the way in which they have both been blinded by the sudden, intense brillance of their desire for one another; the words "mirror" and "face" suggest the way in which they have unmistakably signaled this desire to one another; and the idea of "play" links this moment to those other moments in the text where a character's imag-

161

Dreadful Games

ination takes hold of an as yet unrealized possibility. By using this kind of language, James encourages the reader to participate in the "play of feeling" between the characters, at the same time that the text emphasizes the risks and dangers inherent in the actions they contemplate.

The Golden Bowl is less about the specific problem of adultery than it is about the more abstract problem of "equilibrium"—a word that Maggie uses in her own mind to characterize the characters' relationships, and a word that links the circumstances of these relationships to Lévi-Strauss's discussion of the structure of ritual.[22] As Maggie waits for the Prince to return from Gloucester, she considers the delicate balance that exists between the characters: "That was at the bottom of her mind, that their equilibrium was everything, and that it was practically precarious, a matter of a hair's breadth for the loss of the balance" (24:17). In this novel, James has deliberately chosen a small number of characters; his intention, as he explains in the preface to *The Golden Bowl* is "to play the small handful of values really for all they are worth" (23:viii). As the novel begins, the Ververs are about to add a third party to what has been for so long a "couple," Maggie and her father. The problem with Maggie's marriage to the Prince, despite its apparent happiness, is that it leaves her father open to the dangers represented by women who no longer see any reason why he should not marry. The beginning of the second volume finds Adam Verver spending his time in maneuvers to avoid women like Mrs. Rance, "as in some childish game or unbecoming romp" (23:132). Maggie finds herself unable to choose between being with her husband or being with her father; the birth of the principino serves more to bring father and daughter together than husband and wife. Adam's marriage to Charlotte seeks to solve these problems, but instead creates another: Charlotte and the Prince often find themselves in the position of being a "couple." When Maggie begins to suspect that Charlotte and Amerigo have become too much of a couple for her own or her father's comfort and happiness, she seeks to reconstitute the relationships between them and to provide them all with a new kind of balance or equilibrium.

Of all the characters in *The Golden Bowl* Fanny Assingham most clearly follows and expresses the logic of game playing. Like Mrs. Tristram in *The American,* Fanny is a spectator to the major events of the novel, someone who, in Mathiessen's words, plays "that Jamesian game of scrutinizing the motives of her friends."[23] But she does more than merely comment on other people's motives, she meddles in their affairs. She has initiated and guided the Prince's "pursuit" of Maggie,

Games as Rituals

and she sanctions, however reluctantly, the Bloomsbury shopping trip just before the Prince's marriage. Fanny is the character most often and most likely to play the game of concealment, by concealing from Maggie what she knows about Charlotte and the Prince, and by concealing from Charlotte what Maggie knows. Just as Mrs. Tristram helps to frame Christopher Newman's actions in *The American* as a game, Fanny Assingham helps to highlight the play of relationships in *The Golden Bowl.*

In contrast to the emphasis on "plots" in *The Wings of the Dove,* the interest in this novel lies not in the circumstances of adultery, or in the lies and deception that make it possible, but in Maggie's gradual recognition of it and response to it. Maggie's recognition of her husband's adultery—her recognition of "something wrong and dreadful," something that Charlotte and her husband "cover up" (24:109)—does not shatter her marriage the way it does in so many nineteenth-century novels; the lack of anger and violence in her response can be contrasted to those scenes of strife and conflict in *Anna Karenina* where Dolly discovers Stiva's infidelity and Karenin finally speaks out about Anna's affair with Vronsky. Responses like these, Maggie's own response seems to suggest, are instinctual responses to the recognition of betrayal, and they reflect a desire for vengeance.[24] The damage that results from such moments of unsuppressed vengeance is often irreparable. Not unlike Milly's response to Kate's and Densher's deception and betrayal, Maggie's response sacrifices the instinctual satisfaction of revenge in favor of a plan that gives each of the characters the time and space to imagine new possibilities for the form of their lives. Just as Milly does, Maggie begins with the awareness that the "dangers" she faces can be guarded against by "the proper playing of one's part" (24:8). In order to transform the "strangeness" of their various relationships, Maggie must first of all pretend that she finds nothing strange in them.

But unlike Milly, Maggie must do more than merely adhere to that version of the arrangement she finds expedient; she must find an active way to fulfill the possibilities suggested by this version of the truth, this "fiction," without appearing to *do* anything. What is clear as the second volume of the novel begins is that Maggie is "no longer playing with blunt and idle tools" (24:9) as she had been in the earlier portions of the novel. As her suspicions grow, Maggie uses the metaphor of the game to describe her options. As she explores her alternatives, one thing becomes clear to her: "there was a card she could play, but there was only

163

Dreadful Games

one, and to play it would be to end the game" (24:34). To "end the game," in other words, to reveal her knowledge and to shatter the very structure of their lives, would be to achieve a hollow, vengeful victory over her betrayers.

Consequently, Maggie must restrain herself from seeking the satisfaction that such a revelation would no doubt give her. She must instead find a way to avoid playing the card, even though the possibility keeps coming back to her. She later recalls "that hideous card she might in mere logic play" (24:107). "Mere logic," here, is the logic of rational game playing, where options are judged by the amount of instinctual satisfaction they guarantee. Maggie knows that she must defer, probably forever, the satisfaction of her desire for revenge; she must forgo any kind of immediate instinctual gratification. The language of games links Maggie's decision to the bridge game at Fawns, where she recognizes that she is "presumably more present" to the four players at the table—the Prince, Charlotte, her father, and Fanny Assingham—"than the next card to be played" (24:232). She has distracted the others from playing their own cards and, in the process, has begun to integrate them into the fiction of their lives that she seeks to realize.[25]

Maggie permits Charlotte and Amerigo to believe that they continue to deceive her, but she also begins to do something more than play the part they have assigned her. In effect, she begins to violate their expectations about the way in which they are all "arranged together" (24:45). Maggie demonstrates that she can take positive action in order to bring about a new equilibrium. In order to revise the "false equilibrium"[26] that she believes has evolved, she begins to realign the balance between the characters—a realignment that she signals by waiting alone for the Prince to return from Gloucester, rather than waiting at her father's house. She then encourages her husband to spend more time with her father, to take the principino to see his grandfather, while she arranges to spend more time alone with Charlotte, the two of them becoming "again very much the companions of other days" (24:37). When Amerigo asks about Adam's plans for going to Fawns, Maggie assures him that whatever her father's plans, it "needn't in the least entail your and my going" since Adam and Charlotte are "perfectly happy together" (24:62). Maggie demonstrates her intention not only to separate the "lovers," but to reunite the husbands and wives.

In this way, a new "form" for the characters' lives is proposed not only by means of what Maggie conceals, but also by means of the events she orchestrates. The trip to Fawns, where the bridge game takes place, provides Maggie with an opportunity to confirm the realignment of their relations, and to balance off, as in a pair of scales, the relationship that Charlotte and the Prince have created for themselves. Significantly, Maggie seeks not to destroy that relationship, or even to punish Charlotte and her husband for their transgression, but to impose another kind of logic on their experience. Fanny Assingham becomes important to Maggie because of "this friend's power to cover, to protect and . . . even showily to represent . . . her relation to the form of life they were all actually leading" (24:100). Fanny proves her ability to adhere to the fiction that governs their lives when she smashes the golden bowl, insisting that there has been no intrigue between Charlotte and the Prince. By smashing the bowl, Fanny Assingham seeks to destroy the implication of Maggie's knowledge. But, in fact, her action succeeds in making the Prince aware of what Maggie knows.

The image of the golden bowl echoes a moment toward the end of *The Portrait of a Lady* where Mme Merle and Gilbert Osmond struggle to understand the circumstances that they have created for one another. Grasping one of "his delicate specimens of rare porcelain," Osmond tells Mme Merle, "you always see too much in everything." Telling him how much more clearly she understands him since his marriage to Isabel, she begs him, "Please be very careful of that precious object." Accusing her of having "put [him] into such a box," he puts the porcelain cup down, telling her, "It already has a wee bit of a crack."[27] Like the smashing of the golden bowl, this moment shows the way in which ostensibly unimportant objects and gestures take on a deeper significance. What Mme Merle has once been, Isabel is now—part of Osmond's collection of "delicate specimens;" when Mme Merle calls the cup a "precious object," she links her past injuries to Isabel's present dangers. The crack in the porcelain cup, which only Osmond perceives, signifies the defects in both his past relationship with Mme Merle and his present marriage to Isabel. In much the same way, the flaw in the golden bowl links present and past, marriage and adultery.

The smashing of the golden bowl provides the Prince with evidence that Maggie knows of his affair with Charlotte. At the same time his silence to Charlotte on the subject of Maggie's knowledge seems to signal both the erosion of his intimacy with her and his own decision to agree to Maggie's fiction of their relationships. Silence similarly marks the change in Kate and Densher's relationship: when she leaves Venice, they can no longer exchange letters. Language, the ability to communicate with one another, cements both of these secret relationships, and when that communication fails or is cut off, the relationships fail. But in *The Golden Bowl,* the erosion of Charlotte and Amerigo's relationship

Dreadful Games

begins to open up the possibilities that Maggie has been seeking from the moment she began the process of transformation. By resisting the temptation to play her card, Maggie avoids the necessity of a direct confrontation with Charlotte.

On two separate occasions, Charlotte tries to confront Maggie directly, and both times Maggie formulates a lie that protects them both from the consequences of such an event. Both confrontations are implicitly framed by the ritual message, "let us believe." Both of these occasions show that Maggie senses the ways in which a lie can "facilitate the truth."[28] The kind of lies that Maggie tells in these confrontations with Charlotte become self-fulfilling prophecies. The first lie prevents Charlotte from knowing for certain whether Maggie knows about the affair. As the others are absorbed in the bridge game, Charlotte joins Maggie on the terrace at Fawns. Charlotte chooses this opportunity to ask Maggie if she has wronged her in any way, and when Maggie denies that she has, Charlotte takes the opportunity to embrace Maggie just as the others are leaving the card table. This gesture suggests to the others that there is nothing wrong between them; it helps to further the "fiction of felicity"[29] that Maggie has encouraged. Maggie's second lie grants Charlotte the dignity of seeming to choose to return to American City with Adam. She even allows Charlotte to assert that it is her idea—even though Maggie and Adam have already discussed this course of action—and to claim that Maggie has failed in her efforts to separate Charlotte from Adam.[30] In both of these episodes, Maggie sacrifices the right to speak the truth in order to promote the new equilibrium.

Although it could be argued that Maggie exiles Charlotte to America, much as it can be argued that Isabel Archer banishes Mme Merle at the end of *The Portrait of a Lady,* she asks of Charlotte no more than she is willing to give up herself—a love that by virtue of its irregularity has become more damaging than productive. The blessings and sacrifices of the new arrangement are exacted more or less equally from the characters. Maggie lets Charlotte go, gives her freedom, rather than insisting on the gratification offered by revenge.[31] Even at the end, when Maggie's lies and deception have accomplished their purpose, she objects to Amerigo's desire to tell Charlotte the truth; she objects to putting Charlotte in the "unprecedented situation" in which Mme Merle finds herself with Isabel Archer. What is never spoken between Maggie and either Charlotte or Adam—the accusations and suspicions never voiced—because never voiced, seem never to have existed. Maggie manages to "win" her husband back without "defeating" Charlotte—a feat she accomplishes by suspending her initial desire to reveal her knowledge and by playing a special game that creates, through dissimulation and silence, an acceptable new order for all their lives. And even though Maggie serves her own interests by creating this new equilibrium, the fiction that she has asked the others to share is the one that promises "the most accommodating arrangement for the group as a whole."[32] The novel moves toward an end that, rather than offering the rewards and punishments of victory and defeat, promises the least amount of pain to the largest number of characters.

Both *The Wings of the Dove* and *The Golden Bowl* seek resolutions that avoid the consequences of defeat, and that provide each character with a measure of victory. In the process, James seems to reevaluate the ideas of good and evil. The "evil" character in these novels is the one who seeks to benefit at the expense of another, to mold another to his or her own will; the "good" character, on the other hand, sees "the greatest variety of moral possibilities" and wants "to give them free play in others."[33] Rather than making Charlotte suffer publicly for transgressing some legal or moral principle, Maggie's efforts actually free Charlotte to create a new life for herself, albeit without the Prince's love and companionship. Even asking her to wear the "silken halter" (24:287), suggests a greater degree of freedom than that chosen by Isabel Archer, who is to spend her life in Osmond's prisonlike palace. Charlotte's new life, of course, lies beyond the scope of the novel, but is implied much more clearly than Isabel Archer's hope for the future. Charlotte, at least—unlike Isabel Archer—has the satisfaction of a fiction worth maintaining.

The ending of the novel uses the language of ritual to suggest that Charlotte has been able to find some peace in her fate: to Maggie, Charlotte and Adam seem "conjoined for a present effect," and she notes how "resplendent a show of serenity" Charlotte succeeds in making (24:357). Even if these are mere performances, there is something more intrinsically valuable in such performances than in the deceptions promoted by so many other characters in nineteenth-century novels. The fiction that all the characters find themselves attempting to realize at the end of *The Golden Bowl*[34] is not a fiction that closes itself off once the winners and losers have been determined, but one that opens itself up to the play of possibilities, in much the same way that James's text opens itself up to the play of possible interpretations. Unlike so many of the novels that typify nineteenth-century Realism, in the later James both the game of the characters and the game of the text reflect, in a variety of ways, the essential qualities of play.

Conclusion: Old and New Novels

■ The game that every novelistic text eventually plays is a game with other texts that share or dispute its thematic concerns and linguistic techniques. A useful "fiction" in recent critical theory is that of "intertextuality"—the notion that texts conduct a rational dialogue with one another, and that "every text echoes another text into infinity."[1] As one critic defines this process, "Intertextualilty is the recognition of a frame, a context that allows the reader to make sense out of what he or she might otherwise perceive as senseless."[2] Any collection of literary texts is capable of creating its own context in this way. For example, nineteenth-century novels respond in special ways to one another, echoing the themes and methods of earlier novels, and raising questions for subsequent novels to explore.

What such a critical fiction suggests is that Henry James could not have written *The American* or *The Portrait of a Lady* without responding, in some conscious or intuitive way, to novels he had read and studied—to novels by Laclos, Balzac, Stendhal, or Dostoevksy—just as he could not have written *The Wings of the Dove* or *The Golden Bowl* without echoing and revising the concerns of his own early novels. And to take the development of the novel form a step further, the open-endedness of much twentieth-century fiction—like that of Joyce or Beckett or Gide, or like the textual games of the postmodernist novel—arises out of a context created in part by Henry James's experiments with the fictional status of the characters and events of his later novels.

Conclusion

Perhaps even more importantly, the twentieth-century novel can be seen as a response to James's ideas about the nature of play and to the way that he explains the idea of play not only as power and destruction, but also as knowledge and reconciliation. Twentieth-century novelists turn once again to what had interested the eighteenth-century novelist—the "ontological import" of play.[3] Characters once again play the game of hidden being in order to gain insight and knowledge rather than simply to achieve mastery and power over one another. There are, in effect, two Henry Jameses whose novels participate in this rational discourse among texts: the nineteenth-century novelist who wrote *The American* and *The Portrait of a Lady*, novels about games of ambition and revenge, and a twentieth-century novelist, who in his last novels, moves beyond the Realist formulas for presenting reality, and who suggests that the play of desire need not engender irreconcilable conflicts.

What, then, are Realist and Proto-Realist novels saying to one another about the play of desire and about the nature of "dreadful games"? By tracing the language of games in each text, many of the major thematic and philosophical concerns of the nineteenth-century Realist novel begin to emerge. First, the Realist novel almost always echoes the fictional world of Cervantes, inasmuch as there is always something distinctly "quixotic" about the desires that characters articulate and the projects they pursue. Then too, nineteenth-century Realists' interpretation and reshaping of Cervantes's world is guided by their responses to the Romantic heroes of their immediate past. The Realist hero and heroine emerge as part Don Quixote, as well as part Werther, part Pechorin, even, perhaps, part Jane Eyre. But the Realist often ridicules the kind of heroic character that the Romantics held in awe or horror. Not only are the desires of characters in Realist fiction unmistakably mediated, arising out of a character's perception of the possessions or accomplishments of others, but they are impossibly, embarrassingly extravagant, and the world of the novel provides no means of satisfying them.

Stendhal's Julien Sorel, Balzac's Hulot, Dostoevsky's Raskolnikov, even James's Christopher Newman—none of these characters is ever satisfied with modest accomplishments; they all seek to accomplish

Conclusion

great deeds, even as the circumstances of their lives limit their opportunities to do so. For Stendhal, Balzac, and Dostoevsky, the legendary figure of Napoleon, himself a kind of quixotic hero, lurks in the shadows of the fictional world, reminding characters and readers alike of both the opportunities for success and the possibilities of failure in life—a puzzlingly contradictory commentary on the value of individual efforts. By the end of the century, individual failure seems far more likely than success: the ambitions of Hardy's Jude can be called quixotic, but only because his opportunities are so circumscribed, and the principles that govern his world so immutable. In every case, desire remains not only unsatisfied, but incapable of ever being satisfied, just as the eventual failure of individual efforts, remains inescapable. The language of play and games often underscores the futility of individual effort in a world where even modest dreams seem arrogant.

The metaphor of the game in nineteenth-century novels also tends to indicate an increasingly problematic ambivalence toward the rationalistic social and philosophical tendencies of the age. For all that nineteenth-century literary Realism proposed, as a general movement, to incorporate the methods of science into the practice of fiction, and for all that the fictional world relies heavily on empirical "evidence" taken directly from the material world, the texts themselves seem to question time and again the validity of "logic" and "reason." It is, for example, the "logic" of Mephistopheles and "the language of Hell" that marks the course of Julien Sorel's downfall. A "utilitarian" ethic leads Victorin Hulot to exact a dreadful form of revenge from his enemies in Balzac's *La Cousine Bette*. Logic also helps Crevel to rationalize his manipulative schemes. In both Balzac and Laclos, the rational "games" that structure the characters' experiences cloud the distinction between good and evil, since even one who "plays fair" is capable of committing evil. This ambivalence toward reason continues into the world James describes, where characters must learn to avoid judging their relationships according to a utilitarian logic. The emphasis, in the Realist novel, on human reason can be tied to the absence or suppression of the play spirit in so many fictional worlds: excessive rationalization undermines the spontaneity and freedom inherent in the playful exchange of human desire.

The logic of the "rules" of everyday life is questioned as well, when the metaphor of the game compares such social codes to the rules of games. In almost every novel, society's legal principles prove hopelessly inadequate when individuals are faced with a moral dilemma: law and

Conclusion

morality compete to govern the play of desire. in *La Cousine Bette,* moral transgressions like those of Crevel and Valérie—transgressions that undermine Church and family—are punished not by the legal system, or even by the authority of religion, but by the criminal side of Paris itself. Laclos's characters learn that the social code often fails to serve justice. In much the same way, both Christopher Newman and Isabel Archer learn that the rules that govern social life can sanction evil, provided that appearances are preserved.

The failure of the rules to effectively regulate human desire receives its fullest expression, perhaps, in Dostoevsky and Hardy—in those fictional worlds governed less by competition than by chance. In a world of contingencies, logic fails to provide an adequate explanation of the problems of human desire. In *Jude the Obscure,* human misfortune is beyond the power of reason to explain. And in *Crime and Punishment,* logic is more than simply inadequate; in Raskolnikov's case, it inspires evil, and only through the mediating power of a faith that defies even the logic of human language, can the individual transcend this evil. These novels suggest that even if the methods of scientific research do reveal the "truth" about the world, as the proponents of nineteenth-century positivism contended, they also, just as often, help people to find a rationale for the evil unleashed in the play of human desire.

Finally, the language and attitudes of game playing also help to raise and explore the "Woman Question" in Realist fiction. Child psychologists have observed that girls play differently than boys, for a variety of reasons, and in the social life of adults, as reflected in the novel, women often play differently than men. Interestingly, few of the classic Realist texts—with the possible exception of novels by George Eliot and Edith Wharton—that explore the woman question are written by women writers, as if addressing the woman question permitted even male novelists to explore the more confusing aspects of human experience. Balzac and Laclos—and for that matter Henry James—show women often pursuing their desires surreptitiously, by indirect methods, manipulating others to secure their own ends. As in *Les Liaisons dangereuses* and *La Cousine Bette*—and, in a more benign, but no less dangerous environment in Jane Austen's *Emma*—the woman's creative impulse is often sublimated through the creation of a protégée through whom she can vicariously play the social games that she ostensibly disdains.

But even more important than the sublimation of the creative impulse in these novels is the extent to which women respond differently than men to the rules of social discourse. Female characters, like Dos-

Conclusion

toevsky's Sonya, for instance, sometimes seem to live outside or beyond the law, and as Isabel Archer's playful attitude toward society's rules implies, prostitution alone cannot explain this privileged relationship to the law. And it is often unclear whether this "privilege" is granted or seized. Perhaps because women are disenfranchised—they do not participate at any level in the legislation of the rules of social life—they feel less bound to honor those same rules than men do. An archetypal Eve, who tempts an otherwise obedient Adam to break the Law, recurs in these novels, as Mme Merteuil, as Valérie Marneffe, as Jude's cousin Sue, and as Mme Merle. But as Jane Austen's *Mansfield Park* suggests, women can expect to suffer a punishment equal to or greater than the punishment men suffer for breaking the rules. And the Fanny Prices and Sonyas are handsomely rewarded not only for obeying the rules but avoiding the game altogether. The plight of female characters highlights the more general problem of playing by the rules in the games that structure social experience.

Closely connected to these philosophical issues are the novel's formal problems, especially the problems of character and plot. Using the language of games in constituting character poses certain problems for a novelist, like Balzac, who seeks to present a coherent and consistent image of life. Several nineteenth-century texts echo the problem outlined in Jane Austen's *Mansfield Park:* the game player's charm often masks his or her moral defects. In *La Cousine Bette,* the game players, particularly Crevel and Valérie, often appear charming and witty and sophisticated when compared with those who lack their skills, even though they are so clearly the agents of evil. "Virtue" in Balzac is often represented by characters who are almost incapable of eliciting the reader's sympathy, at the same time that many of those who represent "vice" create themselves for the reader in the play of language. The same thing is true, of course, in *Les Liaisons dangereuses*—Merteuil and Valmont are so dangerous because they are, to all appearances, so charming—but Laclos is less intent on making the kinds of moral distinctions that Balzac makes. Dostoevsky attempts to solve this problem by removing his hero from the influence of game players like Porfiry. Even if Porfiry persuades Raskolnikov to give up the life of a game player, he plays no part in the character's "regeneration." What

Conclusion

appears, in so many nineteenth-century novels, to be an antipathy toward play, is, in fact, a fear of the way that game playing distorts the nature of both virtue and vice, making these opposites almost indistinguishable.

Characters become so ambivalent—what some might even call "amoral"—because the process of game playing in these novels tends to transform individual strengths into fatal, often even self-destructive weaknesses. Julien's determination to succeed, in itself a strength, nevertheless consistently prevents him from evaluating his actual opportunities. The extravagance of his ambitions leads him into failure. Even Christopher Newman's ambitions are extravagant enough to bring him to the brink of disaster. Raskolnikov's intellectual prowess—his ability to participate in rational discourse, in the playful exchange of ideas—rather than enabling him to make his life successful, leads him to commit murder, almost destroying himself in the process. In much the same way, Victorin Hulot's pride in family and sense of responsibility—the very traits for which Balzac asks the reader to admire him—justify his participation in a murder of vengeance, orchestrated by the primitive and instinctual Henri Montès and the criminal Mme Nourisson. In *The American,* Christopher Newman's involvement in the Bellegardes' game, causes him to question the value of being "good-natured," since it makes him vulnerable to the deception and manipulation of others. Isabel Archer similarly learns that high spirits are easily manipulated. As the experience of these characters shows, game playing not only brings out the worst in human nature, it undermines the best.

Both competitive games and games of chance consistently illustrate the futility of individual efforts. If the nineteenth-century "invented" the notion of progress, the novel refuses to make much sense out of the characters' own attempts to rise in life. Even novelists who would hardly be called "determinists" seem to portray a world of inscrutable forces. Both *Le Rouge et le noir* and *Jude the Obscure* are structured by decidedly circular plots. The characters' efforts return them to the point from which they began, and only death resolves their endless, pointless mobility. Stendhal shows the futility of competing against others for the "prizes" life has to offer; what Julien manages to "win," is just as easily "lost" in the next moment. Hardy's novel seems to demonstrate the futility of struggling against anything, as the forces that pit themselves against human progress remain insurmountable. It is not other competitors who undermine Jude's attempts to succeed, but "society"

Conclusion

itself—those mysterious forces of biology and history that dictate individual choices. Even Balzac, in the fictional life of Lisbeth Fischer, shows how unforeseen contingencies work against individual goals. Skill or merit alone is never enough to ensure an individual's success.

The performance of self in the classic Realist text always proves itself compromised by the kinds of goals that characters set for themselves. The creative power of individual performance is diminished by the strategies to which it is subjected. In *Le Rouge et le noir,* Julien's performance of self—along with the "charm" he holds for the reader of the novel—falters, when he replaces his initial fiction of "napoleonic" success, first, with the fiction implicit in Korasoff's game of love and manipulation, and finally, with Mathilde's fiction of Boniface de La Mole. In *La Cousine Bette,* none of the characters ever reveals a "true self" either to the reader or to other characters; all that emerges from the text is the posturing of characters who must conceal and deceive in order to achieve victories over one another. The text grants them no inner life in which such a "true self" might flourish. Balzac seems to insist that appearance and reality coincide, even in those characters who have mastered the game of hidden being. *Crime and Punishment* joins this discussion by dramatizing, through the characters of Raskolnikov and Svidrigaylov, the failure of the self's attempt to create itself through language and gesture, or in other words, the failure of the individual to will a fiction of himself. Unlike the game of hidden being as it is played in a text like Marivaux's *The Game of Love and Chance,* where a false identity reveals the essence of a character's true nature, the games characters play in realist fiction ultimately disguise, rather than reveal, their essential identities.

Thus, a number of European and American novels written in the Age of Realism share certain characteristics as well as certain problems. The problem of individual desire in these novels most often emerges as the problem of unrealizable aspirations, which lead to endless, futile, and ineffective efforts on the part of characters conceived by novelists who can find no humor, only a threat to others, in this plight. These novels, written in an age that worships science, also share an ambivalence about human reason—seeming to prefer it, on the one hand, to the sentimentality and imagination cultivated by the Romantics, but fearing, on the other hand, the costs and consequences of excessively regulated and mechanized social, political, and economic systems. Similarly, a belief in the importance of rules and regulation does not prevent the Realist from questioning how rules are legislated and how effec-

Conclusion

tively they do manage to regulate the play of desire. The issue of legislation gives rise, in turn, to questions about enfranchisement in the rule-making process—questions that novels about women explore so carefully. And finally, these ideological questions no doubt define and determine the special formal problems of the Realist novel.

How, then, would the novelists who succeeded the Realists respond to the concerns and experiments of the nineteenth-century Realist novel? Would the next novelist, as Marthe Robert suggests in *Origins of the Novel,* be free to disclaim himself or herself as a "maker" of stories and "to become a 'maker' of sentences solely intent on creating new figures of speech and startling juxtapositions"? Would the novel free itself of the play of characters only to become absorbed in the infinite play of language and association? Can the novel ever really "dispense with the conflicts of interest, desire, and emotion" that have almost always been its essential subjects?[4]

Henry James intuitively responds to these questions in his later novels, recognizing the power and presence of dreadful games in human experience, but nevertheless showing the characters' attempts to salvage the creative and mediating power of play. In *The Wings of the Dove* and *The Golden Bowl,* the game of hidden being does not so much facilitate the self-interested lie as it prevents a greater evil and creates a more universally satisfying, harmonious "equilibrium." In the characters of Densher and Amerigo, these novels point out the fallacy of the utilitarian ethic that attempts to justify the actions of characters like Balzac's Victorin Hulot or Dostoevsky's Raskolnikov; they provide an alternative logic that denies the necessity of making arbitrary, mutually exclusive decisions. The "either-or" logic underscored by the metaphor of the game in the nineteenth-century novel, is refuted in these later novels. Neither James novel offers a "closed fiction;" rather, both texts argue that individual efforts need not fail, and that human virtues do not always compromise themselves in the play of desire.

The Realist ideology—both its philosophical basis and its theory of fiction—especially as it is reflected in the language of games in the novel, clearly does not die with the passing of the nineteenth century; contemporary novels cast in the realist mode continue to describe a world of "dreadful games," in which the metaphor of the game stands

Conclusion

for everything from international terrorism (Joan Didion's *A Book of Common Prayer*) to marriage and divorce (John Updike's *Couples*). The play of language is hardly the major concern of much mainstream contemporary fiction; novelists persist in acting as makers of stories. But despite its continuing popularity, the realist novel often seems old-fashioned, the relic of an earlier age whose concerns were made almost irrelevant by 1918. But can the "newer novel" become anything more than a parody, as in Robbe-Grillet's *Snapshots,* highlighting the limitations of the Realist vision?

In a book of essays entitled *The Novel of the Future* (1968), Anaïs Nin argues that realism "discounts the possibility of all change or transformation"; it fails to "show the way out of situations which trap human beings."[5] What she proposes to counter this ethos is a "new novel," in which the "magic use of words . . . is intended to sweep you along like a ritual." Fusing poetry and prose, the new novel "could point the way to all the *potentialities* of life." What already exists becomes less important in such a novel that what might be created. The "poet-novelist" would be "concerned with creating new patterns, discarding the old, finding life inacceptable and seeking to transform it." Henry James, as illustrated by his fictional representative Maggie Verver, is, in effect, just such a poet-novelist, who seeks to transform the old patterns, and to create a new form for the life of the characters. When compared with the nineteenth-century novels that preceded it, *The Golden Bowl* can be said to advance the cause of just such a "new novel."

Notes

Notes to Introduction

1. M. M. Bakhtin, *The Dialogic Imagination: Four Essays*, trans. Caryl Emerson and Michael Holquist (Austin, Tex., 1981), p. 262. Bakhtin identifies five "compositional-stylistic unities" into which the languages of the novel enter: (1) "direct authorial literary-artistic narration"; (2) variants of "oral everyday narration"; (3) "semi-literary (written) everyday narration," as for example, the letter or the diary; (4) various forms of "extra-artistic authorial speech"; and (5) the "stylized" speech of individual fictional characters.
2. Bakhtin, p. 275.
3. Henry James, "The Future of the Novel," in *The House of Fiction*, ed. Leon Edel (London, 1957), pp. 50, 54.
4. Mark Shorer, "Fiction and the 'Matrix of Analogy,'" *The Kenyon Review* 11 (1949): 539–60.
5. See Roman Jakobson, "Two Aspects of Language and Two Types of Aphasic Disturbances," in *Fundamentals of Language* by Roman Jakobson and Morris Halle (The Hague, 1956), pp. 55–82. Jakobson argues that realist fiction is less metaphorical than metonymic: "Following the part of contiguous relationships, the realistic author metonymically digresses from the plot to the atmosphere and from the characters to the setting in space and time" (p. 78). For other discussions about the distinction between metaphor and metonymy, see Terry Eagleton, *Literary Theory: An Introduction* (Minneapolis, 1983), pp. 99–100; Rosalind Coward and John Ellis, *Language and Materialism: Developments in Semiology and the Theory of the Subject* (Boston, 1977), pp. 99–100; Jonathan Culler, *The Pursuit of Signs: Semiotics, Literature, Deconstruction* (Ithaca, N.Y., 1981), pp. 187–210; and Terence Hawkes, *Structuralism and Semiotics* (Berkeley and Los Angeles, 1977). The key distinction between metaphor and metonymy, which are both "figures of equivalence" (Hawkes, p. 77), is that in metaphor, the relationship between the literal subject and the term substituted for it is one of similarity or analogy,

Notes to pages 3–7

whereas in metonymy this relationship is one of contiguity or adjacency. In the novels that I am interpreting, the relationship between "game" and whatever it stands for in the text is sometimes intended by the speaker to be analogical and sometimes more clearly contiguous. Perhaps even more importantly, the relationship in the context of the *text* reveals neither similarity or contiguity, but an essential distinction or opposition. In other words, the text often repudiates the relationship of similarity or adjacency that the figure of speech suggests.

6. Tvetzan Todorov, *The Poetics of Prose*, trans. Richard Howard (Ithaca, N.Y., 1977), p. 126.

Notes to Chapter 1

1. For a discussion of the "playful" personality and of "playfulness" in human behavior, see J. Nina Lieberman, *Playfulness: Its Relationship to Imagination and Creativity* (New York, 1977).

2. Roger Caillois, *Man, Play, and Games*, trans. Meyer Barash (New York, 1961), pp. 11–37 [originally published in French as *Les Jeux et les hommes: le masque et le vertige* (Paris, 1958)]. Competition, chance, mimicry, and vertigo are the four categories that Caillois uses to distinguish between different kinds of games, based on powerful instincts. Caillois's study, along with Johann Huizinga, *Homo Ludens: A Study of the Play Element in Culture* (London, 1949), remain the classic works on the nature of play. For a critique of these earlier studies see, Jacques Erhmann, "Homo Ludens Revisited," in *Game, Play, Literature*, ed. Jacques Erhmann (Boston, 1968), pp. 31–57.

3. Peter Farb, *Word Play: What Happens When People Talk* (New York, 1974), p. 6.

4. See, for example, Henry Hamburger, *Games as Models of Social Phenomena* (San Francisco, 1979), pp. 4–11; and Andrew M. Colman, "Experimental Games," in *Cooperation and Competition in Humans and Animals* (Berkshire, England, 1982), pp. 116–17. Daphne Patai defines games theory in her essay on George Orwell and contrasts it to a "play concept of games." See "Gamesmanship and Androcentrism in Orwell's *1984*," *PMLA* (1982): 856–70. The limitations of game theory as a way of interpreting a literary text would seem to outweigh the advantages, since, in Patai's words, game theory "assumes the rational pursuit of strategies" (p. 861), and, of course, many authors and characters do not pursue their strategies rationally. For a useful overview of different theories of play and of games (and the differences between them), see David L. Miller, *Gods and Games: Toward a Theology of Play* (New York, 1970).

5. Manfred Eigen and Ruthild Winkler, *Laws of the Game: How the Principles of Nature Govern Chance*, trans. Robert and Rita Kimber (New York, 1981), p. 3.

6. See James P. Carse, *Finite and Infinite Games: A Vision of Life as Play and Possibility* (New York, 1896). Carse begins his book by defining an "infinite game" as one played "for the purpose of continuing play" (p. 3). "The joyfulness of infinite play," he says, "lies in learning to start something we cannot finish" (p. 26).

7. See Hans-Georg Gadamer, *Truth and Method* (New York, 1975), p. 93 [originally published in German as *Wahrheit und Methode* (Tübingen, 1965)]. See also Jacques Derrida, "Structure, Sign and Play," in *Writing and Difference*, trans. Alan Bass (Chicago, 1978), p. 289 [originally published in French in *L'Ecriture et la différence* (Paris, 1967)]. For an analysis of the similarities and differences between these two writers on the subject of play, see David Couzens Hoy, *The Critical Circle: Literature, History, and Philosophical Hermeneutics* (Berkeley, 1978), pp. 77–84.

Notes to pages 7–11

8. Eugen Fink, "The Oasis of Happiness: Toward an Ontology of Play," in *Game, Play, Literature*, ed. Jacques Ehrmann (Boston, 1968), p. 22. The selection for this volume (originally published as volume 41 of *Yale French Studies*) is derived from Fink's book on play entitled *Spiel als Weltsymbole* (Stuttgart, 1960).
9. Friedrich Schiller, *On the Aesthetic Education of Man in a Series of Letters*, trans. Reginald Snell (New York, 1965), p. 82. The selection is from letter 16.
10. Schiller, *Letters*, p. 80 (letter 15).
11. Paul Ricoeur, "Existence and Hermeneutics," in *The Conflict of Interpretations: Essays in Hermeneutics*, ed. Don Ihde (Evanston, Ill. 1974), p. 20 [originally published in French in *Le Conflit des interprétations* (Paris, 1969)].
12. For other discussions of the relationship between language and desire, see Robert Solokowski, *Presence and Absence: A Philosophical Investigation of Language and Being* (Bloomington, Ind., 1978), p. 25; Wesley Morris, *Friday's Footprint: Structuralism and the Articulated Text* (Columbus, Ohio, 1978), p. 124; Jacques Lacan, *The Language of the Self: The Function of Language in Psychoanalysis*, ed. Anthony Wilden (Baltimore, 1968), pp. 31, 83; Robert Young, *Untying the Text: A Post-Structuralist Reader* (Boston, 1981), p. 13; and Julia Kristeva, *Desire in Language: A Semiotic Approach to Literature and Art*, ed. Leon S. Roudiez (New York, 1980). For a comprehensive discussion of recent critical theories about language and the problems of desire, see Rosalind Coward and John Ellis, *Language and Materialism: Developments in Semiology and the Theory of the Subject* (Boston, 1977); and James S. Hans, *The Play of the World* (Amherst, Mass., 1981), pp. 51–110.
13. William James, *The Principles of Psychology in Three Volumes* (Cambridge, Mass., 1981), pp. 1044–46.
14. L. S. Vygotsky, "Play and Its Role in the Mental Development of the Child," in *Play: Its Roles in Development and Evolution*, eds. Jerome S. Bruner, Alison Joly, and Kathy Sylva (New York, 1976), pp. 538–39.
15. Sigmund Freud, *Beyond the Pleasure Principle, Group Psychology, and Other Works*, trans. James Strachey (London, 1955), pp. 17–21, 35, Vol. 18 of *The Standard Edition of the Complete Psychological Works*.
16. Plato, *The Symposium*, trans. W. Hamilton (London, 1951), p. 77. Socrates says to Agathon, "Everyone who feels desire [*eros*], desires not what is in his present power or possession, and desire and love have for their object things or qualities which a man does not at present possess but what he lacks."
17. See Erving Goffman, *Encounters: Two Studies in the Sociology of Interaction* (Indianapolis and New York, 1961), pp. 19, 25.
18. James Joyce, *A Portrait of the Artist as a Young Man*, ed. Chester G. Anderson (New York, 1968), p. 205.
19. Gadamer, *Truth and Method*, p. 92.
20. Stendhal, *Racine and Shakespeare*, trans. Guy Daniels, foreword by André Maurois (New York, 1962), pp. 30–31.
21. René Girard, *Deceit, Desire and the Novel*, trans. Yvonne Freccero (Baltimore, 1965) [originally published in French as *Mensonge romantique et vérité romanesque* (Paris, 1961)]. The essence of Girard's theory of "mimetic desire" is found in his first chapter.
22. For an examination of the play element in fantasy literature, see W. R. Irwin, *The Game of the Impossible: A Rhetoric of Fantasy* (Urbana, Ill., 1976).
23. Huizinga, *Homo Ludens*, p. 210.

Notes to pages 11–18

24. See, for example, Edward Norbeck, "Man at Play," *Natural History* 80, no. 10 (1971): 48; David Chaney, *Fictions and Ceremonies: Representations of Popular Experience* (New York, 1979), pp. 91–98.

25. For a discussion of rules as "roles," see George Herbert Mead, *The Social Psychology of George Herbert Mead*, ed. Anselm Strauss (Chicago, 1956), pp. 228–29. See also Vygotsky, "Play and Its Role," p. 542; Susanna Millar, *The Psychology of Play* (Baltimore, 1968), p. 188; Goffman, *Encounters*, p. 26.

26. Jean Piaget, *Play, Dreams, and Imitation in Childhood*, trans. C. Gattegno and F. M. Hodgson (New York, 1962), pp. 110–13, 145.

27. Ludwig Wittgenstein, *The Blue and Brown Books* (New York, 1958), p. 13.

28. Immanuel Kant, *Critique of Judgment*, trans. James Creed Meredith (Oxford, 1911), pp. 199–201. The passage is from Book II, "Analytic of the Sublime."

29. For the idea of the way that a "ludic" text "invites" the reader to share in the play of the text, I am indebted to an essay by Anna K. Nardo, "The Play of and the Play in Literature," to be published in the proceedings of the 1983 conference of the Association for the Anthropological Study of Play.

30. Peter Hutchinson, *Games Authors Play* (London and New York, 1983), pp. 18, 23, 42. See also Martin Price, *Forms of Life: Character and Moral Imagination in the Novel* (New Haven and London, 1983), p. 5.

31. Piaget, "The Game of Marbles," in *The Moral Judgment of the Child*, trans. Marjorie Gabain (Glencoe, Ill., 1948), pp. 10–108.

32. On the question of the "boundaries" or "limits" of play, see Gadamer, *Truth and Method*, p. 96; Norbeck, "Man at Play," p. 52; Irwin, *Game of the Impossible*, p. 197; and John R. Bowman, "The Organization of Spontaneous Adult Social Play," in *Play: Anthropological Perspectives*, ed. Michael A. Salter (West Point, N.Y., 1978), pp. 239–50.

33. Chaney, *Fictions and Ceremonies*, p. 93.

34. Gregory Bateson, Don D. Jackson, Jay Haley, and Jon Weakland, "Toward a Theory of Schizophrenia," and Bateson, "A Theory of Play and Fantasy," in *Steps to an Ecology of Mind* (New York, 1975).

35. These extremes of behavior are characterized as "boundary diffuseness" (people who riot at football games) and "boundary rigidity" (game addicts) by R. E. Herron and Brian Sutton-Smith, *Child's Play* (New York, 1971) pp. 103–5.

36. Caillois, *Man, Play, and Games*, p. 44.

37. Eric Berne, *Games People Play* (New York, 1964), p. 48. What one generation views as the humorous foible of human nature, another may take as serious and highly consequential. This notion of "ulteriority" in playing may have its origins in the work of Stephen Potter, an English humorist credited with coining the term "gamesmanship." See Potter, *The Theory and Practice of Gamesmanship* (New York, 1948). Stuart H. Walker, *Winning: The Psychology of Competition* (New York and London, 1980), uses Berne, and relies on the term "gamesmanship" to describe the adverse effects of competition. Walker distinguishes Berne's "ulterior" games from the practice of "gamesmanship," where a player *consciously* plays these "ulterior" games (pp. 14, 246).

38. The literature on ritual—in particular, on its relationship to play and on the feelings that rituals engender—is vast. See, for example, Don Handelman, "Play and Ritual: Complementary Frames of Meta-Communication," in *It's a Funny Thing, Humor*, ed. Anthony J. Chapman and Hugh C. Foot (Oxford, 1977), pp. 185–92; Richard F. Hardin, "'Ritual' in Recent Criticism: The Elusive Sense of Community," *PMLA* 98 (1983): 846–62; "The Ritual Dimension of Play: Structure and Perspective," collection of essays in

Play and Culture: 1978 Proceedings of the Association for the Anthropological Study of Play, ed. Helen B. Schwartzman (West Point, N.Y., 1980), pp. 49–82; Scott Kilmer, "Sport as Ritual: A Theoretical Approach" in *The Study of Play: Problems and Prospects,* ed. David F. Lancy and B. Allan Tindall (West Point, N.Y., 1977), pp. 44–50; and Victor Turner, *The Ritual Process: Structure and Anti-Structure* (Chicago, 1969), and "Liminal to Liminoid in Play, Flow, and Ritual: An Essay in Comparative Symbology," *Rice University Studies* 60, no. 3 (1974): 53–92.

39. Claude Lévi-Strauss, *The Savage Mind* (Chicago, 1966), pp. 30–31 [originally published in French as *La Pensée sauvage* (Paris, 1962)].

40. Lévi-Strauss, *Savage Mind,* p. 32.

Notes to Chapter 2

1. Johann Huizinga, *Homo Ludens: A Study of the Play Element in Culture* (London, 1949), p. 192.
2. Thomas Carlyle, *Past and Present,* in *Collected Works* (London, 1882), p. 185, 244.
3. Priscilla Robertson, *An Experience of Women: Pattern and Change in Nineteenth-Century Europe* (Philadelphia, 1982), pp. 534–35.
4. Max Weber, *The Protestant Ethic and the Spirit of Capitalism,* new edition trans. Talcott Parsons (New York, 1930; 1958), p. 26.
5. Frank E. Manning, "The Rediscovery of Religious Play: A Pentecostal Case," in *The Study of Play: Problems and Prospects,* ed. David F. Lancy and B. Allan Tindall (West Point, N.Y., 1980), p. 157.
6. Kurt F. Reinhardt, *The Theological Novel of Modern Europe: An Analysis of Masterpieces by Eight Authors* (New York, 1969), p. 31.
7. Victor Turner, "Liminal to Liminoid in Play, Flow, and Ritual: An Essay in Comparative Symbology," *Rice University Studies* 60, no. 3 (1974): 52. See also Sebastian de Grazia, *Of Time, Work, and Leisure* (New York, 1962).
8. James S. Hans, *The Play of the World* (Amherst, Mass., 1981), pp. 51–110. See also Samuel Weber's distinction between "workers" and "gamblers" in *Unwrapping Balzac: A Reading of La Peau de chagrin* (Toronto, 1979), pp. 14–24. Also important to this question is a chapter entitled "The Politics of Enjoyment" in Mihaly Csikszentmihalyi, *Beyond Boredom and Anxiety: The Experience of Play in Work and Games* (San Francisco, 1975). The goal of Csikszentmihalyi's research is to find ways to bring the rewards of play into activities that tend to be grim and unrewarding: in other words, to make work more like play.
9. Lionel Trilling, "The Fate of Pleasure," in *Romanticism Reconsidered: Selected Papers for the English Institute,* ed. Northrop Frye (New York and London, 1963), p. 74. Trilling quotes from Wordsworth's preface to *Lyrical Ballads.* As I do here, Trilling has contrasted the Romantic ideology to that of Carlyle, who thought that man's dignity arose from "the resistance which man offers to the impulse to pleasure" (77).
10. Harry Levin, *The Gates of Horn: A Study of Five French Realists* (New York, 1963), p. 163.
11. Turner, "Liminal to Liminoid," p. 70.
12. Henry James, "The Art of Fiction," in *The House of Fiction,* ed. Leon Edel (London, 1957), pp. 25–26. See also William Nelson, *Fact or Fiction: The Dilemma of the*

Notes to pages 26–35

Renaissance Storyteller (Cambridge, Mass., 1973), p. 65–67. Nelson compares James's position to that of Ian Watt, *The Rise of the Novel* (Berkeley, 1967), and argues that, in contrast to Watt's theory of fiction, the Renaissance "makers of fiction" recognize that "the story is play and not history."

13. Linda Nochlin, *Realism* (New York, 1971), p. 58.

14. Robert Alter, *Partial Magic: The Novel as a Self-Conscious Genre* (Berkeley, 1975), p. 98.

15. Franz Stanzel, *Narrative Situations in the Novel*, trans. James P. Pusack (Bloomington, Ind., 1971), pp. 38–39 [originally published in German as *Die typischen Erzahlsituationene im Roman* (Vienna, 1955)].

16. Ernest Renan, "The Future of Science," in *Realism, Naturalism, and Symbolism: Modes of Thought and Expression in Europe 1848–1914*, ed. Roland N. Stromberg (New York, 1968), pp. 25–26. The original "L'avenir de la science" is included in Renan, *Pages choisies* (Paris, 1925), pp. 232–33. For a summary of the characteristics of French Positivism see Wladyslaw Tatarkiewicz, *Nineteenth Century Philosophy*, trans. Chester A. Kisiel (Belmont, Calif., 1973), pp. 7–10.

17. Levin, *Gates of Horn*, p. 25.

18. Marthe Robert, *Origins of the Novel*, trans. Sacha Rabinovicth (Bloomington, Ind., 1980), p. 16 [originally published in French as *Roman des origines et origines du roman* (Paris, 1972)].

19. Nochlin, *Realism*, p. 183.

20. For a discussion of the use of symbolism in the novel form, see Julia Kristeva, *Le Texte du roman* (The Hague, 1970), pp. 25–35; Harold H. Kolb, *The Illusion of Life: American Realism as a Literary Form* (Charlottesville, Va., 1969), p. 118.

21. James Guetti, *Word Music: The Aesthetic Aspect of Narrative Fiction* (New Brunswick, N.J., 1980), pp. 7–8.

22. See Roland Barthes, "Introduction to the Structural Analysis of Narratives," in *Image—Music—Text*, trans. Stephen Heath (New York, 1977), pp. 106–7 [published in French as "L'introduction à l'analyse structurale des récits," *Communications* 8 (1966): 16].

23. Leo Bersani, *A Future for Astyanax: Character and Desire in Literature* (Boston and Toronto, 1976), pp. 59–60. See also Arnold Weinstein, *Fictions of the Self 1550–1800* (Princeton, 1981), pp. 3–18. Weinstein compares nineteenth-century fiction to earlier fiction, arguing that "whereas the nineteenth century tirelessly centralizes character . . ., the life-story in early fiction is more precarious and more devious." Early novels are characterized by "the extraordinary malleability of self, the profusion of mask and repertory, the seesaw of enactment through language as opposed to gesture" (p. 14).

24. Huizinga, *Homo Ludens*, p. 133.

25. For examples and discussions of game motifs in pre-nineteenth-century literature, see David Lloyd Stevenson, *The Love Game Comedy* (New York, 1946). It is also interesting to note that the "story" of Marivaux's play is essentially the same story that Pushkin tells in "Mistress into Maid," one of his *Belkin Tales* (1830).

26. Geoffrey Brereton, *French Comic Drama: From the Sixteenth to the Eighteenth Century* (London, 1977), p. 204. See also Peter Brooks, *The Novel of Worldliness* (Princeton, 1972); and Kenneth N. McKee, *The Theater of Marivaux* (New York, 1958), pp. 120–40.

27. In this connection, see English Showalter, *Evolution of the French Novel* (Princeton, 1972), pp. 83–90; Levin, *Gates of Horn*, p. 43; and Walter L. Reed, *An Exemplary*

History of the Novel: The Quixotic Versus the Picaresque (Chicago, 1981), pp. 19–42, 71–92.

28. Robert, *Origins*, p. 163.

29. On the question of "propriety" in *Mansfield Park*, see David Lodge, "The Vocabulary of *Mansfield Park*," in *Language of Fiction: Essays in Criticism and Verbal Analysis*, 2nd ed. (London, 1984), pp. 94–113.

30. See, for example, Darrel Mansell, *The Novels of Jane Austen* (London and Basingstoke, 1973). Mansell calls his chapter on *Mansfield Park* "The Scourging of Irony."

31. Martin Price, *Forms of Life: Character and Moral Imagination in the Novel* (New Haven and London, 1983), pp. 73–75.

32. F. D. Reeve, *The Russian Novel* (New York, 1966), p. 77. See also Kathleen Blake, *Play, Games, and Sport: The Literary Works of Lewis Carroll* (Ithaca, N.Y., 1974), esp. last chapter.

33. Thomas A. Burns, "The Game of Life: Idealism, Reality, and Fantasy in the Nineteenth and Twentieth Century Versions of a Milton Bradley Game," *Canadian Review of American Studies* 9, no. 1 (1978): 61.

34. Thorstein Veblen, *The Theory of the Leisure Class* (London, 1899). See esp. chapters "Conspicuous Leisure" and "Conspicuous Consumption." Veblen argues that "the utility of both [conspicuous leisure and conspicuous consumption] for the purposes of reputability lies in the element of waste that is common to both" (p. 88). See also Richard Godden, "Some Slight Shifts in the Novel of Manners," in *Henry James: Fiction as History*, ed. Ian F. A. Bell (London and New York, 1985), p. 156. Godden points to Veblen to support his argument that in the nineteenth-century novel "leisure is not indolence but a state of high competition."

Notes to Chapter 3

1. Joseph Epstein, *Ambition: The Secret Passion* (New York, 1980), p. 263. Part biographical vignettes, part social criticism, Epstein's book seems to argue that ambition is a positive force, particularly in American society.

2. Henry James, *The Aspern Papers*, in *The Great Short Novels of Henry James*, ed. Philip Rahv (New York, 1944), p. 471. All other references will be to this edition, page numbers inserted parenthetically. For an analysis of James's novel that explores many of the same ideas as my argument, see Susane Kappeler, *Writing and Reading in Henry James* (London, 1980), pp.14–63. Kappeler discusses at length the relationship between the reader and the narrator in the novel, especially the way the narrator distorts the reader's impression of the other characters and events. Kappeler notes that the narrator's strategy is, particularly with regard to Miss Tina, "a secret reenactment of Aspern's life" (30). In this sense, the narrator competes not only with other "critics" who have sought the papers, and with the Misses Bordereau, who possess them, but also with the legacy of Jeffrey Aspern himself. His goal, then, is not just the papers, but Aspern's Juliana, represented for the narrator in the person of Miss Tina. And in still another sense, the narrator "competes" for the reader's sympathy and for the vindication of his actions, by appeals to the reader that seem to contradict what has actually occurred in the novel. See also Kenneth Graham, *Henry James: The Drama of Fulfilment* (Oxford, 1975), p. 61, who argues that the novel "is a sophisticated game of style that contains its seriousness of

import, and leads gradually towards revelation as the end of the game." For an interpretation that places a slightly different emphasis on the imagery in the novel, see Rosemary F. Franklin, "Military Metaphors and the Organic Structure of Henry James' *The Aspern Papers*," *Arizona Quarterly* 32 (1972): 327–40.

3. Stendhal, *Le Rouge et le noir* (Paris, 1964), p. 99. I have translated the cited passages and included the original French of longer passages in the notes, with page numbers referring to this edition. In translating specific passages, I have relied in a few instances on Robert M. Adams's translation of the novel, *Red and Black: A New Translation: Backgrounds and Sources: Criticism* (New York, 1969). Subsequent references to shorter passages from *Le Rouge et le noir* will be to book and chapter numbers, inserted parenthetically.

4. J. Christopher Herold, *The Age of Napoleon* (New York, 1963), p. 434.

5. Herold, p. 412.

6. *Le Rouge et le noir*, p. 53: "Quand Bonaparte fit parler de lui, la France avait peur d'être envahie; le mérite militaire était nécessaire et à la mode. Aujourd'hui, on voit des prêtres de quarante ans avoir cent mille francs d'appointements, c'est-à-dire trois fois autant que les fameux généraux de division de Napoléon. . . . Il faut être prêtre."

7. Herold argues that until 1811, Napoleon "followed events" rather than "shaping them." The change in approach marked the beginning of Napoleon's downfall (*The Age of Napoleon*, pp. 283–88).

8. See Sigmund Freud, *Group Psychology and the Analysis of the Ego* in vol. 18, *The Standard Edition of the Complete Psychological Works of Sigmund Freud*, trans. James Strachey (London, 1955), p. 93. Freud argues that the Church and the army are "artificial groups" because "a certain external force is employed to prevent them from disintegrating and to check alterations in their structure."

9. Gita May, *Stendhal and the Age of Napoleon* (New York, 1977), p. 214. See also Armand Caraccio, *Stendhal*, trans. Dolores Bagley (New York, 1965), p. 151. For other interpretations of the title of the novel, see Wallace Fowlie, *Stendhal* (London, 1969), p. 99; Robert Alter, *A Lion for Love: A Critical Biography of Stendhal* (New York, 1979), pp. 197–200; Henri Martineau, *L'Oeuvre de Stendhal: Histoire de ses livres et sa pensée* (Paris, 1951), pp. 385–86; and F. W. J. Hemmings, *Stendhal: A Study of his Novels* (Oxford, 1964), pp. 115–16. I would agree with Hemmings's argument that it is less important "for a Post-Napoleonic generation that the road to fortune is colored black, not red," than "that the incredible fulfillment of Napoleon's ambitious dream has so dazzled the imaginative adolescent that he cannot conceive of happiness except in terms of the realization of some equally fabulous ambition."

10. René Girard, *Deceit, Desire, and the Novel*, trans. Yvonne Freccero (Baltimore, 1965), p.138. Girard's argument might be compared with Erich Auerbach's in *Mimesis: The Representation of Reality in Western Literature*, trans. Willard R. Trask (Princeton, 1953), p. 466, that "Julien is much more a [tragic] 'hero' than the characters of Balzac, to say nothing of Flaubert." Because Stendhal forces us to take Julien less seriously than we are allowed to take Balzac's characters, I find it difficult to see Julien's plight as "tragic" in any sense. I would agree, however, that Julien *himself* sees his plight as more "heroic" or "tragic"—especially at the end—than would a Balzacian character. Julien clearly *strives* to be a kind of "tragic hero."

11. Leo Bersani, *A Future for Astyanax: Character and Desire in Literature* (Boston, 1969), p. 115. Along these lines, see Alexander Welsh, *Reflections on the Hero as Quixote* (Princeton, 1981), p. 154. Welsh, who sees in Julien an adolescent Don Quixote, believes

that Stendhal is unable to treat Julien objectively, especially in book II: "the failure of objectivity is due to something like the sincerity of insincerity, a confession that role-playing is the only identity available to a hero. . . . [T]he idea of creating a role for oneself has become desperate [by book II of the novel]."

12. Victor Brombert, *Stendhal: Fiction and the Themes of Freedom* (New York, 1968), p. 66.

13. See Peter Brooks, "The Novel and the Guillotine; or, Fathers and Sons in *Le Rouge et le noir,*" in *PMLA* (1982): 348–59. Brooks analyzes the interaction between these two "novels," that of Julien and that of Stendhal. He also discusses the use of the word "monster" as it is used to describe Julien in the novel.

14. D. A. Miller, "Narrative 'Uncontrol' in Stendhal," in *Narrative and Its Discontents: Problems of Closure in the Traditional Novel* (Princeton, 1981), p. 196. Miller's essay connects the events of the novel to Stendhal's role as novelist. He argues that the novel "defers" closure, and also that Julien's failure to advance in a "linear progression" permits Stendhal "an expansion of peripheral possibilities" (p. 243).

15. See *Le Rouge et le noir,* pp. 52–53: "Dès sa première enfance, il avait eu des moments d'exaltation. Alors il songeait avec délice qu'un jour il serait présenté aux jolies femmes de Paris, il aurait attirer leur attention par quelque action d'éclat. Pourquoi ne serait-il pas aimé de l'une d'elles, comme Bonaparte, pauvre encore, avait été aimé de la brillante Mme de Beauharnais?"

16. *Le Rouge et le noir,* p. 66: "Les romans leur auraient tracé le rôle à jouer, montré le modèle à imiter; et ce modèle, tôt ou tard, et quoique sans nul plaisir, et peut-être en rechignant, la vanité eût forcé Julien à le suivre."

17. *Le Rouge et le noir,* p. 134: "Elle croit tuer son fils en m'aimant, et cependant la malheureuse m'aime plus que son fils. Voilà, je n'en puis douter, le remords qui la tue; voilà de la grandeur dans les sentiments. Mais comment ai-je pu inspirer untel amour, moi, si pauvre, si mal élevé, si ignorant, quelquefois si grossier dans mes façons?".

18. *Le Rouge et le noir,* p. 193: "Les gens adroits parmi les séminaristes virent qu'ils avaient affaire à un homme qui n'en était pas aux éléments du métier." In the Norton Critical Edition of *Red and Black,* Robert M. Adams translates the last part of this passage as "a man who didn't have to learn the rudiments of the game" (p. 140). This translation, though not quite faithful to the sense of the word "métier," emphasizes the extent to which the world of the seminary can be perceived as gamelike.

19. *Le Rouge et le noir,* p. 197: "A la vérité les actions importantes de sa vie étaient savamment conduites; mais il ne soignait pas les détails, et les habiles au séminaire ne regardent qu'aux détails."

20. *Le Rouge et le noir,* p. 214: "Le principe invariable du sévère janséniste Pirard était: Un homme a-t-il du mérite à vos yeux? mettez obstacle à tout ce qu'il désire, à tout ce qu'il entreprend. Si le mérite est réel, il saura bien renverser ou tourner les obstacles."

21. Geoffrey Strickland, *Stendhal: The Education of a Novelist* (Cambridge, 1974), p. 158.

22. *Le Rouge et le noir,* p. 224: "Il vit dans toute cette affaire un *bien joué* qui le met de bonne humeur et lui donna la plus haute opinion des talents de l'abbé."

23. *Le Rouge et le noir,* p. 250: ". . . remarquez qu'il n'y a de fortune, pour un homme de notre robe, que par les grands seigneurs. Avec ce je ne sais quoi d'indéfinissable, du moins pour moi, qu'il y a dans votre caractère, si vous ne faites pas fortune vous serez persécuté; il n'y a pas de moyen terme pour vous."

24. *Le Rouge et le noir,* p. 288–89: "Remarquez, ajouta le marquis, d'un air fort

sérieux, et coupant court aux actions de grâce, que je ne veux point vous sortir de votre état. C'est toujours une faute et un malheur pour le protecteur comme pour le protégé. Quand mes procès vous ennuieront, ou que vous ne me conviendrez plus, je demanderai pour vous une bonne cure, comme celle de notre ami l'abbé Pirard, et *rien de plus*, ajouta le marquis d'un ton fort sec."

25. *Le Rouge et le noir,* p. 327: "Au bout de compte, ils ne m'ont point attrape', se disait Julien en préparant son départ. Que les plaisanteries que Mlle de La Mole fait à ces messieurs soient réelles ou seulement destinées à m'inspirer de la confiance, je m'en suis amusé."

26. *Le Rouge et le noir,* p. 312: "Les guerres de la Ligue sont les temps héroïques de la France, lui disait-elle un jour, avec des yeux étincelants de génie et d'enthousiasme. Alors chacun se battait pour obtenir une certaine chose qu'il désirait, pour faire triompher son parti, et non pas pour gagner platement une croix comme du temps de votre empereur. Convenez qu'il y avait moins d'égoïsme et de petitesse. J'aime ce siècle."

27. Peter Brooks, "The Novel and the Guillotine," p. 359, argues similarly that "not only does Julien appear to renounce his model" in the final chapters, but he seems also to move beyond "the control of the paternal narrator."

28. *Le Rouge et le noir,* p. 442: "Après tout, pensait-il, mon roman est fini, et à moi seul tout le mérite. J'ai su me faire aimer de ce monstre d'orgueil, ajoutait-il en regardant Mathilde; son père ne peut vivre sans elle et elle sans moi."

29. See Henri Martineau, *L'Oeuvre de Stendhal,* p. 402: ". . . peut-on admettre que Julien Sorel est un jeune habile? Non, certes: dans tout le livre, il accumule comme à plaisir les maladresses, et la passion chez lui l'emporte constamment sur le calcul."

30. Some critics have argued that by the end of the novel Julien has been "converted," and has become more "authentic." See Mary Elise Ragland-Sullivan, "Julien's Quest for 'Self': Qui Suis-je?," *Nineteenth Century French Studies* 8 (1978): 1–14.

31. *Le Rouge et le noir,* p. 450: "Chacune des espérances de l'ambition dut être arrachée successivement de son coeur par ce grand mot: Je mourrai. La mort, en elle-même, n'était pas *horrible* à ses yeux. Toute sa vie n'avait été qu'une longue préparation au malheur, et il n'avait eu garde d'oublier celui qui passe pour le plus grand de tous."

32. Ramón Saldívar, *Figural Language in the Novel: The Flowers of Speech from Cervantes to Joyce* (Princeton, 1984), p. 94.

33. Bernard N. Schilling, *The Hero as Failure: Balzac and the Rubempré Cycle* (Chicago, 1968), p. 56.

34. Elizabeth Brody Tenebaum, *The Problematic Self: Approaches to Identity in Stendhal, D. H. Lawrence, and Malraux* (Cambridge, Mass., 1977), p. 42.

35. Robert M. Adams, "Liking Julien Sorel," in *Red and Black,* p. 540.

Notes to Chapter 4

1. Georg Lukacs, "Balzac, critique de Stendhal," in *Balzac et le réalisme français,* trans. Paul Laveau (Paris, 1979), pp. 83–87 [my translation from the French]. Lukacs states that Stendhal uses Mosca and Balzac uses Vautrin to enunciate this view of social life as a game.

2. Clearly, I do not want to suggest that Stendhal only wrote novels about ambition while Balzac only wrote novels about revenge. In some ways *La Cousine Bette* is more

completely a novel of revenge than Balzac's earlier novels. In this connection, see Maurice Bardèche, *Une Lecture de Balzac* (Paris, 1964), p. 166. Bardèche argues that a novel like *La Cousine Bette* moves away from some of the concerns of the earlier novels. "Le jugement qu'ils portent sur la vie sociale s'explique par les découvertes faites par les jeunes gens dans les romans de l'ambition. *La Cousine Bette*, à cet égard, suppose *Le Père Goriot*. Les romans de volonté, presque tous écrits entre 1830 et 1840 servent d'explication et pour ainsi dire de socle aux romans de la vie parisienne, presque tous écrits entre 1840 et 1850."

3. Leo Bersani, *Balzac to Beckett: Center and Circumference in French Fiction* (New York, 1970), p. 33.

4. This discussion is from the "Avant-Propos" to *La Comédie humaine*, which Balzac wrote in July 1842. Balzac says: "L'animal a peu de mobilier, il n'a ni arts ne sciences; tandis que l'homme, par une loi que est à rechercher, tend à représenter ses moeurs, sa pensée et sa vie dans tout ce qu'il appropie à ses besoins."

5. For an analysis of the way in which nineteenth-century critics linked Balzac to Zola, see David Bellos, *Balzac in France 1850–1900: The Making of a Reputation* (Oxford, 1976). See esp. p. 183ff., where Bellos notes that left-wing critics at the end of the century were more likely to see Zola as Balzac's literary and political heir, than were right-wing critics. Marion Ayton Crawford also connects *La Cousine Bette* to Zola and the naturalist novel in her introduction to the Penguin translation of *Cousin Bette* (London, 1965), p. 6.

6. André Malraux, "Laclos et *Les Liaisons dangereuses*," in *Le Triangle noir* (Paris, 1970), p. 29: "Les cartes semblent simples, dans ce jeu qui n'a que deux couleurs: la vanité, le désir sexuel. Vanité contre vanité, vanité contre désir, désir contre vanité. Les nuances, les numéros des cartes sont fournis par les personnages." This essay was originally published in 1939.

7. All references to *Les Liaisons dangereuses* are my own translations from the Folio edition, Choderlos de Laclos, *Les Liaisons dangereuses* (Paris, 1972). Quotations are identified by letter number, inserted parenthetically in the text.

8. Nicole Mozet, "*La Cousine Bette*, roman du pouvoir féminin?" in *Balzac et Les Parents Pauvres*, ed. Francoise van Rossum-Guyon and Michiel van Brederode (Paris, 1981), p. 44: "Dans *La Cousine Bette* le 'pouvoir féminin', selon l'expression de *La Fille aux yeux d'or*, est donc un cauchemar plus qu'une réalité. Aucune femme n'y jouit jusqu'au bout de son pouvoir."

9. Peter Brooks, *The Novel of Worldliness: Crébillon, Marivaux, Laclos, Stendhal* (Princeton, 1969), p. 210, makes much the same point in a slightly different way: "society has arranged its rules and relations to valorize a kind of behavior that finds ultimate expression in the erotic, then publicly decreed that such behavior is immoral."

10. See Brooks, *Worldliness*, p. 179; and Roseann Runte, "Authors and Actors: The Characters in *Les Liaisons dangereuses*," in *Laclos: Critical Approaches to Les Liaisons dangereuses*, ed. Lloyd R. Free (Madrid, 1978), pp. 123–36. Runte argues that the characters are "authors of their own fates and the creator of their illusions" (p. 136).

11. William W. Stowe, *Balzac, James, and the Realistic Novel* (Princeton, 1983), p. 111.

12. See Martin Kanes, *Balzac's Comedy of Words* (Princeton, 1975), p. 52: "We observe calculative forces at play between characters, and we may even glimpse the hidden motivations behind them when they are inadvertently revealed. But we never penetrate deeply into psychological interiors—nor do Balzacian creatures themselves."

13. See Leo Bersani, *Balzac to Beckett*, p. 55: "His images of social power work best

when he dramatizes the exhilaration of exercising power, and almost not at all when he attempts to detail the social machinery which presumably made a Vautrin or a Gobseck possible."

14. All references to *La Cousine Bette* are my own translations from the Folio edition, Honoré de Balzac, *La Cousine Bette* (Paris, 1972). Citations are to chapter number and page number of this edition and are inserted parenthetically in the text.

15. Fredric Jameson, "*La Cousine Bette* and Allegorical Realism," *PMLA* 86 (1971): 241–54, makes a related, though somewhat different point about the two-part structure of the novel. He argues that in the prologue all events are generated by "a positive impulse sexual in its nature." In the main section of the novel, after the introduction, "the motive power is negative, that of hatred and the lust for vengeance." Even when this energy turns against the "negative" characters, it remains profoundly negative (p. 246).

16. In his emphasis on the "how" of social life rather than the "why" Balzac might be seen as a precursor of Zola. As Zola said in *Le Roman expérimental*, "La science expérimentale ne doit pas s'inquieter du *pourquoi* des choses; elle explique le *comment*."

17. *La Cousine Bette*, pp. 167–68: "On ne déploie pas plus d'activité, plus d'intelligence, plus d'audace pour faire honnêtement sa fortune que le baron en déployait pour se plonger la tête la première dans un guêpier."

18. *La Cousine Bette*, p. 55: "Ces excès de délicatesse ne se rencontrent que chez ces belles filles du peuple qui savent recevoir des coups sans en rendre; elles ont dans les veines les restes du sang des premiers martyrs. Les filles bien nées, étant égals de leurs maris, éprouvent le besoin de les tourmenter, et de marquer, comme on marque les points au billard, leurs tolérances par des mots piquants, dan un esprit de vengeance diabolique, et pour s'assurer, soit une supériorité, soit un droit de revanche."

19. *La Cousine Bette*, pp. 64–65: "En ceci peut-être consiste toute la différence qui sépare l'homme naturel de l'homme civilisé. Le Sauvage n'a que des sentiments, l'homme civilisé a des sentiments et des idées. Aussi, chez les Sauvages, le cerveau reçoit-il pour ainsi dire peu d'empreintes, il appartient alors tout entier au sentiment qui l'envahit, tandis que chez l'homme civilisé, les idées descendent sur le coeur qu'elles transforment; celui-ci est à mille intérêts, à plusieurs sentiments, tandis que le Sauvage n'admet qu'une idée à la fois."

20. *La Cousine Bette*, p. 61: "Cette fille perdit alors toute idée de lutte et de comparaison avec sa cousine, après en avoir senti les diverses supériorités; mais l'envie resta cachée dans le fond du coeur, comme un germe de peste qui peut éclore et ravager une ville, si l'on ouvre le fatal ballot de laine où il est comprimé."

21. *La Cousine Bette*, p. 73: "Depuis dix mois, elle avait fait un être réel du fantastique amoureux de sa cousine par la raison qu'elle croyait, comme sa mère, au célibat perpétuel de sa cousine; et depuis huit jours, ce fantôme était devenu le comte Wenceslas Steinbock, le rêve avait un acte de naissance, la vapeur se solidifiait en un jeune homme de trente ans."

22. *La Cousine Bette*, p. 428: "Oh! reprit Montès, je ne suis pas de ce pays-ci, moi! je vis dans une capitainerie où je me moque de vos lois, et si vous me donnez des preuves...."

23. Christopher Prendergast, *Balzac: Fiction and Melodrama* (London, 1978), p. 97, makes much the same point about Victorin, arguing that his situation points out "the tragic impossibility of living in that society according to the values of decency and honor" (p. 97). He also describes the impact of Victorin on the structure of the novel: "The choice that Victorin is called upon to make not only undermines his role in the antithetical

Notes to pages 84–88

structure of the novel as the embodiment of high-minded principle but, in a larger perspective, also evokes in dramatic fashion that zone of ambiguity which calls in question any suggestion that there might have been of a tidy, neatly labelled moral universe. . . ."

24. *La Cousine Bette*, p. 78: "Monsieur Hulot fils était bien le jeune homme tel que l'a fabriqué la révolution de 1830: l'esprit infatué de politique, respectueux envers ses espérances, les contenant sous une fausse gravité, très envieux des réputations faites, lâchant des phrases au lieu de ces mots incisifs, les diamants de la conversation française, mais plein de tenue et prenant la morgue pour la dignité."

25. From the "Avant-Propos" to *La Comédie humaine:* "Dans le tableau que j'en fais, il se trouve plus de personnages vertueux que de personnages répréhensibles. Les actions blâmables, les fautes, les crimes, depuis les plus légers jusqu'aux plus graves, y trouvent toujours leur punition humaine ou divine, éclatante ou secrète."

26. Maurice Beebe, *Ivory Towers and Sacred Founts: The Artist as Hero in Fiction from Goethe to Joyce* (New York, 1964), p. 177.

Notes to Chapter 5

A Note on Texts: To simplify matters I have used the best available English translations of the Russian novels discussed in the chapter, with references to the original texts wherever important to my argument. In these notes I have followed the transliteration of Russian names used by individual editors and translators, even if this is inconsistent with the system of transliteration used in the text of my chapter. In transliterating other Russian words and names, I have relied on J. Thomas Shaw, *The Transliteration of Modern Russian for English Language Publications* (New York, 1979). I have used System I for names and System III for words as words.

1. Mikhail Lermontov, *A Hero of Our Time*, trans. Vladimir Nabokov (Garden City, N.Y., 1958), p. 182. All other references will be to this translation and edition; page numbers are inserted parenthetically in the text.

2. Michael Holquist, *Dostoevsky and the Novel* (Princeton, 1977) also examines this passage from *A Hero of Our Time*. He argues that "Pechorin sees that he is not merely alienated from a particular society at a particular time, but that he is cut off from *any* system that will guarantee that his existence has any meaning" (p. 20). Much has been said about whether Pechorin demonstrates fatalism in the novel; my argument is that while Pechorin distinguishes himself from Vulich, their acts demonstrate a similarity that Pechorin, as a character, chooses to ignore. See also, C. J. G. Turner, *Pechorin: An Essay on Lermontov's A Hero of Our Time* (Birmingham, England, 1978). As Turner and others note, a few critics of Lermontov's novel have seen "The Fatalist" chapter as the least important in the novel, adding nothing to what the novel has already said. For example, Eikhenbaum's study of Lermontov [B. M. Eikhenbaum, *Lermontov*, trans. Ray Parrott and Harry Weber (Ann Arbor, Mich., 1981)], makes only a slight reference to this chapter of the novel.

3. The "superfluous man" is less a character "type" than a tendency toward characterization in Russian fiction that manifests itself in slightly different ways at different moments in Russian history. Although there is some disagreement as to which characters are most appropriately included in this group, two recent books attempt to define the "superfluous man" and account for his various manifestations. See Ellen B. Chances,

189

Notes to pages 88–93

Conformity's Children: An Approach to the Superfluous Man in Russian Literature (Columbus, Ohio, 1978); and Jesse V. Clardy and Betty S. Clardy, *The Superfluous Man in Russian Letters* (Washington, D.C., 1980). For a discussion of how the character of Pechorin fits into the larger Romantic tradition, see James D. Wilson, *The Romantic Heroic Ideal* (Baton Rouge and London, 1982), esp. pp. 52–54.

4. Fydor Dostoevsky, *The Gambler; Bobok; A Nasty Story,* trans. Jesse Coulson (Harmondsworth, England, 1966), p. 39.

5. Roger Caillois, *Man, Play, and Games,* trans. Meyer Barash (New York, 1961), p. 115. See also Jeremy Bentham, *The Theory of Legislation,* ed. C. K. Ogden (London and New York, 1931), p. 166: the gambler lives "upon chances and hope, and a small fixed income has few attractions for him. The want and idleness of such a condition naturally lead to crime." Bentham introduces the idea of "deep play," or game playing where a person has more to lose than gain in playing a particular game. Bentham believed that gambling was "dangerous." Unlike Dostoevsky, however, Bentham believed that such "pernicious desires" could and should be regulated by agents of society.

6. Several critics compare Raskolnikov to Julien Sorel. See Gary Rosenshield, *Crime and Punishment: The Techniques of the Omniscient Narrator* (Lisse, The Netherlands, 1978), p. 76; and Philip Rahv, "Dostoevsky in *Crime and Punishment,*" in *Crime and Punishment: The Coulson Translation: Backgrounds and Sources: Essays in Criticism,* ed. George Gibian (New York, 1975), p. 550–52.

7. All references to *Crime and Punishment* are from Jesse Coulson's translation in the Norton Critical Edition of the novel, ed. George Gibian. Page numbers are inserted parenthetically in the text. I have often included a Russian word or phrase in the text of my chapter as a way of clarifying Coulson's translation, and in some cases I have included an endnote on the translation. References to the Russian text are from F. M. Dostoevsky, *Prestuplenie i nakazanie,* vol. 6, *Polnoe Sobranie Sochinenij* (Moscow, 1973), the thirty-volume collection of Dostoevsky's work. Page numbers referring to this edition are inserted parenthetically in these notes, where appropriate.

8. Thomas Hardy, *Jude the Obscure* (New York, 1895, 1923). All references are to this edition; page numbers are inserted parenthetically in the text.

9. Many critics have commented on the Russian title of the novel and the way that both *prestuplenie* and *nakazanie* convey something a little bit richer in meaning than their English equivalents "crime" and "punishment." Edward Sagarin, *Raskolnikov and Others: Literary Images of Crime, Punishment, Redemption, and Attonement* (New York, 1981), p. 20, notes that the French title uses the word *châtiment* ("chastisement"), which more accurately conveys the sense of the Russian word *nakazanie.* Edward Wasiolek, *Dostoevsky: The Major Fiction* (Cambridge, Mass., 1965), p. 83, argues that the Russian word *prestuplenie* conveys both of "the antithetical poles of Dostoevsky's dialectic: human logic and divine logic."

10. Mikhail Bakhtin, *Problems of Dostoevsky's Poetics,* trans. Caryl Emerson (Minneapolis, 1984), p. 170, emphasizes the importance of the image of the threshold in the novel: ". . . absolutely nothing here ever loses touch with the threshold"; the novel provides no interiors "where biographical life unfolds." The "threshold" image also echoes the use of *prestuplenie* in the title, since one entering a room must "step over" (i.e., the Latin *transgressio*) the threshold.

11. Rosenshield, *Crime and Punishment,* p. 21.

12. The Russian text reads *"on ešče vce voobražal, čto delo ešče, mozet vyt, sovsem ne poterjano"* (234). Luzhin does not use the word "game." *Delo* might best be translated as

"affair" or "project." But since he uses the word for "lost," Luzhin reflects the logic of the game.

13. See, A. D. Nuttall, *Crime and Punishment: Murder as Philosophic Principle* (Sussex, England, 1978), p. 59: "Svidrigaylov simply refuses to play the philosophic game. He will not theorize. Instead his reply is almost idiotic, artlessly appalling." Svidrigaylov's attitudes are echoed by Nietzsche: "When you are exalted above praise and blame, and your will wants to command all things as the will of a lover: that is when your virtue has its origin and its beginning." *Thus Spoke Zarathustra,* trans. R. J. Hollingdale (Harmondsworth, England, 1961), p. 101.

14. Nuttall, *Crime and Punishment,* p. 40, uses the phrase "utilitarian arithmetic" to describe the conversation that Raskolnikov overhears.

15. Again, Coulson's translation makes my point a little bit more clearly than the original. The porter says *"i vprjam' vyžigra"* (135), which means something like "you're a cunning rogue indeed."

16. The Crystal Palace may have been an actual tavern in Dostoevsky's Petersburg, but the image of the Crystal Palace (at the London Exhibition) runs through Dostoevsky's writing. In *Notes from Underground,* it serves as a metaphor for the impossible dreams and desires that men refuse to relinquish, even when something less fabulous will satisfy their basic needs. The image is also used ironically to mock the nihilists who saw the Crystal Palace as symbol of reason and science.

17. Razumikhin says: *"čego ty komedii-to razygryvaeš"* (89), which might also be translated as "what kind of a farce is this."

18. Rosenshield, *Crime and Punishment,* p. 21.

19. See Bakhtin, *Problems,* p. 261: "Porfiry speaks in hints, addressing himself to Raskolnikov's hidden voice."

20. Rosenshield, *Crime and Punishment,* p. 29–30, notes that because Dostoevsky denies an inner view of Porfiry, the character remains an enigma for both the reader and Raskolnikov.

21. The cat and mouse images are literal translations of the Russian text: *"ne igaĭte, kak koška c myšyju"* (195).

22. Several critics have explored Porfiry's methods here. Temira Pachmuss, "Dostoevsky's Porfiry: A New Socrates," *New Zealand Slavonic Journal* (1980), pp. 17–24, argues that Porfiry's method is Socratic, and that he serves as Raskolnikov's "counsellor and spiritual deliverer" (p. 18). Bakhtin, *Problems,* p. 61, says something very close to this when he says that Porfiry uses a "special *dialogic intuition* that allows him to penetrate the unfinalized and unresolved soul of Raskolnikov." I would argue that while these explanations highlight some important aspects of Porfiry's *technique,* both explanations give Porfiry too much credit for what he tries to do—in other words, that his intentions are not quite so noble and altruistic as these analyses suggest they are.

23. The Russian text not only uses the expression *"igru Porfirija,"* or "Porfiry's game," it also uses the word *rassudka* where Coulson uses the phrase "powers of judgment." Edgar H. Lehrman, *A "Handbook" to the Russian Text of Crime and Punishment* (The Hague, 1970), p. 67, notes that Dostoevsky characteristically used *razum* (as in Razumikhin) to mean "reason with God's guidance" and *rassudok* to mean "reason without God's guidance." This distinction underlines the gamelike quality of Raskolnikov's actions here. As Lehrman notes, Luzhin mistakenly calls Razumikhin Rassudkin in part 4, chapter 2.

24. Oddly enough, Raskolnikov does not use the word for game in this context, though

191

Notes to pages 101–119

he has referred to "Porfiry's game" on numerous occasions. The phrase he uses is *"prežnjuju kazenščinu prinimaetsja"* (343), which might also be translated as "take the same old approach" or "go through the same formalitites."

25. Dostoevsky, *Notes from Underground; The Double,* trans. Jesse Coulson (Harmondsworth, England, 1972), p. 40.

26. Holquist, *Dostoevsky,* p. 93.

27. David M. Bethea, "Structure vs. Symmetry in *Crime and Punishment,*" in *Fearful Symmetry: Doubles and Doubling in Literature and Film,* ed. Eugene J. Crook (Tallahassee, Fla., 1981), p. 60, also refers to this nonverbal quality of the text: "Dostoevski willingly mixed levels of meaning in the name of a higher structure. Because he perforce used words to project a non-verbal dimension of understanding, there is, to be sure some sense in which his attempt is imperfect."

28. J. Hillis Miller, *Thomas Hardy: Distance and Desire* (Cambridge, Mass., 1970), p. 39.

29. Albert Pettigrew Elliott, *Fatalism in the Works of Thomas Hardy* (New York, 1966), p. 70: "The Fateful Incident is the most obvious of the motifs of Fate in Hardy's work." Donald Davidson, "The Traditional Basis of Thomas Hardy's Fiction," in *Hardy: A Collection of Critical Essays,* ed. Albert J. Guerard (Englewood Cliffs, N.J., 1963), p. 18, notes the use of coincidences in Hardy's novels: "Superstitions are used in the background of his narrative; coincidence in the actual mechanics."

30. Peter J. Casagrande, *Unity in Hardy's Novels: 'Repetitive Symmetries'* (Lawrence, Kan., 1982), p. 217: "The triumph of Arabella shows that cruelty and cunning can triumph over love and enlightened intelligence."

31. Joseph Warren Beach, *The Technique of Thomas Hardy* (New York, 1962), p. 239. Beach also notes the "tense dramatic play of feeling between them."

32. Carol Edwards and Duane Edwards, "*Jude the Obscure:* A Psychoanalytic Study," *Hartford Studies in Literature* 13 (1981), p. 88. The Edwardses compare Jude to Hardy's Tess and see the characters' situations as essentially reversed.

33. Elliott, *Fatalism,* p. 92. Elliott uses an extended game metaphor here to make his point: "Fate has marked the cards against Man in that he is endowed with an irresistible instinct for [Woman's] charms. The aces and kings are all in Woman's hand in this fascinating but ruinous game. Man cannot play at chess; whist is the game."

Notes to Chapter 6

1. William W. Stowe, *Balzac, James, and the Realistic Novel* (Princeton, 1983), p. 8.

2. Henry James, "Honoré de Balzac (1902)," in *Notes on Novelists* (New York, 1969), p. 139.

3. For an example of James's use of "biographer" as a metaphor for the novelist, see the beginning of chapter 13 of *The American* or chapter 6 of *The Portrait of a Lady*.

4. Review in *The Literary World,* July 1877; reprinted in Henry James, *The American: An Authoritative Text: Backgrounds and Sources: Criticism,* ed. James W. Tuttleton (New York, Norton Critical Editions, 1978), p. 397. Cf. James's own argument in "The Art of Fiction" (1882) about the "old-fashioned" distinction between the "novel of character and the novel of incident" [*The House of Fiction: Essays on the Novel,* ed. Leon Edel (London, 1957), p. 34–35].

5. Leon Edel and Oscar Cargill both make much the same argument about the influence of French fiction on James in essays collected in the Norton Critical Edition of *The American*. Edel says that James's goal was to "write a novel about an American businessman and his seige of Paris, of that Faubourg St. Germain about which Henry had read in Balzac, and of which he himself was having only a passing glimpse" (p. 417). Cargill argues that James's "knowledge of the Bellegardes was derived largely, it would appear from his reading of French novels and from the presentation of French nobility on the Parisian stage" (p. 429).

6. See Mariana Torgovnick, *Closure in the Novel* (Princeton, 1981), who argues that James sought to create endings that were "rigorously aesthetic and intellectual"; he moves in his career from "a playful manipulation of nineteenth-century conventions for ending to a full-scale alternative in the scenic ending" (p. 123). I would argue that James had both formal and philosophical reasons for reformulating the endings of those novels he knew and read. See Morris Roberts, *Henry James's Criticism* (New York, 1965), who attributes to James a belief that "the French, however mature their sense for form, were in other respects but gifted and perverse children;" James found, for instance, the treatment of the theme of adultery "monstrously vicious and arid" (p. 41).

7. Letter from Henry James to William Dean Howells, October 26, 1876, reprinted in Norton Critical Edition of *The American*, p. 344.

8. Henry James, *The American*, Norton Critical Edition, p. 104. All references will be to this edition (the London edition of 1878); page numbers inserted parenthetically in the text.

9. James, *The Portrait of a Lady: An Authoritative Text: Henry James and the Novel: Reviews and Criticism*, ed. Robert D. Bamberg (New York, Norton Critical Editions, 1975), p. 67. All references will be to this edition (the New York edition of 1908); page numbers inserted parenthetically in the text. [I have chosen the New York edition because, as I argue elsewhere, some of the revisions clarify the author's ideas about games and play, but also because the editor of the Norton Critical Edition has included a textual appendix that lets the reader compare variants. I have used this appendix to identify important variants and have provided page numbers in parentheses, which refer to this appendix.] With regard to this conversation between Mrs. Touchett and Isabel, see Elizabeth Allen, *A Woman's Place in the Novels of Henry James* (London, 1984), p. 67, who calls Isabel's pronouncement a "theoretical moral freedom"; and Susan Reibel Moore, *The Drama of Discrimination in Henry James* (St. Lucia and London, 1982), p. 49, who calls Isabel's "theory" here "presumptuous" because it fails to take into consideration circumstances that dictate choices.

10. See J. A. Ward, *The Imagination of Disaster: Evil in the Fiction of Henry James* (Lincoln, Neb., 1961). While I agree with Ward's argument that a character like Newman faces in Europe "the alternate possibilities of being betrayed by Europe and of losing his native integrity" (p. 36), I disagree with the implication that evil in James is associated with a particular place or a specific culture. James is not talking about actual European civilization when he exposes the dangers faced by Christopher Newman and Isabel Archer.

11. With regard to the theme of interpretation in *The American*, see Stowe, *Balzac, James*, pp. 37–41; an early version of this argument can be found in Stowe, "Interpretation in Fiction: *Le Père Goriot* and *The American*," *Texas Studies in Literature and Language* 23 (1981): 248–67. Stowe compares Newman to Balzac's Rastignac, arguing that "Parisian society presents itself to both men as a text to be interpreted; its language

Notes to pages 124–137

and manners form a code which these socially ambitious outsiders must crack" (p. 250).

12. See James's preface to the New York edition of *The American,* Norton Critical Edition, p. 4.

13. For a discussion of the theme of honor in James, see Manfred Mackenzie, *Communities of Honor and Love in Henry James* (Cambridge, Mass., 1976), esp. p. 65.

14. Ellen Douglas Leyburn, *Strange Alloy: The Relation of Comedy to Tragedy in the Fiction of Henry James* (Chapel Hill, N.C., 1968), p. 21.

15. Preface to *The American,* Norton Critical Edition, p. 2.

16. Henry James refers to the "tall stone walls which fatally divide us" in a letter to Howells, March 30, 1877, reprinted in Norton Critical Edition of *The American,* p. 348.

17. On this question of Newman's "renunciation" see May 5, 1877, review in *The Nation,* reprint in Norton Critical Edition of *The American,* p. 392. See also Carren Kaston, *Imagination and Desire in the Novels of Henry James* (New Brunswick, N.J., 1984), p. 23. Kaston argues that "the revenge and the obsession with lost love that [Newman] gives up do not seem to be great losses," and that the more "typical" Jamesian renunciation is Claire's renunciation of Newman's love. I think that this argument raises some interesting points, but that it overestimates Claire's importance in the whole scheme of the novel, and underestimates Newman's pride. What, in fact, he gives up when he forsakes revenge is not so much an "obsession with lost love" as it is an opportunity to make others feel his power, not to be thought of as a dupe.

18. Nina Baym, "Revision and Thematic Change in *The Portrait of a Lady,*" *Modern Fiction Studies* 22 (1976): 183–200. More convincing to me than Baym's argument are the following: Kaston, *Imagination and Desire,* p. 40–41 (both versions mourn "the melodramatic imbalance of power in human relationships"); Harriet Blodgett, "Verbal Clues in *The Portrait of a Lady*: A Note in Defense of Isabel Archer," *Studies in American Fiction* 7 (1979): 28–35 ("James strengthens his intentions; he does not change them.").

19. Among the more distressing revisions James made to *The American* is the ending. In the revised version Mrs. Tristram, rather than suggesting, as she does in the original version, that Newman has not done much to make the Bellegardes frightened of him, tells him that "I like you as you are." She is also given the last word in the novel, lamenting "poor Claire."

20. For a discussion of the ways in which James made the theme of freedom more important in the revision, see Anthony J. Mazzella, "The New Isabel," in the Norton Critical Edition of *The Portrait of a Lady,* p. 599. Mazzella argues that the two portraits are different literary experiences and, like Baym, that "the Isabel Archer who faces her destiny is not the same girl in both versions, nor is the quality of her destiny the same" (p. 597). While I would agree that the process by which the reader interprets Isabel's destiny is different in the revision—since the style is so much closer to that of the later novels—I would disagree that either Isabel's choices, or the decisions she makes, are changed by the revision.

21. James, *Notes on Novelists,* p. 187.

22. James, *Notes on Novelists,* p. 224.

23. James, *House of Fiction,* p. 198.

24. Alexander Welsh, *Reflections on the Hero as Quixote* (Princeton, 1981), p. 116, argues that Ralph and his father "play an unfortunate joke" on Isabel in giving her the money.

25. In the original version, Ralph "would not have forgiven himself if he had not been able to find a great deal in the society of a woman in whom the social virtues existed in

polished perfection" (529).

26. See Baym, "Revision and Thematic Change," p. 189. Baym argues that by making Isabel's intelligence finer in the 1908 revision James was compelled to alter the characters of Osmond and Merle. According to Baym, in the revision James stresses Mme Merle's "artificial and exploitative nature." Again, I think that there is a difference between changes that "stress," or "emphasize," or "refine," and ones that alter the author's theme or intentions. Mme Merle is sufficiently exploitative in the London edition to warrant the changes James makes in the revision.

27. See Susan Reibel Moore, *Drama of Discrimination,* p. 42, who compares Mme Merle's "methods of destruction" to those used by Kate Croy in *The Wings of the Dove* to entrap Milly Theale.

28. Again, James makes a change here that emphasizes his intentions with regard to Mme Merle. In the original edition he says "Isabel suspected that her friend had esoteric views" (546); in the revision he makes it clear that Mme Merle's views are more than merely different: "Our young woman had a sense in her of values gone wrong or, as they said at the shops, marked down" (275).

29. Paul B. Armstrong, *The Phenomenology of Henry James* (Chapel Hill, N.C., and London, 1983), p. 119. See also E. A. Sklepowich, "Gilded Bondage: Games and Gamesplaying in *The Awkward Age, Essays in Criticism* 5 (1978): 187–93, who argues that "games, ambiguous because of their association with both frivolity and aesthetics, are appropriate vehicles to convey James's own ambivalent response to the 'gilded bondage' of social life" (p. 187).

30. Laurence B. Holland, *The Expense of Vision: Essays of the Craft of Henry James,* 2nd ed. (Baltimore and London, 1982), p. 26, argues that the themes of "marriage as a hollow and factitious form" and "marriage as a form of fulfillment and creative possibilities" are brought together in the end by the connection made between Isabel's and Pansy's destinies.

Notes to Chapter 7

1. Claude Lévi-Strauss, *The Savage Mind* (Chicago, 1966), pp. 30–32.
2. See Don Handelman, "Play and Ritual: Complementary Frames of Meta-Communication," in *It's a Funny Thing Humor,* ed. Anthony J. Chapman and Hugh C. Foot (Oxford, 1977), pp. 185–92: "If the bypass to play is predicated upon a premise of 'make-believe,' that to ritual is predicated upon a premise of 'let us believe,' thus controlling the kinds of metacommunication each can sustain. From the perspective of the ordinary social order, human beings recognize the 'inauthenticity' of one and the 'truth' of the other" (p. 187).
3. For good summaries of the debates over whether the major characters of *The Golden Bowl* are "good" or "evil," see Walter Wright, "Maggie Verver: Neither Saint nor Witch," in *Henry James: Modern Judgments,* ed. Tony Tanner (London, 1968), pp. 316–27; R. B. J. Wilson, "A History of Critical Response," chap. 2 of *Henry James' Ultimate Narrative: The Golden Bowl* (St. Lucia, 1981); and Daniel Mark Fogel, *Henry James and the Structure of the Romantic Imagination* (Baton Rouge and London, 1981), pp. 85–89.
4. Leo Bersani, *A Future for Astyanax: Character and Desire in Literature* (Boston and Toronto, 1969), p. 132.
5. For a good technical analysis of the stylistic "difficulties" of the Henry James's late

195

prose, see Seymour Chatman, *The Later Style of Henry James* (Oxford, 1972).

6. Nicola Bradbury, *Henry James: The Later Novels* (Oxford, 1979), p. 145.

7. Elizabeth Stevenson, *The Crooked Corridor: A Study of Henry James* (New York, 1949), p. 24.

8. Bradbury, *Henry James*, p. 7: "The highly formal situation of a game of cards, which images relationships for us, also provides an opportunity for Maggie to consider, not only these liaisons, but their formal (social and moral) contexts. This prepares both her and us for the shifting and complex exploration of both social and literary form in the encounters with Charlotte which ensue."

9. Chatman, *Later Style*, p. 110, argues that James's use of low-grade metaphors is deliberate, since they represent the language of contemporary speech, but that James did reanimate these clichés "by extension and elaboration." Alexander Holder-Barell, *The Development of Imagery and its Functional Significance in Henry James' Novels* (Bern, 1959), pp. 52–53, does not find the game images used to describe Kate and Densher's relationship of "particular significance," but believes that "the frequency of their occurrence has the effect of putting a strong emphasis on the successful cooperation between them in reaching their egotistical goal."

10. Holder-Barell, *Imagery*, p. 50. See also, Robert L. Gale, *The Caught Image: Figurative Language in the Fiction of Henry James* (Chapel Hill, N.C., 1954), pp. 183–84.

11. In addition to Holder-Barell and Gale, see the discussions of figurative language in R. W. Short, "Henry James's World of Images," *PMLA* 68 (1953): 943–60 (discussion of drama images); and Daniel Schneider, *The Crystal Cage: Adventures of the Imagination in the Fiction of Henry James* (Lawrence, Kan., 1978) (discussion of images of warfare and aggression, acting images).

12. All citations to *The Wings of the Dove* or *The Golden Bowl* are from the New York edition, *The Novels of Henry James* (New York, 1909). Volume and page numbers are provided in parentheses.

13. Many critics sympathize with Kate, either because they see in her a willingness to act, which is more commendable than Densher's passivity, or because they believe she is both a product and a victim of her environment. An argument that links both these threads can be found in Sallie Sears, *The Negative Imagination: Form and Perspective in Henry James* (Ithaca, N.Y., 1963), p. 95: "The bravery of her risk coupled with her refusal to rationalize her behavior, while most of Merton's energy is devoted to rationalization, helps account for our greater sympathy for Kate."

14. Kenneth Graham, *Henry James: The Drama of Fulfillment* (Oxford, 1975), p. 203. Graham points out that Densher's assertion of will at this point only commits him more completely to Kate and her plan.

15. John Goode, "The Pervasive Mystery of Style: *The Wings of the Dove*," in *The Air of Reality: New Essays on Henry James*, ed. John Goode (London, 1972), p. 251.

16. Graham, *Drama*, p. 200.

17. Bradbury, *Henry James*, p. 218.

18. The extremes in this range of interpretations might be represented by, at one end, Robert C. McLean, " 'Love by the Doctor's Direction': Disease and Death in *The Wings of the Dove*," *Papers on Language and Literature* 8 supp. (1972), p. 148, who believes that Milly's disease is "hysteria," her death suicidal, and her gift to Densher a "vengeful bequest . . . [which] accomplishes the rupture of the lovers . . . smothering their capacity for the life of love and sexuality Milly herself was denied"; and in contrast, Lawrence B. Holland, *The Expense of Vision: Essays on the Craft of Henry James*, 2nd ed. (Baltimore

and London, 1982), p. 319, who says that Milly "bequeaths to Densher an image of her love for him [which] redeemed their enterprise by transforming it into a gift, making her loving surrender to her tragic fortune."

19. Tony Tanner, *Adultery in the Novel: Contract and Transgression* (Baltimore and London, 1979), p. 15.

20. F. O. Mathiessen, *Henry James: The Major Phase* (London, 1944), p. 52.

21. Donald D. Kummings, "The Issue of Morality in *The Golden Bowl*," *Arizona Quarterly* 32 (1976): 384.

22. M. L. Krupnick, "*The Golden Bowl:* Henry James's Novel About Nothing," *English Studies* 57 (1976): 536: "As the novel proceeds it appears that the aggression has not been renounced so much as displaced. The natural rage, the simple instinctual response, is turned into a silent ecstasy of managing, handling, containing, and appropriating—various acts of the mind which have as their motive and aim restitution for Maggie's loss."

23. It is interesting to note that Todorov uses the word "equilibrium" to describe the relationships between characters at the beginning and at the end of a novel: "The two moments of equilibrium, similar and different, are separated by a period of imbalance which is composed of a process of degeneration and a process of improvement." Tvetzan Todorov, "Structural Analysis of Narrative," *Novel* 3 (1969): 75. Edwin Muir, *The Structure of the Novel* (New York, n.d.), also uses the word "equilibrium" to talk about the structure of events that the ending of a novel produces.

24. Mathiessen, *Major Phase*, p. 95. For another discussion of Fanny Assingham's role in the novel, see Ruth Bernard Yeazell, *Language and Knowledge in the Late Novels of Henry James* (Chicago, 1976), p. 89: "Fanny puzzles out meaning by playing with the implications of language: one assertion leads to the next by a kind of verbal logic as she expands and qualifies her statements, repeats a former phrase with new emphasis, or makes comparatively more explicit the connotations of words."

25. Fogel, *Romantic Imagination,* p. 103.

26. Gabriel Pearson, "The Novel to End All Novels: *The Golden Bowl*," in *Air of Reality,* ed. Goode, p. 347: Maggie's "most extreme form of pleasure is the overwhelming temptation that almost conquers her—to play the card that will crack the whole system apart as Fanny had cracked the golden bowl itself. She might so easily become a palpable focus of terror and anguish for all the others and assume an appalling substance in their gaze. It represents a supreme sacrifice that she does refrain from playing this last card."

27. Henry James, *A Portrait of a Lady: An Authoritative Text: Henry James and the Novel: Reviews and Criticism,* ed. Robert D. Bamberg (New York, Norton Critical Editions, 1975), p. 436 (chapter 49).

28. Paul B. Armstrong, *The Phenomenology of Henry James* (Chapel Hill, N.C., and London, 1983), p. 140; for other discussions of James's fictional use of the lie, see Pearson in *Air of Reality,* ed. Goode, p. 302: "The lie in James is sanctified by what it salvages and the disaster it postpones"; Wilson, *Golden Bowl,* p. 56. Cf. Sears, *Negative Imagination,* p. 204, who argues that Maggie, in lying becomes like Charlotte and the Prince: "Like them she operates now under the dictates of expediency and necessity, not morality, and the ensuing events resemble a chess game played by civilized people for the most unholy of stakes." Sears also uses the chess game metaphor to describe *The Wings of the Dove:* "There is something reminiscent of a hellish chess game in the book's presentation of the mathematics of narrowing alternatives" (p. 74).

29. Armstrong, *Phenomenology,* p. 175.

Notes to pages 166–176

30. Carren Kaston, *Imagination and Desire in the Novels of Henry James* (New Brunswick, N.J., 1984), p. 153.

31. Schneider, *Crystal Cage*, p. 92.

32. Catherine Cox Wessel, "Strategies for Survival in James's *The Golden Bowl*," *American Literature* 35 (1983): 587. Wessel also argues, however, that the novel explores the "most primitive impulses" of human beings—"the lust for conquest and the will to possess" (p. 577), and that James sees life as "painfully provisional and compromised" (p. 585). Cf. Gore Vidal, "Return to *The Golden Bowl*," *New York Review of Books* 30 (January 19, 1984): 8–12. Vidal argues that Charlotte and the Prince are far more sympathetic as characters than either Maggie or Adam, seeing them as willing "to devour the whole great world" (p. 9) in order to satisfy their desires. He also sees the novel not as one of freedom but of bondage, arguing that in the last scene, Maggie and the Prince are both prisoners: "The golden cage has shut on them both" (p. 12).

33. Mathiessen, *Major Phase*, p. 146.

34. See Yeazell, *Language and Knowledge*, p. 125, who argues that the novel provides the reader with "less a closed fiction than a character struggling to will such a fiction." See also Leo Bersani, "The Subject of Power," *Diacritics* (Fall 1977): 2–21.

Notes to Conclusion

1. Jeanine Parisier Plottel, *Intertexuality: New Perspectives in Criticism*, ed. Plottel and Hanna Charney, *New York Literary Forum* 2 (1978): xv.

2. Plottel, p. xix.

3. Ted L. Estess, "Dimensions of Play in the Literature of Samuel Beckett" *Arizona Quarterly* 33 (1977): 19.

4. Marthe Robert, *Origins of the Novel*, trans. Sacha Rabinovitch (Bloomington, Ind., 1980), pp. 229–30.

5. Anaïs Nin, *The Novel of the Future* (London, 1968), pp. 168–69, 199.

Select Bibliography

A. About Games and Play (arranged chronologically)

Friedrich Schiller, *On the Aesthetic Education of Man in a Series of Letters*, trans. Reginald Snell (New York, 1965), esp. Letters 15 and 16.

Immanuel Kant, *Critique of Judgment*, trans. James Creed Meredith (Oxford, 1911), esp. Book II, "Analytic of the Sublime."

Thomas Carlyle, *Past and Present*, in *Collected Works* (London: 1882).

William James, *The Principles of Psychology in Three Volumes* (Cambridge, Mass., 1981; first published 1899); esp. chapter entitled "Instinct," pp. 1044–46.

Sigmund Freud, *Beyond the Pleasure Principle, Group Psychology, and Other Works*, trans. James Strachey (London, 1955); volume 18 of the Standard Edition.

George Herbert Mead, *The Social Psychology of George Herbert Mead*, ed. Anselm Strauss (Chicago, 1956), esp. pp. 220–30.

Johann Huizinga, *Homo Ludens: A Study of the Play Element in Culture* (London, 1949).

Roger Caillois, *Man, Play, and Games*, trans. Meyer Barash (New York, 1961); published in French as *Les Jeux et les hommes: le masque et le vertige* (Paris, 1958).

Ludwig Wittgenstein, *The Blue and Brown Books* (New York, 1958).

Eugen Fink, "The Oasis of Happiness: Toward an Ontology of Play," in *Game, Play, Literature*, ed., Jacques Ehrmann (Boston, 1968; orginally published as Volume 41 of *Yale French Studies*). The selection for this volume is derived from Fink's book on play entitled *Spiel als Weltsymbole* (Stuttgart, 1960).

Select Bibliography

Jean Piaget, *Play, Dreams, and Imitation in Childhood,* trans., C. Gattegno and F. M. Hodgson (New York, 1962).
Claude Lévi-Strauss, *The Savage Mind* (Chicago, 1966); published in French as *La Pensée sauvage* (Paris, 1962).
Eric Berne, *Games People Play* (New York, 1964).
Hans-Georg Gadamer, *Truth and Method* (New York, 1975); published in German as *Warheit and Methode* (Tubïngen, 1965).
Jacques Derrida, "Structure, Sign, and Play," in *Writing and Difference,* trans. Alan Bass (Chicago, 1978); published in French as *L'Ecriture et la différence* (Paris, 1967).
David L. Miller, *Gods and Games: Toward a Theology of Play* (New York, 1970).
Peter Farb, *Word Play: What Happens When People Talk* (New York, 1974).
Mihaly Csikszentmihalyi, *Beyond Boredom and Anxiety: The Experience of Play in Work and Games* (San Francisco, 1975).
L. S. Vygotsky, "Play and Its Role in the Mental Development of the Child," in *Play: Its Roles in Development and Evolution,* ed. Jerome S. Bruner, Alison Joly, and Kathy Sylva (New York, 1976).
J. Nina Lieberman, *Playfulness: Its Relationship to Imagination and Creativity* (New York, 1977).
David Chaney, *Fictions and Ceremonies: Representations of Popular Experience* (New York, 1979).
Manfred Eigen and Ruthild Winkler, *Laws of the Game: How the Principles of Nature Govern Chance,* trans. Robert Kimber and Rita Kimber (New York, 1981).
James S. Hans, *The Play of the World* (Amherst, Mass., 1981).
Peter Hutchinson, *Games Authors Play* (London and New York, 1983).
James P. Carse, *Finite and Infinite Games: A Vision of Life as Play and Possibility* (New York, 1986).

B. About Fiction and Realism

Robert Alter, *Partial Magic: The Novel as a Self-Conscious Genre* (Berkeley, 1975).
Erich Auerbach, *Mimesis: The Representation of Reality in Western Literature,* trans. Willard R. Trask (Princeton, 1953).
M. M. Bakhtin, *The Dialogic Imagination: Four Essays,* trans. Caryl Emerson and Michael Holquist (Austin, Tex., 1981).
Leo Bersani, *A Future for Astyanax: Character and Desire in Literature* (Boston and Toronto, 1976).
Peter Brooks, *The Novel of Worldliness* (Princeton, 1972).
Harry Levin, *The Gates of Horn: A Study of Five French Realists* (New York, 1963).

Select Bibliography

D. A. Miller, *Narrative and Its Discontents: Problems of Closure in the Traditional Novel* (Princeton, 1981).

Linda Nochlin, *Realism* (New York, 1971).

Marthe Robert, *Origins of the Novel,* trans. Sacha Rabinovitch (Bloomington, Ind., 1980); originally published in French as *Roman des origines du roman* (Paris, 1972).

Walter L. Reed, *An Exemplary History of the Novel: The Quixotic Versus the Picaresque* (Princeton, 1972).

Franz Stanzel, *Narrative Situations in the Novel,* trans. James P. Pusack (Bloomington, Ind., 1971); originally published in German as *Die typischen Erzahlsituationene im Roman* (Vienna, 1955).

Roland N. Stromberg, *Realism, Naturalism, and Symbolism: Modes of Thought and Expression in Europe 1848–1914* (New York, 1968).

Mariana Torgovnick, *Closure in the Novel* (Princeton, 1981).

Arnold Weinstein, *Fictions of the Self 1550–1800* (Princeton, 1981).

Alexander Welsh, *Reflections on the Hero As Quixote* (Princeton, 1981).

Index

Adams, Robert M., 63
Adultery, 160–62, 163, 165
Adventures of Huckleberry Finn, The (Twain), 38
Age of Napoleon, The (Herold), 45
Alice in Wonderland (Carroll), 8, 38
Allen, Elizabeth, 193 n. 9
Alter, Robert, 27
Ambition, theories of, 40–42
American, The (James), 18, 41, 119, 120–31, 132, 133, 134, 137, 142, 144, 145, 149, 160, 162, 163, 168, 169, 171, 173, 194 nn. 17, 19
Anna Karenina (Tolstoy), 20, 21, 24, 160, 163
Aquinas, St. Thomas, 10
"Art of Fiction, The" (James), 26
Aspern Papers, The (James), 42–44; 48, 51
Auerbach, Erich, 184 n. 10
Austen, Jane, 36, 37; *Emma*, 171; *Mansfield Park*, 36–38, 172; *Pride and Prejudice*, 36

Bakhtin, Mikhail, 1, 2, 99, 177 n. 1, 190 n. 10, 191 n. 19

Balzac, Honoré de, 17, 26, 36, 47, 63, 65, 66, 67, 70–86, 106, 118, 120, 147, 150, 168, 171, 172, 173, 174, 186 nn. 1, 2, 187 n. 4, 189 n. 25, 193 n. 11; *La Comédie Humaine*, 36, 67, 85, 187 n. 4, 189 n. 25; *La Cousine Bette*, 17, 66, 67, 69, 70, 71–86, 92, 106, 119, 147, 151, 169, 170, 171, 172, 173, 174, 175, 186 n. 2, 187 nn. 5, 8, 188 n. 15; *Les Illusions perdues*, 63, 65, 147; *Le Père Goriot*, 41, 63, 65
Bardèche, Maurice, 187 n. 2
Bateson, Gregory, 15
Baym, Nina, 132, 195 n. 26
Beach, Joseph Warren, 192 n. 31
Beckett, Samuel, 168
Beebe, Maurice, 86
Bellos, David, 187 n. 5
Bentham, Jeremy, 190 n. 5
Berne, Eric, 16, 17; *Games People Play*, 16, 180 n. 37
Bersani, Leo, 30, 47, 146, 187 n. 13
Bethea, David M., 192 n. 27
Beyle, Marie Henri [pseud. Stendhal], 10, 47, 48, 51, 59, 65, 66, 71, 73, 90, 122, 150, 168, 173, 186 n. 2; *Racine and Shakespeare*, 10; *Le Rouge et le noir*, 18, 44–64, 65, 66, 76, 89, 90, 91, 92, 104,

Index

106, 107, 110, 111, 120, 147, 169, 170, 173, 174
Beyond the Pleasure Principle (Freud), 9
Blodgett, Harriet, 194 n. 18
Book of Common Prayer, A (Didion), 176
Book of Job, The, 111, 116
Bradbury, Nicola, 196 n. 8
Brontë, Charlotte, *Jane Eyre,* 169
Brooks, Peter, 185 n. 13, 186 n. 37, 187 n. 9
Burns, Thomas, 39

Caillois, Roger, 5, 17, 18, 89, 178 n. 2
Cargill, Oscar, 193 n. 5
Carlyle, Thomas, 23, 24, 26; *Past and Present,* 23
Carroll, Lewis. *See* Dodgson, Charles Lutwidge
Carse, James P., 178 n. 6
Casagrande, Peter, J., 192 n. 30
Cervantes Saavedra, Miguel de, 33, 169; *Don Quixote,* 33–36, 38, 48, 63, 91, 169
Chances, Ellen B., 189 n. 3
Chaney, David, 15; *Fictions and Ceremonies,* 15
Chatman, Seymour, 195 n. 5, 196 n. 9
Chernyshevsky, Nikolai Gavrilovich, 24; *What is to Be Done,* 24
Christianity, 24–25
Clardy Jesse V., and Betty S., 190 n. 3
Clemens, Samuel Langhorne [pseud. Mark Twain], 39; *The Adventures of Huckleberry Finn,* 38
Comédie Humaine, La (Balzac), 36, 67, 85, 187 n. 4, 189 n. 25
Competition, 36, 39, 86, 144
Confessions (Rousseau), 49
Couples (Updike), 176
Cousine Bette, La (Balzac), 17, 66, 67, 69, 70, 71–86, 92, 106, 119, 147, 151, 169, 170, 171, 172, 173, 174, 175, 186 n. 2, 187 nn. 5, 8, 188 n. 15
Crawford, Marion Ayton, 187 n. 5
Crime and Punishment (Dostoevsky), 17, 20, 21, 49, 89, 90–105, 106, 107, 108, 111, 115, 116, 117, 118, 121, 146, 147, 154, 169, 171, 173, 174, 175

Critique of Judgement, The (Kant), 13
Crystal Palace, The, 98, 191 n. 16
Csikszentmihalyi, Mihaly, 181 n. 8

Darwinism, 28
Davidson, Donald, 192 n. 29
Dead Souls (Gogol), 38
Deceit, Desire and the Novel (Girard), 11
Derrida, Jacques, 6
Desire, 8–9, 68, 109, 114
Dialogic dimension of fiction, 1, 104
Dickens, Charles, *Great Expectations,* 8
Diderot, Denis, 27, 18, 30; *Jacques le fataliste,* 27
Didion, Joan, *A Book of Common Prayer,* 176
Dodgson, Charles Lutwidge [pseud. Lewis Carroll], *Alice in Wonderland,* 8, 38
Don Quixote (Cervantes), 33–36, 38, 48, 63, 91, 169
Dostoevsky, Fyodor Mikhaylovich, 17, 21, 47, 49, 88, 89, 90, 93, 94, 104, 105, 106, 121, 150, 168, 170, 171, 172, 190 n. 5, 192 n. 27; *Crime and Punishment,* 17, 20, 21, 49, 89, 90–105, 106, 107, 108, 111, 115, 116, 117, 118, 121, 146, 147, 154, 169, 171, 173, 174, 175; *The Gambler,* 89, 95; *Notes from Underground,* 191 n. 16
Dudevant, Amandine Aurore Lucie (née Dupin, Baronne) [pseud. George Sand], 133

Edel, Leon, 193 n. 5
Éducation sentimentale, L' (Flaubert), 50
Edwards, Carol and Duane, 192 n. 32
Effie Briest (Fontane), 160
Eliot, George. *See* Evans, Mary Ann
Elliott, Alert Pettigrew, 192 n. 29
Emma (Austen), 171
Eugene Onegin (Pushkin), 88
Evans, Mary Ann [pseud. George Eliot], 20, 21, 171; *Middlemarch,* 20, 21
"Existence and Hermeneutics" (Ricoeur), 8
"Extraordinary Man" Theory, 93

Index

Farb, Peter, 5; *Word Play*, 5, 10
Fate, 58, 87–89, 113, 115, 153, 157
Fathers and Sons (Turgenev), 88
Faust (Goethe), 64
Fiction and Ceremonies (Chaney), 15
"Fiction and the 'Matrix of Analogy'" (Shorer), 2
Fink, Eugene, 7
Flaubert, Gustave, 47, 133; *L'Éducation sentimentale*, 50; *Madame Bovary*, 47, 133, 160
Fogel, Daniel Mark, 195
Fontane, Theodor, 160; *Effie Briest*, 160
Freud, Sigmund, *Beyond the Pleasure Principle*, 9; *Group Psychology*, 184 n. 8
"Future of the Novel, The" (James), 2
Future of Science, The (Renan), 28

Gadamer, Hans-Georg, 6, 10
Gambler, The (Dostoevsky), 89, 95
Gambling, 89–90, 95, 190 n. 5
Game of Hidden Being, 30–35, 38, 48, 78, 174
Game of Life, The (board game), 39
Game of Love and Chance, The [Le Jeu de l'amour et hasard] (Marivaux), 30–33, 174
Game Theory, 5, 178 n. 4
Games Authors Play (Hutchinson), 12
Games People Play (Berne), 16, 180 n. 37
Gide, André, 168
Girard, Réne, 11, 47; *Deceit, Desire and the Novel*, 11
Goethe, Johann Wolfgang von, 64; *Faust*, 64; *Werther*, 169
Gogol, Nikolai Vasilievich, 27, 29, 30, 38–39; *Dead Souls*, 38
Golden Bowl, The (James), 18, 19–20, 145–51, 159–67, 168, 175, 176
Gospel According to St. John, The, 105
Graham, Kenneth, 154, 196 n. 14
Great Expectations (Dickens), 8
Group Psychology (Freud), 184 n. 8
Guetti, James, 29

Handelman, Don, 195n
Hardy, Thomas, 18, 47, 90, 106, 117, 171;

Jude the Obscure, 18, 47, 90, 91, 92, 105–17, 118, 129, 150, 170, 171, 172, 173
Hemmings, F. W. J., 184 n. 9
Hero of Our Time, A, (Lermontov), 87–88, 189
Herold, Christopher, 45; *The Age of Napoleon*, 45
Herron, R. E., 180 n. 35
Holder-Barell, Alexander, 150, 196 n. 9
Holland, Laurence B., 195 n. 30, 196 n. 18
Holquist, Michael, 189 n. 2
Howells, William Dean, 41; *The Rise of Silas Lapham*, 41
Huizinga, Johann, 11, 22, 23, 30, 36, 106
Hutchinson, Peter, *Games Authors Play*, 12

Illusions perdues, Les (Balzac), 63, 65, 147
Intertextuality, 168–69

Jacques le fataliste (Diderot), 27
Jakobson, Roman, 177 n. 5
James, Henry, 2, 9, 20, 21, 26, 47, 118, 119, 120, 122, 125, 132, 134, 137, 145, 147, 149, 150, 151, 162, 167, 168, 169, 171, 175; *The American*, 18, 41, 119, 120–31, 132, 133, 134, 137, 142, 144, 145, 149, 160, 162, 163, 168, 169, 171, 173, 194 nn. 17, 19; "The Art of Fiction," 26; *The Aspern Papers*, 42–44; 48, 51; "The Future of the Novel," 2; *The Golden Bowl*, 18, 19–20, 145–51, 159–67, 168, 175, 176; *The Portrait of a Lady*, 18, 119, 120, 121, 131–43, 144, 145, 147, 149, 150, 151, 154, 155, 156, 159, 160, 165, 166, 168, 169, 171, 172, 173, 194 n. 25, 195 n. 26; *What Maisie Knew*, 9; *The Wings of the Dove*, 4, 20, 145–59, 160, 161, 163, 167, 168, 175, 195 n. 27
James, William, *Principles of Psychology*, 8
Jameson, Fredric, 188 n. 15
Jane Eyre (Bronte), 169
Josephine de Beauharnais (1st wife of Napoleon I), 57
Joyce, James, 10; *A Portrait of the Artist as a Young Man*, 10

Index

Jude the Obscure (Hardy), 18, 47, 90, 91, 92, 105–17, 118, 129, 150, 170, 171, 172, 173

Kanes, Martin, 187 n. 12
Kant, Immanuel, 13; *The Critique of Judgement*, 13
Kappeler, Susane, 183 n. 2
Kaston, Carren, 194 n. 17
Krupnick, M. L., 196 n. 22

Laclos, Pierre-Ambroise-François Choderlos de, 17, 70, 71, 77, 79, 118, 150, 168, 170, 171, 172, 187; *Les Liaisons dangereuses*, 17, 67–71, 79, 83, 85, 120, 126, 137, 171, 172
Lermontov, Mikhail, 87, 88, 89, 189; *A Hero of Our Time*, 87–88, 189 n. 2
Letters on the Aesthetic Education of Man (Schiller), 7
Lévi-Strauss, Claude, 19, 144; *The Savage Mind*, 19, 144, 162
Liaisons dangereuses, Les (Laclos), 17, 67–71, 79, 83, 85, 120, 126, 137, 171, 172
Lukács, Georg, 65

Mackenzie, Manfred, 194 n. 13
McLean, Robert C., 196 n. 18
Madame Bovary (Flaubert), 47, 133, 160
Malraux, André, 68, 187 n. 6
Mansfield Park (Austen), 36–38, 172
Marguerite de Navarre, 58
Marie Louise (2nd wife of Napoleon I), 57
Marivaux, Pierre Carlet de Chamblain de, 30, 31; *The Game of Love and Chance*, 30–33, 174
Martineau, Henri, 186 n. 29
Marxism, 25, 28
Matthiessen, F. O., 161–62
Mazzella, Anthony, 194 n. 20
Measure for Measure (Shakespeare), 30–33
Metaphor, 2, 29, 65, 177 n. 5
Middlemarch (Eliot), 20, 21
Miller, D. A., 48, 185 n. 14

Miller, J. Hillis, 106
Moore, Susan Reibel, 193 n. 9, 195 n. 27
Mozet, Nicole, 187 n. 8

Napoleon Bonaparte, 44, 46, 47, 62, 74, 91, 123
Nardo, Anna K., 180 n. 29
Nelson, William, 181 n. 12
Nin, Anaïs, 176; *The Novel of the Future*, 176
Nochlin, Linda, 27
Notes from Underground (Dostoevsky), 191 n. 16
Novel of the Future, The (Nin), 176
Nuttall, A. D., 191 n. 13

Origins of the Novel (Robert), 175

Pachmuss, Temira, 191 n. 22
Past and Present (Carlyle), 23
Patai, Daphne, 178 n. 4
Pearson, Gabriel, 197 n. 26
Père Goriot, Le (Balzac), 41, 63, 65
Piaget, Jean, 12, 14, 91
Plato, *The Symposium*, 9, 179 n. 16
Play, Theories of, 6–12
Playfulness, 4, 59
Poetics of Prose, The (Todorov), 3
Portrait of the Artist as a Young Man, A (Joyce), 10
Portrait of a Lady, The (James), 18, 119, 120, 121, 131–43, 144, 145, 147, 149, 150, 151, 154, 155, 156, 159, 160, 165, 166, 168, 169, 171, 172, 173, 194 n. 25, 195 n. 26
Positivism, 28
Potter, Stephen, 180 n. 37
Prendergast, Christopher, 188 n. 23
Pride and Prejudice (Austen), 36
Principles of Psychology (William James), 8
Protestant Ethic, The (Weber), 24
Pushkin, Aleksander Sergeevich, 88, 89; *Eugene Onegin*, 88

205

Index

Racine and Shakespeare (Stendhal), 10
Realism, 4, 22–23, 26, 38, 118, 147–49, 169, 174
Reeve, F. D., 38
Reinhardt, Kurt, 24
Renan, Ernest, 28; *The Future of Science*, 28
Ricoeur, Paul, "Existence and Hermeneutics," 8
Rise of Silas Lapham, The (Howells), 41
Ritual, 18–21, 25, 46, 52, 110, 160, 162, 167
Robbe-Grillet, Alain, 176
Robert, Marthe, 175; *Origins of the Novel*, 175
Roberts, Morris, 193 n. 6
Robertson, Priscilla, 23
Romanticism, 25–26, 27, 88, 169, 174, 190 n. 3
Rouge et le noir, Le (Stendhal), 18, 44–64, 65, 66, 76, 89, 90, 91, 92, 104, 106, 107, 110, 111, 120, 147, 169, 170, 173, 174
Rousseau, Jean Jacques, 49; *Confessions*, 49
Rules, 12–15, 34, 52, 69, 70, 72, 121, 130, 142, 152, 170
Runte, Roseann, 187 n. 10

Sagarin, Edward, 190 n. 9
Sand, George. *See* Dudevant, Amadine Aurore Lucie
Savage Mind, The (Lévi-Strauss), 19, 144, 162
Schiller, Johann Christoph Friedrich von, 7, 8, 23; *Letters on the Aesthetic Education of Man*, 7
Science, 28–29, 101
Shakespeare, William, 30, 33; *Measure for Measure*, 30–33
Shorer, Mark, "Fiction and the 'Matrix of Analogy'," 2
Sklepowich, E. A., 195 n. 29
Stanzel, Franz, 28
Stendhal. *See* Beyle, Marie Henri
Sterne, Laurence, 27, 29, 30; *Tristram Shandy*, 27
Stevenson, Elizabeth, 149
Stowe, William W., 118, 193

Superfluous Man, The, 189 n. 3
Sutton-Smith, Brian, 180
Symposium, The (Plato), 9, 179 n. 16

Tanner, Tony, 160
Theory of the Leisure Class, The (Veblen), 39, 183 n. 34
Thousand and One Nights, The, 96
Todorov, Tsvetan, 3, 197 n. 23; *The Poetics of Prose*, 3
Tolstoy, Leo, 20, 21; *Anna Karenina*, 20, 21, 24, 160, 163
Torgovnick, Mariana, 193 n. 6
Trilling, Lionel, 25, 181 n. 9
Tristram Shandy (Sterne), 27
Trollope, Anthony, 26
Turgenev, Ivan Sergeevich, 88, 89; *Fathers and Sons*, 88
Turner, Victor, 25, 26
Twain, Mark. *See* Clemens, Samuel Langhorne

Updike, John, *Couples*, 176
Utilitarianism, 28, 97, 190 n. 5

Veblen, Throstein, 39; *The Theory of the Leisure Class*, 39, 183 n. 34
Vidal, Gore, 198 n. 32
Vygotsky, L. S., 9

Ward, J. A., 193 n. 10
Weber, Max, 24; *The Protestant Ethic*, 24
Weinstein, Arnold, 182 n. 23
Welsh, Alexander, 184 n. 11, 194 n. 24
Werther (Goethe), 169
Wessel, Catherine Cox, 198 n. 32
Wharton, Edith, 171
What is to Be Done (Chernyshevsky), 24
What Maisie Knew (James), 9
Wilson, James D., 190 n. 3
Wings of the Dove, The (James), 4, 20, 145–59, 160, 161, 163, 167, 168, 175, 195 n. 27

Index

"Woman Question," 79–80, 171–72, 187 n. 8
Word Play (Farb), 5, 10
Wordsworth, William, 25
Work, 23–25, 89–91, 107–8, 123
Wright, Walter, 195 n. 3

Yeazell, Ruth Bernard, 197 n. 24, 198 n. 34

Zola, Émile, 28, 67, 187 n. 5, 188 n. 16